Charles Schwab's
New Guide to
Financial Independence

Other Books by Charles R. Schwab

You're Fifty—Now What?
It Pays to Talk
How to Be Your Own Stockbroker

Charles Schwab's
New Guide to
Financial Independence

Practical Solutions for Busy People

COMPLETELY REVISED AND UPDATED

Charles R. Schwab

THREE RIVERS PRESS • NEW YORK

A complete list of permissions appears on page 285.

Published by Three Rivers Press, New York, New York.

Member of the Crown Publishing Group, a division of Random House, Inc.
www.crownpublishing.com

THREE RIVERS PRESS and the Tugboat design are registered trademarks of Random House, Inc.

Originally published in different form in hardcover by Crown Publishers, a division of Random House, Inc., in 1997 and subsequently in paperback by Three Rivers Press, a division of Random House, Inc., in 1998.

Printed in the United States of America

Design by Debbie Glasserman

Library of Congress Cataloging-in-Publication Data
Schwab, Charles.
Charles Schwab's new guide to financial independence : practical solutions for busy people / Charles R. Schwab.— Completely rev. and updated.
Rev. ed. of: Charles Schwab's guide to financial independence. c1998.
Includes index.
1. Finance, Personal.   2. Stocks.   3. Investments.   I. Title: New guide to financial independence.   II. Title.
HG179.S334   2004
332.024—dc22   2003022195

ISBN 1-4000-4679-3

10 9 8 7 6 5 4 3 2 1

First Revised Edition

*I dedicate this book to my beloved wife, Helen,
who has encouraged and supported me
through my lifelong pursuit of investing,
and to my kids and grandkids, who are
my biggest dividend.*

Contents

Acknowledgments 9

Preface: About the Second Edition 11

Prologue 13

PART I: INVESTING MADE EASY 17

  1. The Wise Investor 19

  2. Getting Started 42

PART II: CHOOSING INVESTMENTS 75

  3. Investing in Individual Stocks and
     Stock Mutual Funds: The Basics 77

  4. Investing in Individual Stocks and
     Stock Mutual Funds: The Details 91

  5. Choosing Bonds 118

  6. Choosing Cash-Equivalent Investments 130

PART III: CREATING YOUR PLAN 137

  7. Putting Your Plan into Action 139

  8. The Taxing Side of Investing 157

  9. Planning Ahead for Your Second Half 167

  10. Families and Investing 197

PART IV: STAYING INVOLVED   **213**

11. Monitoring Your Results   **215**

12. Staying on Track   **236**

APPENDIXES   **255**

Appendix A: The Mathematics of Performance
                    Measurement   **257**

Appendix B: The Language of Investing   **263**

Appendix C: Important Legal Information   **279**

Epilogue   **281**

Permissions   **285**

Index   **287**

Acknowledgments

As anyone who has attempted it knows, writing a book is hardly a solitary activity. In writing and revising this book, I owe thanks and acknowledgment to several sources of help. Nicole Young helped me determine the concept for the first edition of this book, Joanne Cuthbertson guided every aspect of this new edition, and Bo Caldwell helped shape and polish the prose for both editions. My thanks also go to the Schwab Center for Investment Research—especially Bill Swerbenski—for their assistance, and to all of the employees of Charles Schwab & Co. for their dedicated customer service and their commitment to acting as the custodians of our clients' financial dreams. Lastly, my thanks go to our clients, the millions of people who have trusted us with those dreams.

About the Second Edition

Five years have passed since the first edition of this book was published, and it has been a turbulent time. Our economy has suffered, as have millions of individual investors. Our trust in our financial markets has been seriously breached, and as a result of these events, many Americans have been forced to scale down and delay the retirement they'd counted on. In the late 1990s, the stock market produced record highs almost daily, while the early years of the new millennium brought the worst bear market since the Depression. Investor confidence sank to new lows, thanks in large part to the corporate wrongdoings of a relatively few individuals.

Yet we've seen positive changes as well. The way people invest has changed dramatically: Thanks to the Internet, investing has become more accessible than ever before, and thousands of individuals have become active investors. The tools available to help investors develop and monitor their portfolios are both easier to use and more sophisticated. And, as a result of the market downturn, a lot of people have learned or relearned the value of balance and perspective, and of not jumping on the bandwagon.

It is my hope that by the time you read these pages, we will be well into a recovery. While there are several positive factors at work, one of the things that makes me feel most optimistic is the new tax legislation recently signed by Congress. The Jobs and Growth Tax Relief Reconciliation Act of 2003 not only reduces the federal income tax brackets and the long-term capital gains tax rate from 20% to 15%; more important, it lowers the dividend tax rate from a maximum of 38.6% down to 15%. I have every confidence that these tax cuts will encourage investment, particularly in dividend-paying stocks and equity mutual funds, and that we will see a significant boost to the stock market as a direct result.

In response to all of these changes, I've included new information in these pages, such as how to create a portfolio that will see you through down as well as up markets, and how you can objectively monitor your performance and understand your results. There's also much in these pages that hasn't changed, for the simple but very important reason that the fundamentals of investing haven't changed. Investors haven't always embraced those fundamentals, and many have paid dearly for that lapse. The combination of the accessibility brought about by online investing and an amazing bull market created a euphoria that was hard to resist, and an atmosphere that caused a lot of people to ignore time-tested investing basics and throw discipline out the window.

Those basics are more important now than ever. They are our investing compass points, and I urge you to take them to heart. If you do, they will stand you in good stead. I strongly believe that the American stock market is still the best place for long-term investing, and that with a wise investing plan, you can meet your financial goals. It is my hope that this book will help those goals become a reality.

Prologue

Dear Reader,

I've heard it said that people are motivated by hope of reward or fear of punishment—the carrot or the stick. That's as true in investing as in any other area of life, for both are present—the carrot and the stick. The stick, or punishment, in investing is what your future looks like if you ignore your financial life; the carrot, or reward, is the choice you have later if you pay attention and do what it takes to plan for that future now.

I like to concentrate on the rewards of investing, but it's important to look at the dangers as well. Sadly, there are reminders all around us: elderly people who have worked hard for most or all of their adult lives but have nothing to show for it in terms of retirement, leaving them in their sixties or seventies or eighties with financial pressures they shouldn't have at this stage of life. They have no financial safety net, and now they're truly on their own, in a very frightening way. It's a relatively new phenomenon, the result of diminishing Social Security and pension plans. And it's a very real and sobering cautionary tale about what can happen if you don't put your financial house in order.

A national news story from several years ago has stayed with me vividly because what is happening to these people is at the very heart of my passion about investing. The story described a 73-year-old man who worked stocking the shelves and delivering food for public schools. *Seventy-three years old*—and his retirement was not in sight. His wife's health was failing, and his job was hard on him physically, not to mention emotionally.

The more I read his story, the more wrenching it became. He didn't set out to end up like this. Thirty years ago he was a branch manager, with salary and commissions reaching to $500 a week, an income that was more than adequate. He and his wife and children lived in a home they'd built, and they even had some of the extras: a boat, a camper, a motor home, vacations. It was, in many ways, the good life.

But he had no pension, savings, or retirement plan, which meant that after years of hard work, because of the harsh economic realities of our times, he took a job that paid six dollars an hour, a job younger men were turning down. Even with that, he didn't have enough.

This was not a man who was unemployed year after year, someone who just couldn't hold down a job. This was a man who had a good job but who had little to show for those years of hard work. His story pulls at me, and I find it sobering, to say the least.

That's the negative way to look at investing: what happens if you don't do it. But there's a positive side, too, and it's just as important. Investing is about your life, and the reward it offers you is *having enough* and being able to live the way you want. It's about choice, and while this book and others on the shelf may seem as if they're explaining a sequence of tasks, what we're really talking about are keys that open doors. Investing is about money in the same way that school is about education. They both offer you choice.

The language of investing can disguise this. The word itself makes us think of stock certificates, financial reports, brokerage statements. It all seems so removed from the stuff of our daily lives—dinnertime, and the kids going to college, and retirement. But dinnertime and our hopes for our kids and our dreams of a good life are *exactly* what investing is all about.

If you're just starting out, don't let yourself become overwhelmed and feel as though you have to learn everything in a day. You don't. We don't expect our children to mature overnight; we don't ask ourselves to become proficient at a new sport or skill in a day. Many of the important endeavors in life take time, and this one may take time as well. It's fine to let the investor side of you mature gradually.

Truth be told, we're all investors. Each day we invest time and energy and intelligence in our children and our work. Investing for our future is just another aspect of it, but a crucial one.

If I sound passionate about this, I am. When I see elderly people lining up for a free lunch at a senior center, my heart goes out to them. I remind my employees that we are the custodians of our customers' financial dreams, and it's not something I take lightly. I've spent more than 40 years living and breathing investing; I know what to do, and I'm eager to pass on what I've learned. I could explain most of what you need to know over a long lunch.

Think of this book as everything I would share with you during that lunch. Read it. Try out the suggestions. But please, do *something,* because the biggest risk in investing is doing nothing. You've got to start; as soon as you do, you're two steps closer to your hopes of financial security. I wish you the best as you begin.

With my best regards,

Charles R Schwab

Part I

INVESTING MADE EASY

1

The Wise Investor

What do you think it takes to be a wise investor? An Ivy League MBA? A sixth sense about market timing? Years of 60-hour weeks on Wall Street? Maybe it's talent, a certain ability that some people are just born with, leaving those who aren't without a chance. Or maybe it's just luck.

The answer is none of the above. Anyone can become a wise investor. To do so, you need to do only two things: learn the basics, and build your investing strategy with those basics as its foundation. That's it; no magic, no degrees. And that's what this book is about: learning the basics of wise investing, and developing an investing strategy that's as timeless and dependable as it is simple.

I have every confidence that the approach explained in these pages will work for you and see you through all types of market conditions *if*—and this is an important *if*—you make the commitment to become a serious investor for the rest of your life. Not for a month or a year. Investing is a lifelong commitment, which means you stick with it. If that sounds serious, it is. Investing isn't a game. It's about the things that matter most to you, like buying your first home, or educating your kids, or being able to travel once you've retired. Plain and simple, investing is about what's important in your life, and anybody—*everybody*—can do it the right way.

The key is understanding the basics. Once you do, you'll always be able to handle the financial part of your life, for the simple reason that the basics never change. The economy changes, and the market changes, and our needs and goals change, but the strategies you use to meet those goals and handle those market fluctuations remain the same. Learn them once, and you've learned them for good.

So here they are, the basics of your investing plan:

1. INVEST FOR GROWTH

When you invest your money, what do you want most? You want it to grow. In fact, that's probably your first objective: growth, meaning a positive, real return on your investments after inflation and taxes have taken their toll. Without growth, you lose ground every year; with growth, the value of your portfolio increases and stays ahead of inflation. All of this means that the first step of a good investing plan is to invest for growth—and *that* means your portfolio should include stocks.

2. DIVERSIFY YOUR PORTFOLIO

Investing for growth has its potential rewards, but it also has its potential risks. Therefore, while I firmly believe that investing in stocks is the best road to long-term growth, I'm also the first to admit that it can be a pretty bumpy ride, thanks to the nerve-racking phenomenon we call market volatility. So how do you reap the rewards of investing for growth without being thrown overboard? Diversification, which simply means spreading your investments across a range of investments—including stocks, bonds, cash equivalents, and possibly hedge funds, real estate investment trusts (REITs), or other investments—and finding the mix that best suits your particular situation. That mix helps to guard you against dramatic declines while at the same time helping your portfolio grow. You get the benefit of growth potential tempered by the safety of diversification.

3. KNOW YOURSELF

No two investors are the same. We all have our individual needs, personalities, and priorities. Therefore, as you create and maintain your investing plan, it is essential that you pay attention to things like your specific financial objectives (do you want to buy a house, start a college fund, retire at age 50?), your age, and your tolerance for risk. Don't expect your portfolio to look like your neighbor's portfolio. It should reflect you and your family—and no one else. Also realize that as your personal circumstances change, your portfolio may need to change as well.

4. KEEP YOUR PERSPECTIVE

Perspective is an investor's best friend and strongest defense. Keeping your perspective means maintaining an even keel, so that you stay calm and level-headed during those euphoric highs as well as the downbeat lows. If you lose perspective, you can really get into trouble. But once you learn to keep your emotions in check and invest strategically rather than emotionally, you can ride out the lows and be objective about the highs.

5. STAY INVOLVED

Investing is not a one-time thing. To be a successful investor you can't just set everything in place and then go on autopilot and expect to reach your destination. Staying involved doesn't mean you should redo your game plan every month. But it does mean that you need to periodically check your progress and make sure you're still on track. You do that by comparing your results to reliable industry yardsticks. That's the best way of knowing whether you need to reexamine your plan and make adjustments.

■ ■ ■

That's it; those are the basics. Learn them and put them into practice, and you'll know how to invest for the rest of your life. Each of them is essential to achieving long-term success as an investor; together they'll stand you in good stead over decades. This is a time when the whole is definitely larger than the sum of its parts.

1. Invest for Growth

You may not associate the word *growth* with investing, but for me, growth is at the very heart of the matter. What do I mean by growth? Strange as it may sound, I mean the kind of growth that's all around us, the growth we see every day in trees and plants and our kids.

Think of biology. Maybe you've looked through a microscope and seen an amoeba dividing itself into two. There it is, this tiny one-celled organism that reproduces by dividing itself right before your eyes. All of a sudden where there was one now there are two. You keep watching, and soon the two become four, and the four become eight, and the eight sixteen—an incredible example of growth.

THE GENETICS OF STOCKS

What does all that have to do with investing? A lot. Like an amoeba, a company is an organism that grows. In fact, that's exactly what it's designed to do—so much so that management's main job is to encourage and enable that growth. In the four decades I've spent in the business world, I've never heard a management team announce that their company would strive to remain static for the upcoming year, that no growth was planned. The company may not meet its goal or it may exceed its mark; the point is that business is about growth.

And companies do grow. They get bigger, in so many ways: the number of employees and services offered, the number of customers, the number of products produced and shipped, revenues, net worth, operating plants or factories, and—most important—

earnings. Suppose a company starts out with 5 employees, 1 product, 20 customers, and a rented building. The next year it might have 12 employees, 3 products, and 50 customers; and the year after that, it grows again! Companies even grow physically.

Companies need fuel for all that growth, and amazingly, they fuel themselves. Although I believe that it is important to reward investors with dividends (especially in light of the recent reduction in dividend taxes; see Chapter 4 for more details), a company can also reinvest a sizable portion of its profits in itself, thereby feeding its own growth. A company that paid out 100% of its earnings in dividends couldn't sustain growth—it would have no fuel. But if it paid 25% in dividends, it could put 75% of its net income back into its own growth. And *that's fuel*—the company puts that money right back to work so that it continues to compound, feeding the company, helping it to grow. That's growth on top of growth.

Let's say an average American company grows at the rate of 11% per annum. Maybe 3% of that is inflation and 8% is real growth. At 11% growth, shareholders might be paid a 2% dividend, and the company reinvests 9% back into growing the company. The reinvestment fuels the company as it expands by building new plants and new equipment and by offering new services. Over time shareholders probably get an average of 9% to 11% *compounded* return. No other financial instrument features this same genetic engineering.

PARTICIPATING IN LONG-TERM GROWTH

So how do you as an investor take part in all that growth? Simple. If companies are what grows, you invest in companies by buying stock, which means that you own a very small part of that company. That's the best way I know to achieve growth: by buying stock (either as individual stocks or as a group of stocks called a mutual fund, which we'll discuss in Chapter 3). Your share of ownership may be a very small portion, but you're still part owner of something that has the potential to grow, and as the company grows, so does your share of its wealth. Your investment may not grow overnight; it may take two steps forward and one step back. It may even reach a plateau now and then. But over a five-to-ten-year period, chances are that it will grow. You just have to be patient.

THE PROOF IS IN THE PAST

The basis for my strong belief in the power of stocks is this historical fact: *Over time, stocks have outperformed all other kinds of investments, including bonds, CDs, and U.S. government securities.* We know this by taking a look at the stock market's track record. As you can see in the following figure, when you look back as far as 1925, stocks have outperformed all other types of assets. One dollar invested and reinvested in stocks since 1925 would have accumulated to $1,775 by the end of 2002, far outperforming other investments.

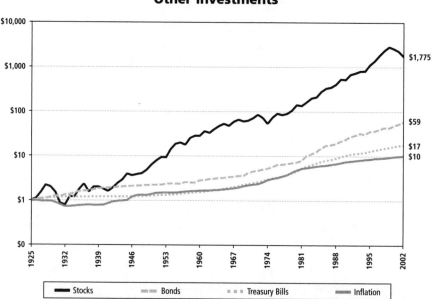

Over the Long Term, Stocks Have Outperformed Other Investments

Note: This chart illustrates the growth in value of $1 invested in various financial instruments from 1925 through 2002. Figures above indicate the value of that same $1 at the end of 2002. **Source:** Stocks, Bonds, Bills & Inflation, 2003 Yearbook, Ibbotson Associates, Inc. Based on copyrighted works by Ibbotson and Sinquefield. All rights reserved. Used with permission. The indexes representing each asset class are: S&P 500 Index (stocks), Ibbotson Intermediate U.S. Government Bond Index (bonds), and 30-day Treasury bills (cash). The Consumer Price Index for All Urban Consumers (CPI-U), which is not adjusted seasonally, is used to measure inflation. Indexes are unmanaged, do not incur fees or expenses, and cannot be invested in directly. Results assume reinvestment of stock dividends and bond coupons and do not include taxes. Past performance is no indication of future results.

As you can see, the long-term trend of the stock market in the United States has always been upward. Yes, there have been up periods and significant down periods, including the dramatic decline from the market peak in 2000, but over the long haul the trend is up. That simple fact alone—*over time, stocks have outperformed all other kinds of investments*—makes an excellent case for investing in stocks. But how do we know that upward trend will continue?

We come back to growth, the one thing that distinguishes stocks from all other investments. Growth is the reason stocks have proved to be such solid investments over time. Even now, having experienced one of the worst bear markets in history, I still believe that stocks will continue to outperform other kinds of investments over the long term.

COMPARING APPLES AND ORANGES

What about other investments? How do stocks compare to bonds or CDs? Let's start with bonds. Suppose a company offers investors the opportunity to invest not only in its stock but in its corporate bonds as well. The bonds would provide investors with a 7.5% return, so after paying personal taxes, investors might net 5%. The person interested in investing in that company would then have a choice between investing in stocks—which have the potential to grow at 10% or even 12% per annum after taxes—and bonds that pay 5% after taxes.

The corporate bond would probably pay its interest every year right on time, but the bond itself would never grow. In contrast, the company's stock value would change from year to year, appreciating or declining generally in line with the company's growth rate. Stocks carry much more upside potential than bonds, but they're also more volatile, a factor that alarms a lot of people. But I believe that such variations provide the opportunity for those who understand the genetics of stocks to become confident and lifelong investors. And while I've oversimplified this theoretical example, in reality it's very close to what happens. Bonds are made to pay interest, while stocks are made to grow.

CDs are like bonds in this regard: They pay interest, but they don't really grow. When you put your money into a CD or a money market account in a bank, you aren't buying anything. You're simply loaning your money to someone who's willing to pay you some interest on it. (If the bank then takes your money and loans it out to other people or companies, it makes a profit off the difference.) Your interest rate is predetermined and limited, and generally it runs slightly higher than inflation.

But with a company, the whole idea is for it to get bigger, and that makes stocks fundamentally—almost *genetically*—different from all other investment alternatives, including money market funds, CDs, government bonds, and corporate bonds. If you want the value of your money to follow a nice straight line with a very slight upward tilt and no dips, put it into a savings account and leave it there. If, on the other hand, you want your money to have the ability to grow, put it into something that's designed to grow: stocks.

THE INFLATION FACTOR

Inflation: It sounds relatively harmless, but when it comes to investing, that's far from the truth. Inflation is always there, and it always will be, like a small leak you can't fix—only it gets bigger with time because it compounds every year. Even at the low rate of 3% per annum, inflation eats up more than a quarter of your money's purchasing power every ten years. In 24 years, your money will be worth only half as much as it is now. That's a pretty big number, and that's inflation at a conservative 3%. Watch what happens when that number begins to climb: At 5% your purchasing power is cut in half in 14 years, and at 6%, it's 12 years.

Startled? A lot of people are when they hear about inflation's corrosive effect, and with good reason. When you get a sneaking suspicion that your money just isn't going as far as it used to, you're right. It *isn't* going as far, simply because it has less purchasing power. (Interestingly enough, although inflation usually captures the headlines, in 2003 we also started to hear more about a new problem— the danger of *deflation,* or falling prices. In a nutshell, deflation discourages capital spending as buyers wait for prices to decline—and as a result, economic growth can come to a grinding halt. We've seen this happen in Japan. However, in my opinion, the threat of serious deflation in the United States is remote, not only because of the underlying strength of our economy but also because the Federal Reserve has the tools it needs to nip deflation in the bud.)

Inflation is another area where stocks win out over other investments in the long term. Bank-paid interest and bonds will often match or almost keep up with inflation, but over time, good companies can change their prices or cut their costs to stay ahead of inflation. For example, look at Coca-Cola. The cost of a bottle of Coke was about five cents back in 1950; now that same soft drink

Equities Have Been the Best Defense Against Taxes and Inflation
(1970–2002)

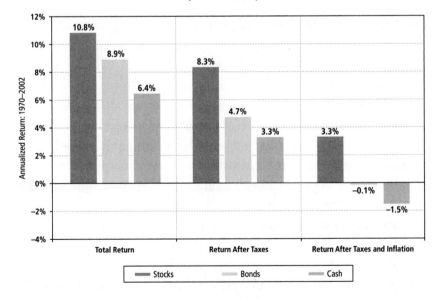

Source: Schwab Center for Investment Research with data from Ibbotson Associates, Inc. Indexes representing each asset class are S&P 500 Index (stocks), Ibbotson Intermediate Government Bond Index (bonds), and U.S. 30-day Treasury bills (cash). Historical maximum income tax rates and inflation rates were used to adjust "Return After Taxes" and "Return After Taxes and Inflation" for the period 1970–2002. Dividend payments were taxed annually at historical maximum income tax rates, and capital gains were calculated at the end of the period at the long-term capital gains rate (20% as of 2002). Indexes are unmanaged, do not incur fees or expenses, and cannot be invested in directly. Past performance is no indication of future results.

sells for around a dollar a bottle, which means that through the years, its price has been adjusted for inflation.

For all of these reasons, I view stocks as offering investors the best potential for long-term growth. You may not make money overnight, and you may experience some unsettling downs. But with patience, you stand a good chance of making your financial dreams a reality. History suggests that when you consider the effect of inflation in your investing equation, stocks are the best way to obtain a long-term return that is substantially above the rate of inflation. Add in the effect of taxes and the picture becomes even clearer. To be a successful long-term investor, it's crucial to be invested for growth. I believe that there's simply no other way to meet your long-term goals, to stay ahead of inflation, and to have your money outlive you.

2. Diversify Your Portfolio

So how can you take advantage of the power of growth and still sleep at night? By diversifying your portfolio, perhaps the most important investing move you can make.

Diversifying your portfolio simply means not putting all your eggs in one basket, but rather dividing your investing dollars among a variety of investments. It means finding just the right mix of investments, given your particular situation, and it's what helps you earn a positive long-term return while at the same time protecting you from dramatic declines. Diversification is the cornerstone of wise investing.

Diversification has two essential levels. First, you want to diversify *among* asset classes—in other words, to include a mix of stocks, bonds, and cash equivalents in your portfolio. Second, and equally important, you need to diversify *within* asset classes—which means, for example, including in the stock part of your portfolio a variety of stocks, such as a mix of large and small companies, companies from several industries, and international as well as domestic firms.

THE PIECES OF THE PIE

As you look at potential investments, think of your portfolio as a pie, with each type of investment—stocks, bonds, and cash equivalents—as a piece of that pie. Let's look at the pieces of the pie more carefully.

As we've said, stocks represent ownership of shares in a company. Bonds are like IOUs from a municipal or federal government or from a corporation: You loan the borrower money, and in return, it promises to return the full amount on a specific date and pay you interest in the meantime. Cash-equivalent investments are investments that can be so easily converted into cash that they're almost like cash—and they pay a low rate of interest. These investments include money market funds, Treasury bills, and CDs.

A well-diversified portfolio includes a mix of these types of investments. The mix you choose—the percentage of stocks, bonds, and cash equivalents—is called your *asset allocation,* which simply means how you spread your assets among types of investments. There's no one-size-fits-all asset allocation; it's very much a custom fit, so that what's right for one person might be totally wrong for another. The good news is that finding the right mix isn't difficult. It's not magic—it takes a little time and effort—but it's pretty easily done once you put your mind to it.

One of the most important aspects of that mix is that it includes each asset class—stocks, bonds, and cash. Each type of investment plays a certain role. You don't just buy one type of asset when it's doing well (say, stocks), then sell it when it goes down and move your money to another asset class (bonds). That sort of approach is based on the idea that it's possible to time the market—to know with a pretty high degree of accuracy exactly when one asset class is going to outperform another. The truth is that timing the market accurately is difficult, to say the least, and closer to impossible.

What that does mean, in terms of asset allocation, is that a buy-and-hold strategy is a wise approach. You've probably heard of *buy-and-hold* in terms of stocks or individual investments—the idea that you buy an investment and then hang on, in good times and bad. (This assumes, of course, that you have carefully selected your investments. We'll talk more about that in Chapter 12.) Buy-and-hold in terms of asset allocation means that you include each asset class in your portfolio all the time, never moving completely out of one class (selling all of it) in an attempt to time the market. But why not simply invest all of your money in the investment you think offers the best potential?

Too risky. William F. Sharpe, a 1990 Nobel laureate in economics and professor of finance at Stanford University, provides a simple example: "At one time, each ship sent from London to bring back spices from the Orient was financed by one merchant. If the ship happened to sink, the investor lost everything. But if several merchants pooled their resources, with each taking partial interests in several ships, risk could be greatly reduced, with no diminution in overall expected return. Such pooling could be accomplished in a number of ways. One of the simpler procedures involved the issuance of 'ownership shares' (not surprisingly), with each investor holding a *diversified portfolio* of shares in several ships."

In Sharpe's example, some ships did better than others. Some investments do better than others, too; in fact, different kinds of investments do well or poorly at different times, and it's impossible to predict which will outperform another at any given time. This is true of both asset classes (stocks, bonds, and cash equivalents) and different investments within each of these classes. Diversification not only helps to protect you from being overly invested in stocks during a bear market, it also protects you from those sinking ships we call *market fluctuations* in any one sector of the market. For example, if you put 90% of your investing dollars into tech stocks—sad to say, something a lot of people did just a few years ago—you wouldn't be diversified, and sooner or later, you'd be in trouble (as a lot of people found out).

RISK AND RETURN

Mention the stock market and a lot of people immediately think *risk*. But risk isn't something to fear; it's something to deal with, and the first thing to understand is that it's a part of investing, just as it's a part of life. You have to take on some level of risk to succeed. Your goal isn't to eliminate risk altogether, but to eliminate *unnecessary* risk and take only calculated, intelligent risks. We take a risk every time we drive on a freeway or ski down a mountain, but it's a calculated risk. Some risk is actually good, for the simple fact is that to have growth, you have to take on some risk. The trick is to avoid unwise risk.

Each type of investment—stocks, bonds, and cash equivalents—entails particular risks and offers a particular kind of return. *Risk* refers to how much danger there is of losing your investing dollars, while *return* refers to your profit—how much money you make on an investment. The two are closely linked: In very general terms, the greater the potential return, the higher the risk. The table on the following page shows the relationship between risk and return for each type of investment.

Ask investors what they fear most, and they'll almost always say losing the money they invested. That's a very real concern—so much so that entire financial industries have been built on counteracting it. As a category, stocks certainly carry the greatest short-term risk. Banks tout savings accounts and CDs as "risk free," while government bond brokers promote "risk-free" Treasury securities.

But wise investors understand that capital loss is only one kind of risk; there are plenty of others. You probably won't lose the money you place in a savings account, but when it comes to preserving purchasing power (after inflation and taxes take their toll), savings accounts are almost as risky as you can get. Treasury bonds may be free from default risk, but not from inflation risk, interest rate risk, or yearly taxes.

Each particular investment is subject to investment-specific risks as well. For example, stock prices rise and fall with the stock market cycle, making stocks subject to market psychology risk. If you buy a stock, you also inherit a certain amount of cyclical economic risk. If you buy a bond, you inherit the inflation risk—or the risk that the interest you earn doesn't keep up with the rise in prices—that comes with all bonds.

Three Basic Investments: Stocks, Bonds, and Cash

Lower ◄— Risk and Return —► Higher

Cash-Equivalent Investments	Bonds	Stocks (Equities)
Investments that are easily converted to cash, thus often known as "liquid assets."	Issued by a borrower, such as a public entity or corporation, seeking to raise funds.	Ownership of shares in a company. Categories include small-capitalization (small-cap)[3] stocks, large-capitalization (large-cap) stocks, and international stocks.[4]
Treasury bills (T-bills)	Corporate bonds • High-Yield Bonds • Investment-Grade Bonds	Common stock
Short-term certificates of deposit (CDs)	Municipal bonds	Preferred stock
Money market mutual funds[1,5]	Government bonds • U.S. Government Bonds • Zero-Coupon Treasuries (STRIPs)	Stock mutual funds[5]
	Bond mutual funds[2,5]	

[1]Money market funds are managed to maintain a stable $1 share value. Investments in these funds are not insured or guaranteed by the U.S. government or the FDIC, and there can be no assurance that the funds will be able to maintain a stable net asset value.

[2]Investment value will fluctuate, so shares, when redeemed, may be worth more or less than their original cost.
[5]Mutual funds are sold by prospectuses, which contain more complete information, including management fees, charges, and expenses. Read the prospectus carefully before investing or sending money.

[3]Small-cap companies are subject to greater volatility than those in other asset categories.
[4]International investing may result in higher risk due to political instability, currency exchange fluctuation, and differences in acccounting methods.

Shorter ◄— Time Horizon —► Longer

Source: Adapted from the Charles Schwab & Co., Inc., publication *Plan for Success.*

Let's go a step further: Each investment is also subject to a specific risk that other investments of its type may not have. Every stock has its own risks unique to that company. In addition, every stock is exposed to the business cycle, but not all corporations suffer from complacent management or an antiquated product. Also, some sectors, such as tech stocks, tend to be more volatile than others. Every bond undertakes inflation risk, but not all bonds have equal risk of default.

What does this mean to you as an investor? First, you have to understand that you can't eliminate risk. In fact, if you altogether avoid what you perceive as high-risk investments, you're really just shooting yourself in the foot. By omitting a whole class of investments, you lose the potential returns that that class generates. The chances are that a hard-line, low-risk approach will produce low-reward results.

But you can take a very important step toward eliminating *unnecessary* risk, which you do by being adequately diversified. By holding part of your portfolio in stocks and part in bonds, and by owning a broad mix of stocks and bonds, you don't avoid the risk of stocks and bonds but you do diminish your overall volatility.

In addition to the level of risk they entail, investments differ in the type of return they can offer—growth or income. Capital *growth* results from increases in the market price of a security. Common stocks are probably the best-known growth investment. *Income* investments, on the other hand, provide current cash payments in the form of interest and dividends. Bonds, mortgage-backed securities, and CDs are examples of income investments.

How do you find that perfect mix of investments? It all starts with understanding yourself as an investor.

3. Know Yourself

Wise investors understand that their portfolios must reflect who they are and what they want to accomplish. Therefore, when you first become an investor, one of your primary orders of business should be to do some serious soul-searching. What is important to you? What financial objectives do you and your family have for the next 5, 10, 15, or even 50 years? How much volatility can you tolerate?

Of course, there are no right and wrong answers to any of this.

The point is that you have to be honest and realistic. Following are some things to consider as you start to create your plan:

• *Be specific about your goals and time frame.*

When a business executive puts together a business plan, he or she doesn't say something like "I'd like to increase sales" or "I'd like to cut expenses." Rather, a successful executive sets specific targets such as "By 2005 I plan to increase revenues by 5%, decrease expenses by 5%, and increase the profit margin by 10%."

Successful investors take the same approach. Instead of simply saying "Someday I'd like to have a comfortable retirement," think in specific terms of what this really means. Does "comfortable" mean that you want to maintain your current income? Is "someday" 10 years from now, 15, 20? Answering these questions is the first step in making your plan a reality.

• *Think about how involved you want to be.*

Before you begin selecting investments, take some time to think about how involved you want to be with the day-to-day management of your accounts. For example, monitoring a portfolio of individual stocks is much more time-consuming than investing in mutual funds. Therefore, before you decide on your approach, be honest about how much time you can commit.

• *Think about how much risk you can tolerate.*

Earlier in this chapter we talked about different kinds of risk and what that means for investors. Before you buy any investment—and I can't emphasize this enough—you *must* understand how much and what kind of risk is appropriate for your circumstances, goals, and time frame. Avoid risk altogether, and you'll pay the penalty with subpar returns. On the other hand, some of the worst investment decisions come when investors have assumed more risk than they can handle. Finding the proper balance is key. This is as basic as it gets.

You'll learn the specifics of creating your portfolio in Chapter 2, but it all starts with what we've discussed here: understanding your priorities, your time frame, and your temperament. Only then can you develop a custom-fit asset allocation that addresses your unique situation in terms of your time horizon and your comfort level with risk, and that gives you the best chance of meeting your financial goals.

4. Keep Your Perspective

Perspective is invaluable to an investor. Without it, you run the risk of letting your emotions get the best of you at the market's every turn. There are a lot of ups and downs in investing, and if you don't keep a cool head, they can very easily throw you off-balance.

Maintaining your perspective is a two-part harmony between fact and emotion. First, the facts, which you've just read: A little knowledge about the stock market goes a long way. When the bumps come, you're able to put them in context, and they don't mean the end is near. For example, once you understand that stocks are by nature somewhat volatile, the ups and downs don't throw you as much. Second, the emotions: You have to stay objective. In the highs, that means not buying all the hype and moving everything over to whatever's hot just then. And in the lows, it means not selling out of fear.

Keeping your perspective isn't always easy; it can be one of the hardest things you ever do. But if you stay the course, your confidence will grow as you achieve your goals. Some of the tricks of keeping your perspective apply to both the good times and the bad. The following will stand you in good stead whatever the mood in the market.

• *Keep a long-term view.*

Perspective means knowing that investing is not an overnight phenomenon but a long-term commitment. Once you have a long-term view, market volatility doesn't get to you as much because you know it's part of the deal. If you learn to hold on through the down periods, after the first couple of business cycles, you'll gain some confidence and the fluctuations won't throw you.

• *Keep your emotions in check.*

Where investing is concerned, you have to learn to moderate your mood swings, not only in the bad times when selling is the worst thing you can do but also in the good times, as in March 2000, when everyone was jumping into tech stocks. The euphoria can tempt you to do things you'd never consider under normal circumstances, and the downturns can make you want to cash everything in. Don't be swayed by either extreme; take a deep breath and remain objective.

• *Be prepared.*

Don't be caught off guard by the market's ups and downs. By keeping an eye on what's going on in the financial world, you can become better prepared to react in a rational way. Staying current gives you context for whatever's going on, making you less tempted to jump to conclusions.

In an up market, being prepared means anticipating the hype and euphoria that accompany a really strong bull market. It can mean holding back a little and not jumping on the bandwagon and investing in whatever sector is hot just then. A wait-and-see attitude can be very helpful here. If you see a stock that just looks terrific, holding off for a few months and keeping your eye on things can be a very wise move. (We'll talk about what to look for in stocks in Chapters 3 and 4.)

A down market is tougher, which means it's all the more important to be prepared mentally, emotionally, and fiscally. If you anticipate down periods, you'll worry about them less because you'll know that, as history has shown, the market won't stay down forever. The U.S. economy is robust and growing, and chances are the market will recover and eventually gain new highs. I believe it's just a matter of time. If down periods are really going to bother you, you can take steps to reduce your exposure by putting a portion of your holdings into something that won't go down in value. But in these times, remember that you're in this for the long term; don't lose sight of your goals.

• *Don't follow the crowd.*

It's hard to be the one person around who isn't buying or selling along with everyone else, but that person often looks pretty good when the dust settles. Stick to your strategy and don't follow the herd. Just about the worst thing you can do as an investor is chase past performance.

If you don't have a strategy, now is the time to develop one, whether that just means doing your homework or getting some professional help. That strategy is what will see you through those dramatic times.

• *Be patient.*

Continuing to be patient in any kind of extreme market is much easier said than done. In a bull market, when it seems that everyone but you is getting richer by the hour, it's hard to sit back and stay objective. But patience is critical. Not only that: In a down market, patience can even be painful. The market conditions of the recent bear market tried my patience to the breaking point. After a while, you feel completely worn out, and it gets tougher to hold on by the day. But you have to keep going and learn to hang on. I strongly believe that your patience will be rewarded.

5. Stay Involved

The fifth step is staying involved. Unfortunately, this step is often overlooked, which is like ignoring a warning light in your car. Keep driving, and you may end up in trouble.

As you'll see in later chapters, I'm a big fan of a buy-and-hold approach to investing. That means that you choose your investments thoughtfully, after doing some careful research or getting good, unbiased advice, and then ideally you hang on to those investments for years and sell only if, over time, they don't stand up under close scrutiny. You don't sell the moment one of your stocks or mutual funds goes down a little. But *buy-and-hold* doesn't mean *buy-and-do-nothing*. You still have to keep your eye on things; you don't just file your brokerage statements in a drawer and forget all about your portfolio. To do so is foolish.

Still, the monitoring part of investing is something a lot of people ignore. We should know better; when we ignore the monitoring or maintenance tasks in any part of our lives—whether that means going to the dentist, or keeping an eye on our kids' activities, or getting the car tuned up—we can get into trouble because, while those maintenance tasks can be tedious, they're crucial.

The maintenance required in investing is knowing how you're doing and making adjustments as needed. You do this in the same way you do it in other areas of your life: You compare your progress to some sort of yardstick. That's what grades are about—a letter grade indicates how a student is doing relative to other students. The grading scale is a yardstick for measuring academic progress. In investing, we have yardsticks, too, and we can use them to gauge our progress. You can't know how well you did until you decide relative to what.

As an example, let's look at one yardstick commonly used for stocks: the S&P 500® Index. (We'll look at other yardsticks, or *benchmarks,* for all investments in Chapter 11.) The S&P 500 Index includes the country's 500 largest companies, based on market capitalization, which account for approximately 80% of the market value of the U.S. equity markets, and it's a pretty good measuring stick for large-company stocks. If the S&P 500 is down, that probably means the economy is in a slump, so it's not necessarily alarming if your portfolio is down. But if the S&P 500 is down 10%, and your portfolio is down closer to 20%, that's a different story. If the S&P 500 is down 20%, and your portfolio is down only 10%, you can take that as a positive result.

The key is knowing where you stand relative to something. By regularly comparing your return on your investments, you can see if you're outperforming the market (which is great, but could be a red flag for the future), tracking it (which is fine—you don't have to outperform the market to do well in investing), or underperforming it (which could mean a couple of things). And with that knowledge, you can then make wise decisions about whether or not you need to take action. More on this in Chapter 11.

Another important step is to periodically see how your current portfolio stands up against the asset allocation you chose. Because of market fluctuations, your portfolio can drift away from your original percentages. Checking to see where you are, then asking once again where you want to be, is wise. We'll talk more about this in Chapter 12.

IRVING R. LEVINE ON STAYING INVOLVED

Lots of investors will do anything these days to avoid looking at how their stocks are doing. It's like the child who shuts his eyes at the movies and asks you to tell him when the scary part is over. Ask an investor with a depressed portfolio about the market and you're likely to get the answer "I don't look anymore; it's too scary." The youngster who closes his eyes may miss the best part of the film. The investor who closes his eyes may miss the best opportunities. The expensive stock you've always wanted to buy may now be affordable. The lemon stock you've wanted to sell may have risen so that you can take an acceptable loss or even break even. In the dot-com heyday of the roaring '90s it was fun to follow the market, even on an hourly basis, to watch one's investments climbing. On many days now, it's anything but fun. But the successful investor has to pay attention and not let the scary performance cause him to shut his eyes.

Reprinted from *Nightly Business Report,* January 30, 2003. Used with permission.

Summing Up

In this chapter we've talked about the basics of a wise investing strategy: investing for growth, being well diversified, knowing yourself, keeping your perspective, and staying involved. Learn these basics and you'll be well on your way to developing a successful investing plan that will stand you in good stead for years to come. You'll be able to survive the lows, and you'll be in place to benefit from the highs. And you'll know that you're doing one of the most important things you can do for your future.

The Bottom Line on Being a Wise Investor

• *To become a wise investor, you need to build your investing strategy on the basics: investing for growth, diversifying your portfolio, knowing yourself, keeping your perspective, and staying involved.*

• *Investing is a lifelong commitment, which means you stick with it.*

• *Investing in stock is investing for growth. Companies grow; when you buy stock in a company, you're buying part of something that's like a living organism. As it grows, so will your investment.*

• *Over time, stocks have outperformed all other kinds of investments, including bonds, CDs, and U.S. government securities.*

• *The biggest risk in investing is doing nothing and watching inflation eat up your money. Even at the low inflation rate of 3% per annum, you lose more than a third of your money's purchasing power every ten years.*

• *Diversifying your portfolio means dividing your investing dollars proportionately among asset classes and within asset classes, given your particular situation. It helps you earn a positive long-term return while at the same time protecting you from dramatic declines.*

• *The mix of stocks, bonds, and cash-equivalent investments you choose is called your asset allocation. Each type of investment plays a certain role.*

• *Risk refers to how much danger there is of losing your investing dollars, while return refers to your profit—how much money you make on an investment. The two are closely linked: In very general terms, the greater the potential return, the higher the risk.*

• *Your portfolio should reflect who you are as an investor. Never lose sight of your goals, your time frame, and your ability to withstand volatility.*

• *Be ready for the market's ups and downs. Learn to ignore the hype and euphoria during strong bull markets and to anticipate down periods, knowing that history has shown that the market doesn't stay down forever.*

• *The maintenance required in investing is knowing how you're doing and making adjustments as needed.*

2

Getting Started

Financial goals. Investment plan. Asset allocation. A lot of people are put off by the language of investing. Some find it daunting, and it makes them feel that they're in over their heads. Others find it just plain dull.

If the language of investing turns you off, I hope you'll stay with me, because what's just underneath all that language is something wonderful and very valuable: the commodity we call *choice*. What financial planning is *really* about is taking steps now so that you'll have enough money to do the things you want later, whether that means buying your first home, financing your children's college education, or traveling when you retire. If you think of what you want to be able to accomplish financially as your destination, financial planning is simply the map that gets you there.

In this chapter, we'll talk about the first steps toward making the future you envision a reality: taking control of your financial life, understanding yourself as an investor, choosing an asset allocation plan, and knowing when to get help.

Taking Control of Your Financial Life

Gaining control of the financial part of your life isn't difficult. It simply involves taking a few steps to put things in order, then building a foundation for your investing life. And while doing so isn't hard, it's rewarding. Strange as it may sound, it just *feels* good to take care of this part of your life, or even to take the first steps toward getting things under control. So here we go.

ON LEARNING SOMETHING NEW

Tackling a new subject can be daunting. Maybe it brings back old classroom feelings of dread or apprehension, the way you felt before a math test or English paper. If that's true for you, please keep reading. One thing I truly understand is the anxiety that comes from the prospect of having to learn something you perceive as difficult. And I'm here to tell you that there are ways to get through it and that the rewards are great.

I speak from experience here, for while investing has come easily to me, other things haven't. School was always hard for me. I was good in math and science, but English was slow and painful. I had a hard time taking notes during lectures, and I couldn't memorize more than a few words at once. I figured I was just stupid at certain subjects, and I felt terrible about it, but didn't know how to fix the problem. During my four years in high school, I never read a novel from cover to cover; eventually, rather than struggling through the texts of the classics like *Moby Dick* and *A Tale of Two Cities,* I "read" the Classic Comics versions, which gave me the basics in pictures. Meanwhile, my friends were doing great, picking up this scholarship and that award while I watched with envy. I nearly flunked out of Stanford at the end of my freshman year—I was a unit away.

I struggled for years and never had a name for my condition—until, years later, in 1986, when my son began having the same kinds of difficulties in school, and my wife, Helen, and I were told he was dyslexic. It was only when the school psychologist asked if either of us had had problems similar to my son's that I was able to give my learning problems a name. And my struggles finally made sense.

I can't call dyslexia a blessing, but it has brought some good, for all that time in school, when things were so difficult for me, I was learning other skills. I became a pretty good risk-taker, and I learned what it feels like to fail. Eventually I saw that I had a different way of processing information, a way that gave me a real advantage. I tend to skip some of the minor steps of logic and see a solution to something more quickly than others—sort of like seeing the finish line right from the start. I synthesize differently: I see where I want to end up, and that tells me how I should get there. In an odd way, I attribute much of my success to my learning difficulty because it has helped me to see solutions that others might not see.

And there's been more tangible good. After our son's diagnosis, when Helen and I first began trying to learn about dyslexia, we found the task difficult, to say the least. What helped us, little by little, was information and understanding. As we learned about the disorder and about others like it, we came to see that a lot of kids who were very bright were getting lost along the way, simply because they had difficulty learning. What was needed was information, because if a learning disorder is identified, a kid can get help and do just fine. We came to want to share what we'd learned with other parents going through the same struggles. And so, in 1989, we founded Schwab Learning, a place where parents and teachers trying to understand learning disorders can find information, guidance, and community support. (You can visit Schwab Learning online at *www. SchwabLearning.org.*)

Dyslexia has also caused me to learn about how I learn, and I've come to see that people learn in a surprising variety of ways. Some are visual learners, others more auditory. Some learn best by working with a teacher or coach; others do better on their own. So if you find yourself intimidated by the idea of learning about investing, I strongly encourage you to give some thought to how you learn best. This doesn't have to be painful. I hope this book is helpful, but there are other ways in addition to it. You can learn online (at *www.schwab.com,* for example), or you can go to a Schwab branch and meet with someone there to get started. And there are classes available. The trick is to find the way that best suits you, and to use it.

Learning a new skill can be tough, I know, but don't let it overwhelm you. If it's a little uncomfortable at the start, do whatever is necessary to overcome it. Find the way that's best for you, and stay with it. It's the best thing you can do for your future.

Whose Job Is It, Anyway?

A generation or two ago, husbands and wives often divided their responsibilities along pretty predictable lines. Those lines have blurred over the last 20 years, and in many families, finances are now the responsibility of both spouses. There's a reason for that: Saving money to invest requires the commitment of both people. Still, we're all busy, and if one partner is more experienced in the financial arena than the other, the temptation is usually to let him or her handle the money. It saves time, right? Why should two do the work of one?

Wrong. This is an area of your life where both of you have to take responsibility. If you're the one who knows more about investing, I strongly urge you to include your partner or spouse in your planning. If you're the one who knows less, do something about it, and take an active role in planning for your family's future. It's essential for you to understand the family financial picture in case of the untimely death of your spouse. Put bluntly, do all you can to "teach your wife to be a widow"—or, if you, as the wife, are in charge of the finances, "teach your husband to be a widower." Take the saying metaphorically: Don't let yourself, or anyone in your family, be indispensable in terms of understanding family finances.

If you're the reluctant partner, you may have to push yourself to become involved, but it will be well worth the effort. Ignoring the financial aspect of our lives is a big mistake. When you finally do address it, the task is usually easier to handle than you thought it would be. Gail Sheehy, author of *Passages* and *New Passages,* wrote about the fear many women experience about finances in an article titled "Why Women Fear They Will End Up Living in a Box Outside Bergdorf's" (reprinted from the November 1996 issue of *Money* by special permission; copyright © 1996 by Time, Inc.). A lot of women, Sheehy says, secretly fear that they will end up broke. For many, the nightmare is living in a box outside a department store. Such "bag-lady fears," Sheehy says, are prevalent, "particularly among professional women who are beyond economic dependence on a man." The phenomenon astonishes her, yet she hears such fears articulated frequently.

It is one she used to share. Only relatively recently did she herself face the financial responsibilities of her life head-on. The first time she earned more money than she needed to pay the bills, she felt paralyzed. She just didn't want to think about how to manage her financial resources. "Now you'll have to learn how to husband your money well," her accountant told her, and she soon found herself the recipient of all kinds of financial advice. An IRA and a couple of individual investments, she saw, wouldn't be enough. She continues:

It gradually dawned on me that I would have to practice what I preach in my recent book, *New Passages,* to people entering second adulthood: You must be willing to take risks if you're going to shape a new self. So I set out to shape a new "financial self"—not a defeatist bag lady, but an active steward of my own money and an educated partner in joint decisions with my husband.

It meant being willing to expose myself as dumb. I hired a financial advisor. I said to the advisor: "Explain it to me like I'm in kindergarten"—and he did. When he forced me to think about how much risk I could stand, I realized that here was a chance to catch up. I had to think long term, socking away a maximum amount of money to grow and compound in a highly diversified portfolio. And I had to ignore the market when it went down.

To my surprise, I found that investing for growth is exciting. It changes the way I think about myself. My bag-lady fears sometimes recur, but they don't control my actions anymore. The best way I know to counteract anxiety is to turn on the lights and face the bogeyman—or, in this case, bogey-lady. Educating myself about investing is the equivalent of turning on the lights.

Taking Care of the Basics

Before you even begin to invest, it's crucial to take care of the financial basics; that is, to do what's necessary to protect yourself and your family. These steps are as basic as it gets:

1. CREATE A FINANCIAL SAFETY NET

Create a financial safety net by setting aside enough money to cover several months' living expenses and put it in a place where you can access it quickly and easily in case of an emergency, such as illness or a period of unemployment. I suggest putting aside enough to cover your living expenses for at least two months, perhaps as much as six months. Setting aside only enough for two months is an admittedly aggressive approach, but it's my view that many people err on the side of being overly cautious and tie up more money than necessary. Regardless of the amount, keep these funds liquid—an investment that can easily be converted to cash. I suggest a money market mutual fund.

2. MAKE SURE YOU'RE ADEQUATELY INSURED

Insurance is a crucial part of any financial plan. If you have dependents, health and life insurance are essential. Life insurance is the best hedge against that ultimate family crisis, the death of the primary supporter or the primary childcare provider. In most cases, term insurance will satisfy your needs at a much lower cost, but there are times when whole life insurance may make sense. Either way, life insurance is something that every conscientious parent and spouse should consider.

3. CONTRIBUTE THE MAXIMUM AMOUNT TO AN IRA AND A 401(K) OR 403(B) PLAN

Regularly investing in a tax-deferred account is the best long-term investment you can make. The combination of compound growth and deferred taxation has incredible potential to increase your nest egg. I urge you to make this investment a priority in your life, and try to contribute the maximum. In 2004, the maximum IRA contribution allowed is $3,000 per year, plus $3,000 more in an IRA for a husband or wife who doesn't work. Investors age 50 or above can contribute $3,500. The maximum contribution to a 401(k) or 403(b) plan in 2004 is $13,000 for investors under age 50, and $16,000 for those age 50 or older. IRA contribution limits will increase to $5,000 ($6,000 if you are 50 or older) and 401(k)/403(b) to $15,000 ($20,000 if you are 50 or older) by 2008.

4. PAY YOURSELF FIRST

A great way to make investing a priority is by making it a habit, and an easy way to do that is by paying yourself first and signing up for an automatic investment plan (AIP). An AIP allows regular investments to be made through payroll deductions or through automatic transfers from your checking account. The amount you set aside is up to you, but I encourage you to invest as much as you can. Try to start with at least 5% to 10% of your gross (the total amount you earn before taxes), and increase that amount if you are able to comfortably. Use that money to invest for your future.

5. GET STARTED NOW

When you're talking about long-term investing, the real risk isn't the ups and downs in the market. Doing nothing is a far more serious risk, so whatever you do, get started now, whenever that is, wherever you are, whether you are saving for that first home, or investing for college for your kids, or planning for your retirement. The reason is an amazing thing called *compound growth,* a very compelling reason to start investing as soon as possible.

Compound growth has been called the eighth wonder of the world. Why? Because money that is compounding grows remarkably fast. Think of it this way: The money you invest grows; then the combined amount of both the original investment and its new value grows again. It's like that amoeba, growing faster and faster. Your investment grows geometrically rather than arithmetically. With compounding, investments that are allowed to grow over time can increase in value surprisingly fast.

The chart "The Value of Your Investment" on page 50 illustrates how the rate of return on an investment affects compounding. For five different rates of return, it shows how much a $10,000 investment would be worth at various points in the future, before taxes, if earnings are reinvested. For example, $10,000 invested for 20 years at an 8% rate of return would grow to over $45,000. The same $10,000 invested at 12% would grow to over $96,000 in 20 years. *That's* the power of compounding—and the power of the American stock market.

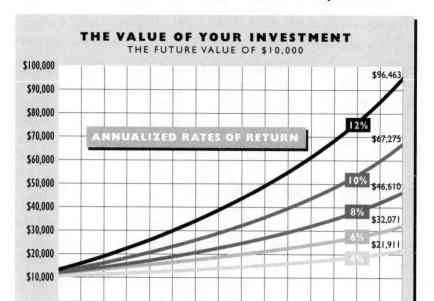

THE VALUE OF YOUR INVESTMENT
THE FUTURE VALUE OF $10,000

ANNUALIZED RATES OF RETURN

12% — $96,463

10% — $67,275

8% — $46,610

6% — $32,071

4% — $21,911

Number of Years Invested

Note: This chart is intended for hypothetical illustration only, and not to project the future performance of any investments. No adjustments have been made for income taxes.

THE RULE OF 72

The rule of 72 comes in handy when you're talking about time and money. This simple formula gives you an approximate idea of how long it will take to double your money at different rates of return. For example, suppose you want to know how long it will take to double your investment at 8%. Simply divide the number 72 by your rate of return. At an 8% rate of return, doubling your money will take 9 years (72 ÷ 8 = 9). At a 10% rate of return, it will take 7.2 years to double your money (72 ÷ 10 = 7.2). And at a 12% rate of return, it will take 6 years (72 ÷ 12 = 6).

GETTING AS FAR AWAY FROM ZERO AS I COULD

When I was 24, I didn't have much money, and that felt like being pretty close to zero. I didn't know everything, but I knew I wanted to get as far away from zero as I could, because I figured that the farther away from zero you were, the better you could handle loss. Say you have $5,000 and you invest the whole thing in the market. Then you lose 50% of it. Well, you're down to $2,500—not much. But if you have $100,000 and you lose half, that's a big loss. But you still have $50,000; you're still doing okay; you can handle a 50% drop because you're so far away from zero.

When you're young, you're usually pretty close to zero—and I wanted to not just put some distance between me and that zero but to do it fast. So I invested pretty aggressively. I looked for high-quality, high-growth stocks because I figured that with them I could get farther down the road—and faster—than by just investing in some laggard utility. Today I'd encourage people on the younger side of things to consider doing the same. What's young? Twenty-five is young. Thirty-five is still young, and I'd even call 45 young. Those are the years to invest for growth and put as many miles as you can between you and zip. You'll be glad you did.

Understanding Your Investing Personality: The Investor Profile

When you make a purchase such as a house or car, your personality plays a huge role in that decision: You look for something that fits you in terms of taste and needs and where you are in life. The same is true for investing: Your personality plays a role in the kind of investing plan you develop. To ignore who you are as an investor is a big mistake. So let's start with looking at two very important parts of your investing personality: your time frame and your attitude toward risk.

IT'S ALL ABOUT TIME: LOOKING AT YOUR INVESTING GOALS

When you buy that house or car, time plays a role, right? If you're planning on remaining in a house for only a few years, that influences which houses you look at. Same with a car. If you think you're going to sell it before it reaches 40,000 miles or so, that narrows your search.

Time is an important factor in investing, too: How much time you have to invest your money before you'll need it is a big factor in choosing investments. Money you'll need two years from now should be invested differently from money you'll need in 20 years. For some investments, such as stocks, your risk decreases as your time frame expands, so the longer your time frame, the more risk you can take. For example, if your child is 17, and you'll need the money for college tuition, you don't want that money invested in stocks because if there's a downturn in the market, you won't have time to make up for any losses. If your child is 7, that's a different matter; investing the money in stocks will give you more potential growth, thanks to compounding, with less downside risk because of your longer time frame.

Before you can develop an investing plan, you need a sort of investing timeline—an idea of when you'll need to withdraw money from your portfolio. To determine your investing timeline, you start by looking at how you imagine your future. Do you want to help your kids through college? How about work? Are you nearing retirement or still in the middle of things? What do you dream of? Owning a home? A vacation getaway? Traveling around the world? Maybe you just want to have enough money to keep doing what you're doing and preserve your current lifestyle.

For any of those goals, begin to think about how much time you have to make them real. You can start by looking at your financial responsibilities. For many of us, owning a home is one of the first things on our list. The next big item is often our children's futures, a concern that takes considerable planning. (Chapter 10 discusses the effects of a family on investing.) And then, well before our own retirement, our parents retire. We may feel personal responsibility for their care, and stepping up to that can involve a great deal of money. Having been there, I have to say that it's a big responsibility.

Finally, and most important, there's your own retirement. Even if you're fortunate enough to be in love with your work and you plan on working forever, you still need to have something put aside so that you can slow down if you want to—or if you have to.

■ ■ ■

A lot of people try to address these responsibilities sequentially, but they can get into trouble that way. Here's what happens: They think, "Well, it's the house first, that's what I'm saving for," so they save for the house and then finally buy it. Then they save for college for the kids, and when it's over, they cross that one off the list. When their parents start needing their help, they squirrel away enough for them. Finally, after they've paid for the house, the kids, and the parents, they figure they'd better start saving for their retirement. They could easily be 50 by this time, and they figure they've got plenty of time—another 20 years to save. Right?

Wrong. Addressing financial responsibilities sequentially simply doesn't work. The easier way, and it's a way that works, is to think of your responsibilities as a continuum. It's not a question of choosing the kids' education over your own retirement. These are both things you want to provide for. You don't have to figure out which one to save for first, and often you can't. You won't always know the *when*—when you'll retire, when your parents might need your help—but you do know a few of the *what*'s, and you can plan to meet those responsibilities as they arise.

Once you've planned for your responsibilities, you can think about the frills you want—the extras that you dream about before you fall asleep. Maybe you long for a boat. Maybe you want to travel. Or maybe you've always wanted a vacation home. It's possible and desirable to start saving for those as well by putting aside a little at a time.

So before you move on, think about time: When will you first need to withdraw money from your investments?

THE RISK FACTOR

The other half of your investing personality deals with risk: How comfortable are you with risk? It's an important question because your attitude toward risk—how you approach uncertainty—is one of the biggest issues you'll face as an investor. We call this "risk tolerance," and it varies widely from person to person.

In our everyday lives we make decisions all the time based on our tolerance for risk. You may be willing to ski and risk breaking a leg, for example, but you may not be willing to hang-glide because the possibility of injury is greater. Or you may be willing to fly in a small plane, but you wouldn't consider skydiving. Where investing is concerned, your risk tolerance means how much of a downturn in the market you can handle without bailing out. How much would your portfolio have to drop in value before you'd sell it all? That's how much risk you can tolerate.

Every investment is associated with a certain amount of risk. There are the possibilities of rising costs, a downturn in the economy, or a sudden upswing in interest rates. You have no way of controlling these kinds of factors. What you can control, to some extent, is the level of risk in the investments you choose.

Maybe you're pretty comfortable with risk; you're willing to risk a little more if there's a chance of greater reward. But maybe you're at the other end of the scale. You're the kind of person who gets nervous about almost any kind of risk. If you're going to lose sleep and be miserable every time the market drops 100 points, you have to take that fact into consideration in your investment planning. In other words, you have to know yourself. Once you know what kind of investor you are, you'll have a clearer idea of what types of investments to choose.

THE ELEMENT OF FEAR

When we talk about risk, it's important to say a word about fear. For many people, fear is an important emotion in investing—they often bring up their fears almost as soon as you mention the word. The idea of losing what we worked so hard for is naturally anxiety pro-voking. But a little fear goes a long way, and if fear goes unchecked, it can really work against you and even become a self-fulfilling prophecy. You lose money because inflation eats it up because you were afraid of losing money if you invested.

Where risk is concerned, it's important to sort out fact from fic-tion. Many people automatically associate investing in the stock market with unacceptable risk, but the fact is that because of the wonder of growth, investing in the stock market is the best way I know to achieve your long-term goals. So if the very idea of invest-ing in stocks sends you into a panic, I encourage you to examine those feelings and see if they're not based on fiction more than fact.

It's certainly true that many people have taken a chance on the market and lost. Maybe they jumped on the high-tech bandwagon of the late 1990s, or maybe they followed a hot tip they picked up at last weekend's cocktail party or tennis game, invested in their brother-in-law's company, or bought into a company they believed in with all their heart. Then they saw it fold, and now they figure once is enough. That fear can be even harder to overcome than the fear that results from inexperience.

But the constructive side of fear is caution, and a little caution is a good thing. Where finances are concerned, there are, of course, reasons for caution. I saw a lot of those reasons the sum-mer I was 19. This was in 1958, a recession year. That summer I drove an old Ford across the country to Chicago and applied for a job at a steel mill. There I found long lines of people who were being told there was no work. These people had no hope of any kind of a secure future. They simply didn't have enough money, not that day or that month, let alone a few years down the pike. A 35-year-old musician who had a wife and two kids worked as a railroad switchman—and I mean he worked really hard—with, as you can guess, almost nothing to show for it. For him, putting something away for the future wasn't a remote possibility. He didn't have much good waiting for him in his future. It shook me up, and I saw that there are no guarantees. You have to take responsibility for your future in terms of your financial security, I realized; no one is going to do it for you.

But you can't let fear stop you in your tracks. If you're not investing now, you're not alone, but start with $500 or $1,000—just something—and keep that fear in check. Be thoughtful, but don't be paralyzed. When you're paralyzed, you lose out, and *that's* something to fear.

THE ROLE OF CHANGE

As you develop an investing plan, it's important to remember that the decisions you make today aren't written in stone. Over time your plan will change in response to your changing needs. In other words, once you decide on a game plan for investing, hold that plan in an open palm and be ready to modify it as you change. That doesn't mean moving investments around every month or two; it means reevaluating your strategy perhaps once a year to see if it still suits your goals and your personality.

I encourage you to be open to change. Many people find that their attitudes toward risk and investing change dramatically with experience. If you find yourself interested in an investment that you wouldn't have even considered last year, don't panic—and don't throw the idea out the window. Chances are that the portfolio that took you comfortably from age 23 to age 43 won't be appropriate when you're 53 or 63 or 73. I've seen myself change a number of times as an investor. As with many endeavors, whether it's skiing or swimming or playing golf or investing, experience breeds confidence. And the more your confidence grows, the more fun you'll have and the better you'll do.

The Investor Profile Questionnaire

Once you've given some thought to your investing timeline and attitude toward risk, you're ready to fill out the "Investor Profile Questionnaire," which is designed to help you determine which mix of assets may best suit your needs right now. The questions address a number of important factors, but key among them are your life stage and your attitude about risk.

When you finish the questionnaire, you'll have two scores that you'll use to determine your investor profile. You may want to make a copy of these pages before you begin, for easier updating.

INVESTOR PROFILE QUESTIONNAIRE

1. I plan to begin withdrawing money from my investments for major needs within:

(Major needs may include retirement, child's college education, home purchase, etc.)

__ Less than 3 years	1 point
__ 3–5 years	3 points
__ 6–10 years	7 points
__ 11 years or more	10 points

Points _____

2. Once I begin withdrawing funds from my investments, I plan to spend all of the funds within:

__ Less than 2 years	0 points
__ 2–5 years	1 point
__ 6–10 years	4 points
__ 11 years or more	8 points

Points _____

Subtotal A

Add your total points from questions 1 and 2 and enter here: _____

If your score is less than 3, STOP HERE.

A score of less than 3 indicates a very short investment horizon. For such a short time horizon, a relatively low risk portfolio of 40% short-term (average maturity of 5 years or less) bonds (or bond funds) and 60% cash is recommended, as stock investments may be significantly more volatile in the short term.

If your score is greater than 3, please continue.

3. **I would describe my knowledge of investments as:**

    ___ None   0 points

    ___ Limited   2 points

    ___ Good   4 points

    ___ Extensive   6 points

                    Points _____

4. **When I decide how to invest my money, I am:**

    ___ Most concerned about the possibility of   0 points
    my investment losing value

    ___ Equally concerned about the possibility of   4 points
    my investment losing or gaining value

    ___ Most concerned about the possibility of   8 points
    my investment gaining value

                                Points _____

5. **Review the following list and select the investments you currently own or have owned in the past. Then choose the one with the highest number of points and enter that number.**

    ___ Money market funds or cash equivalents   0 points

    ___ Bonds and/or bond funds   3 points

    ___ Stocks and/or stock funds   6 points

    ___ International securities and/or   8 points
    international funds

    (***Example:*** *You now own stock funds and have in the past purchased international securities. Your point score would be 8.*)

                    (Maximum possible score = 8)

                                Points _____

6. **Consider this scenario:**

   Imagine that over the past three months, the overall stock market lost 25% of its value. An individual stock investment you own also lost 25% of its value. What would you do?

   I would:

   __ Sell all of my shares   0 points

   __ Sell some of my shares   2 points

   __ Do nothing   5 points

   __ Buy more shares   8 points

   Points _____

7. **Review the chart showing hypothetical investment plans.** We've outlined the average-, best-, and worst-case annual returns of five hypothetical investment plans. Which range of possible outcomes is most acceptable to you or best suits your investment philosophy?

   (The figures are hypothetical and do not represent the best performance of any particular investment.)

INVESTMENT PLANS	AVERAGE ANNUALIZED RETURN (1 YEAR)	BEST-CASE SCENARIO (1 YEAR)	WORST-CASE SCENARIO (1 YEAR)	POINTS
Investment Plan A	7.2%	16.3%	−5.6%	0 points
Investment Plan B	9.0%	25.0%	−12.1%	3 points
Investment Plan C	10.4%	33.6%	−18.2%	6 points
Investment Plan D	11.7%	42.8%	−24.0%	8 points
Investment Plan E	12.5%	50.0%	−28.2%	10 points

Points _____

Subtotal B

Add your total points for questions 3 through 7 and enter here: _____

Now you're ready to determine your personal investor profile.

STEP 1

Enter Subtotal A here: _____

This number represents your time horizon score.

Enter Subtotal B here: _____

This number represents your risk tolerance score.

STEP 2

Now plot your time horizon score and your risk tolerance score on "Your Personal Investor Profile" chart below and locate their intersection point. Then find the corresponding asset allocation plan that might work best for you.

Your Personal Investor Profile

Time Horizon Score

	3–4 points	5 points	7–9 points	10–12 points	14–18 points
0–10					
11					
12	CONSERVATIVE				
13					
14					
15					
16					
17		MODERATELY CONSERVATIVE			
18					
19					
20					
21					
22			MODERATE		
23					
24					
25					
26					
27					
28					
29					
30			MODERATELY AGGRESSIVE		
31					
32					
33					
34					
35					
36					
37					
38					
39			AGGRESSIVE		
40					

Risk Tolerance Score

Choosing an Asset Allocation Pie Chart

What proportion of your money will you invest in stocks? In bonds? How much do you want to keep in liquid investments? Now that you have a better idea of who you are as an investor, you can look at how you'll divide your investing dollars among types of investments. In other words, you'll decide what kind of asset allocation plan will best meet your needs.

An easy way to think of an asset allocation plan is as a pie chart, with each type of investment (stocks, bonds, and cash equivalents) making up a piece of the pie. On pages 63–64 you'll find five possible asset allocation pie charts, from aggressive to conservative.

THE ARGUMENT FOR BALANCE

As you evaluate your choices, I encourage you to make sure you're not overly cautious in the approach you choose. If you find yourself looking at the more conservative pie charts, take a moment to make sure it's a good fit. I say this because I worry about investors not meeting their goals for the simple reason that they haven't taken enough advantage of opportunities for growth. If you decide you simply can't handle a very aggressive approach, then start conservatively. Over time, investors change; you may surprise yourself eventually.

My belief in stock market growth over time is so strong that for most of your prime wage-earning years, I would frankly encourage you to invest primarily for growth—that is, to invest primarily in stocks over bonds and cash equivalents. (Note that that doesn't mean *instead* of them; as we've said, each of the asset classes plays a part in a well-diversified portfolio.) I encourage this approach because of both my strong confidence in the American economy and the historical performance of the stock market (and I say this even as we have just experienced the worst bear market since the Depression). In my opinion, only by investing in the stock market for a sustained period of time can you outpace inflation and allow your money to outlive you.

THE PIE CHARTS

Use your time horizon and risk tolerance scores from the "Investor Profile Questionnaire" to see which pie chart—or asset allocation plan—might best meet your needs. (But bear in mind that the investment plans shown here are only general guidelines, not rigid instructions. You should always feel free to fine-tune depending on your personal situation.)

One final note: Research suggests that the most advantageous balance between risk and return over time may fall somewhere in the moderate range. As the pie charts become more aggressive, the chance for a higher return certainly increases, but that increase in return is associated with an even larger increase in risk. At the other extreme, also note that even the most conservative plan includes some stocks. Why? Once again, it's the value of diversification. Introducing even 20% stocks into a portfolio that is otherwise comprised of bonds and cash equivalents will not only increase the potential return but also reduce the portfolio's volatility. (Also realize that the average annual returns listed here are for the time period 1970–2002. Although this will give you an idea of the type of returns you might achieve in the future, there is certainly no guarantee.)

Aggressive Plan

For long-term investors who want high growth and don't need current income. Substantial year-to-year volatility in value is acceptable in exchange for a potentially high long-term return.

Cash equivalents 5%

Stocks 95%

Bonds 0%

Average annual return (1970–2002): 10.4%   Best year: 36.3%   Worst year: –25.4%

Moderately Aggressive Plan

For long-term investors who want good growth and don't need current income. A fair amount of risk is acceptable, but not as much as if they invested exclusively in stocks.

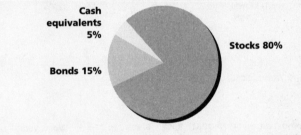

Cash equivalents 5%

Stocks 80%

Bonds 15%

Average annual return (1970–2002): 10.3%   Best year: 32.3%   Worst year: –20.4%

Moderate Plan

For long-term investors who don't need current income and want reasonable but relatively stable growth. Some fluctuations are tolerable, but they want less risk than the risk associated with the overall stock market.

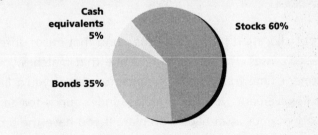

Cash equivalents 5%

Stocks 60%

Bonds 35%

Average annual return (1970–2002): 10.1%   Best year: 28.3%   Worst year: –13.9%

Moderately Conservative Plan

For investors who want current income and stability, with some increase in the value of their investments.

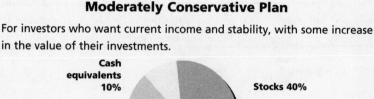

Cash equivalents 10%

Stocks 40%

Bonds 50%

Average annual return (1970–2002): 9.7%   Best year: 23.9%   Worst year: –7.2%

Conservative Plan

For investors who want current income and stability and aren't concerned about increasing the value of their investments.

Cash equivalents 30%

Stocks 20%

Bonds 50%

Average annual return (1970–2002): 8.7%   Best year: 21.9%   Worst year: –1.4%

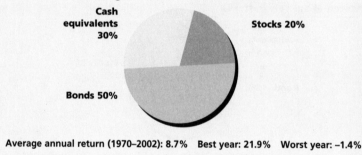

KEEPING IT SIMPLE: STARTING WITH ASSET ALLOCATION FUNDS

An asset allocation fund is a mutual fund that mixes different asset classes. The key is to find one that matches your investment time frame and tolerance for risk. If you'd like more involvement, you can purchase index funds for each category of your asset allocation plan. If you have the time for more involvement, you might purchase a combination of index funds and actively managed mutual funds. (Chapter 3 discusses this approach, which we call Core & Explore®, in greater detail.) And finally, if you have the time and energy to devote to research and ongoing management, you could add individual stocks to your portfolio. But whatever method you choose, remember that it's important for you to understand the basics, even if someone else handles the day-to-day decisions.

From Independent to Delegator: What's Your Investor Style?

We've talked a good deal in this chapter about knowing yourself as an investor—specifically, understanding your time horizon and your attitude toward risk. Another part of that is understanding what kind of investing style you're comfortable with. Some people take to investing like a fish to water, and really enjoy handling the whole thing themselves. They enjoy having complete control of this part of their lives, and wouldn't dream of handing things over to someone else. At the other end of the spectrum are those who try it and find out that it's just not their thing. They just don't have the time or interest. Not only are they comfortable delegating this responsibility; they prefer having someone else at the helm. Many others fall in the middle—they may want to consult with a professional about a portion of their assets, and manage other assets on their own.

Regardless of where you fit, it's very helpful to think about how you like to do things. Understanding that part of yourself will help you determine if and when you need professional help with your investments. While it's true that for most people managing their own investments usually isn't difficult or overly time-consuming, there are times when getting professional help is the wisest move you can make. In fact, most investors can benefit from professional help at some point in their investing lives. It's very normal. Understanding your investing style is a big factor in deciding whether or not professional help is right for you.

People's reasons for seeking investing advice vary. Maybe you've recently taken control of a retirement distribution or received an inheritance, or perhaps your situation is more complicated than most. Maybe you've tried it on your own and found yourself in over your head, especially during the recent bear market. Or maybe you just feel that you don't have time to handle the day-to-day details of managing your money. Or maybe it's just not your thing.

So what kind of an investor are you? You may not find yourself completely in one camp; it's often not that simple, and your feeling about wanting help can certainly change over time. But you may find that one tack may simply be more appropriate at a given time.

INVESTOR TYPES

Generally speaking, investors seem to fall into one of three categories. From those wanting the least help to those wanting the most, investors fall into categories as independents, validators, and delegators. Let's look at each of these individually:

Independents

These people like to have complete control of their portfolios and are comfortable making most of their investment decisions with little or no advice. They get advice only when they feel they need it. They can have as little as $10,000 invested or as much as several million dollars. Some follow a buy-and-hold strategy, but independents can also trade more frequently and be more aggressive. Either way, they like to do it themselves. They're comfortable making their own investment decisions, they have confidence in their ability to do so, and they have enough investing knowledge to do it well. Perhaps most important, they are not discouraged by the time and effort necessary to manage their own portfolios. In fact, they understand that research is part of successful investing, and they take advantage of online research and investment planning tools. They also like to trade and monitor their portfolios online.

Validators

These investors look for more support than the independents, typically in the form of a one-to-one relationship. They usually want advice on an ongoing basis, but they retain control of their portfolios and remain the chief decision makers. Validators may have portfolios valued at $100,000, $500,000, or more, and while they like being involved in the management of their portfolios, they also like some help. They have often managed things themselves in the past, but have reached the point where they want help because of the complexity of their situations, or because they've become more and more successful and therefore affluent. They like access to research and online tools to support them in making their decisions.

Delegators

These investors like the prospect of working with a professional to create a plan for the day-to-day management of their portfolios. An individual financial adviser is often a good match for this type of investor. Generally speaking, these investors usually have portfolios with values of at least $500,000. Not only do they want guidance, they want it in the form of a customized relationship, and they like someone else to make the day-to-day decisions. They are or have become delegators for a variety of reasons—for example, their portfolios have grown and there's more at stake; they're retired and don't want to spend the time managing their portfolios; or there are simply too many demands on their time. Many are successful in their careers and recognize that portfolio management is not their area of expertise.

Delegators are often as focused on preserving their wealth as on making sure their portfolios continue to grow. For many of them, the goal is simply to keep their assets intact for their heirs. Delegators vary in what they want from their advisers. Some want someone to handle everything; others like to take a more gradual, wait-and-see approach, allowing the advisers more control over time.

WHERE DO YOU FIT? THE "FINDING YOUR INVESTING PERSONALITY" QUESTIONNAIRE

Deciding where you fit in may be obvious—you may read the descriptions above and know right away where you stand. Or you may find yourself somewhere in the middle and have to settle on

FINDING YOUR INVESTING PERSONALITY

	A	B	C	D
Which statement best describes your investment goals?	☐ I have specific, written investment goals and clear strategies for achieving them.	☐ I have specific investment goals, but I need help developing strategies to achieve them.	☐ I'd like someone to listen to my situation and help define my goals.	☐ I care about financial success, but not about the specifics of achieving it.
How often do you spend time investing?	☐ More than once a week.	☐ Approximately once a week.	☐ Every six months.	☐ Once a year.
Which statement best describes your interest in investing?	☐ I enjoy keeping track of the market and my investments.	☐ I like to stay informed but don't always have the time.	☐ I rarely open statements and consider monitoring investments a necessary evil.	☐ I'm only interested in the end results.
Which statement best describes your comfort level with making investment decisions?	☐ I am comfortable making decisions without the advice of a professional.	☐ I'd welcome help with investment planning but feel comfortable making decisions on my own.	☐ Before I make a final investing decision, I want the advice of a professional.	☐ I'm more comfortable leaving the day-to-day decision-making to a professional.
How complex is your current financial situation?	☐ I do not feel that my situation is too complex to handle on my own.	☐ My situation is growing more complex, and I may seek advice in the future.	☐ My situation has grown complex, and I could use help to make sense of it all.	☐ My situation requires a professional's ongoing attention.

68

	A	B	C	D
When do you prefer to use a computer for investing?	All the time—in fact, I almost never use the phone.	For just about everything except placing trades.	Only when there's no other alternative.	Never.
Which is your preferred method of making investment decisions?	Do research on my own, and then take action.	Decide on a course of action, then consult with a professional.	Ask a professional for recommendations, then decide.	I feel most comfortable making investment decisions with a professional.
How would you describe your attitude about paying for advice?	I don't see the value in paying for advice—I know what I'm doing.	I'd pay for one-time advice such as financial planning or portfolio consultation.	I am willing to entertain the idea of a fee-based relationship but need to know more.	I'd gladly pay a reasonable fee to have a professional manage my investments for me.

If you answered mostly A and B, you may be:

An Independent Investor: You're probably comfortable making the majority of your decisions without much advice. And when you do need advice, you feel comfortable getting it on an as-needed basis. Independent investors may have as little as $10,000 invested, or as much as several million dollars.

If you answered mostly B and C, you may be:

A Validator: You may be looking for more support and a one-to-one relationship. Validators typically seek more ongoing advice and guidance for their ideas than independent investors, but prefer to stay involved and in control of their portfolios. Many validators have significant wealth to manage, typically upwards of $500,000.

If you answered mostly C and D, you may be:

A Delegator: You're probably comfortable with the idea of working with a professional to develop a strategy for the day-to-day management of your portfolio. The best type of relationship for you may be a dedicated financial adviser who provides full-time management and financial planning. Like validators, delegators typically have assets of more than $500,000.

Reprinted with permission of On Investing Magazine, Fall 2002. © Charles Schwab & Co., Inc.

one approach. Things may also be harder if you find that you're one type and your spouse is another.

To start, think about your personality and what you're comfortable with in other areas of your life. Do you typically like being in control? Are you sometimes comfortable having others handle things for you? Or do you often like to delegate and concern yourself with only the big picture? You may know right away which type you are, but if you don't, the "Investing Personality" questionnaire can help.

STAYING IN SYNC

Once you know what kind of investor you are, you're wise to take a few simple steps to make sure your personality and financial needs stay in sync with your investing style. What follows are some suggestions to help you do that:

Periodically Reevaluate Your Approach

Things change, in terms of both our financial situations and our personalities. And because those changes can't help but affect our financial approach, it's important, once a year or so, to take a look at whether your approach needs some fine-tuning.

Be Open to Change

What you're comfortable with may change, either because of what's happening in the market or because of where you are in life. For example, as your financial situation becomes more complex, you may find that you're more comfortable delegating than you used to be. The trick is to keep your approach in sync with your situation.

Do Your Homework

Finally, remember that even if you're a delegator through and through, it's still important to understand what you're delegating and to be conversant in investing. Don't stop learning just because someone else is handling the day-to-day details for you. You owe it to yourself to understand the basics.

Where to Get Help

If you think professional money management is a good fit for you, the next step is to find the financial adviser who suits your needs and fits your style. That person will help you analyze your current needs, your long-term objectives, and your attitude toward risk, and determine the best investment plan to meet them. Then he or she will go into action and handle your day-to-day business for you: making investment decisions, monitoring your account, and keeping you updated. And you can feel confident that your finances are being managed by someone who understands your investment goals.

Most investment managers base their fees on a percentage of the assets they manage. (Typical annual fees range from 1% to 2% of the assets under their management.) This *fee-based management* is designed to be in your best interest, because your manager is paid based on the service he or she provides, rather than on the basis of trading commissions charged to your account. This means he or she is making recommendations and decisions based on your needs. You'll find more information on finding and working with a financial adviser in Chapter 11.

You're on Your Way

Whether it's in our business lives or our personal lives, good beginnings are important, and that's just as crucial in investing. Taking the steps described in this chapter, and taking them seriously, will help you lay a solid foundation for your investing plan and for your investing life. There are no guarantees in the world of investing, but my decades in investing have taught me that time spent on a solid start is time well spent. And now that you know how to get started, you're that much closer to realizing your financial goals.

The Bottom Line on Getting Started

• *The first steps toward making the future you envision a reality are taking control of your financial life, understanding yourself as an investor, choosing an asset allocation plan, and knowing when to get help.*

• *Before you invest, it's crucial to take care of the financial basics: create a financial safety net, make sure you're adequately insured, contribute the maximum amount to an IRA and a 401(k) or 403(b) plan, pay yourself first, and get started now.*

• *Your personality plays an important role in the kind of investing plan you develop. The two most important aspects to look at are your time frame and your attitude toward risk.*

• *Every investment is associated with a certain amount of risk. You can't eliminate risk, but you can control the level of risk and the kinds of risk that you are willing to bear.*

• *The decisions you make today about your investing plan aren't written in stone. Over time, your plan will change in response to your changing needs.*

• *An asset allocation plan defines what proportion of your money you should invest in stocks, bonds, and other investments.*

• *My belief in stock market growth over time is so strong that for most of your prime wage-earning years, I would encourage you to invest primarily for growth—that is, to invest primarily in stocks over bonds and cash equivalents.*

• *While each of the asset classes plays a part in a well-diversified portfolio, in my experience, only by investing in the stock market for a sustained period of time can you outpace inflation and allow your money to outlive you.*

• *Research suggests that the most advantageous balance between risk and return over time may fall somewhere between the moderate and moderately aggressive plans.*

• *There are times when getting professional help is the wisest move you can make. Most investors can benefit from professional help at some point in their investing lives.*

• *Generally speaking, investors seem to fall into one of three categories. From the group using the least help to the most, those categories are independents, validators, and delegators.*

• *A financial adviser will help you analyze your current needs, your long-term objectives, and your attitude toward risk; determine the best investment plan to help you meet your goals; and then handle your day-to-day business for you.*

Part II

CHOOSING INVESTMENTS

Investing in Individual Stocks and Stock Mutual Funds: The Basics

By now you probably have a good idea of what percentage of your portfolio should consist of stocks. Next you can get more detailed and learn how to build that stock portion of your pie. We'll start with the basics of investing in stocks in this chapter; then in Chapter 4 we'll look in detail at choosing the best mix of stocks for your portfolio.

One Team or the Whole League? Individual Stocks and Mutual Funds

Suppose it's the start of the football season. Everybody knows that come January, only two of those 30 NFL teams will be playing in the Super Bowl, which will have only one winner. So maybe you try to pick the winner; the 49ers have a good shot at it, you say, or maybe the Chiefs, maybe Tampa Bay.

Investing in individual stocks, which means buying shares of stocks of one or more specific companies, is a little like trying to pick a winning team. You see a company that you think has potential, you track it for a while and do some research, and then maybe you invest in it. And maybe you'll be right and your investment will grow, and you'll find that you've picked a winner. That's a great feeling, and it can be rewarding, both psychologically and financially. But it's not guesswork, and it's not buying a lottery ticket. You have to bring experience and analysis, as well as quite a bit of time and hard work, to the vast world of individual stocks.

Trying to pick the winners is one way to invest in stocks. It can be rewarding, but it can also be tough to do. Fortunately, there's a second way—one that's like buying many teams or even the whole league, instead of picking just one team. When you invest in a mutual fund, with one investment you can buy a whole group of different stocks—shares of 100, 500, or even 1,000 companies. That's quite a proposition, and quite an opportunity. It's like acknowledging that you don't have to own the few top performers to be a successful investor.

Both propositions, picking a winner and buying several teams, are attractive. Best of all, you don't have to choose one method or the other. Buying individual stocks and stock mutual funds isn't an either/or proposition: Many investors will want to own both. As you'll see, they can each play an important role in a well-diversified portfolio. Let's take a closer look.

INDIVIDUAL STOCKS

When you buy stocks individually, you're buying shares of a company's stock, which means that you're essentially participating in company ownership. Whether you win or lose on your investment depends on the success or failure of that stock over time. The more successful the company, the better is the chance for a good return on your money. The less successful the company, the greater is your chance of a loss.

The idea of ownership is an important one. Suppose you own stock in Fun & Games, Inc. That means you're part owner of that company. When you go down to the Fun & Games store and buy toys for your kids, you can feel really great because you own a small piece of that company. You're even helping it grow by shopping there. Or maybe you visit it and you're not thrilled with the way things are being run. Well, you can do something about it. You can sell your stock if the trend continues.

Stocks of large, established corporations are usually less risky than stocks of young, smaller firms. There is no question that "proven" companies can suffer setbacks, but because large companies are widely analyzed and tracked (and there is a vast amount of information readily available on financial Web sites such as *schwab.com*), they are less likely to surprise you. However, because not as many analysts follow and report on small-cap stocks, it's a lot harder to find complete information on them. Therefore, small companies may have explosive growth potential, but they are much harder to evaluate. That is, in part, why investments in these stocks are usually considered higher risk.

MUTUAL FUNDS

The downside of buying individual stocks is that choosing them can be tough; there are many thousands of publicly traded companies out there, and picking a few good stocks can be tricky stuff, as anyone who watches the stock market knows. People spend their lives learning how to pick a solid stock, and not even they are always right. But with a mutual fund you don't have to pick stocks; by investing in one fund you can own shares in hundreds of companies. The mutual fund company makes that possible by pooling the money of many investors and buying shares in a variety of companies.

I'm a big fan of mutual funds. I've been involved with them for over 40 years, and my experience includes working for a fund in the 1960s, founding and managing a fund in the 1970s, creating Schwab's Mutual Fund Marketplace® in the mid-1980s, and launching Mutual Fund OneSource® and SchwabFunds® in the 1990s. At the start, only 500 funds existed. Today there are more than 9,000, and we've seen them emerge as possibly the single most important financial asset out there. In 2003, investment dollars in U.S. mutual funds totaled over $6 trillion.

To say that mutual funds are a great way to invest is to put it mildly. In my view, they're the investment of choice for many of us. One reason is that investing in mutual funds is easier than investing in individual stocks because a lot of the work has been done for you; because someone else is choosing the stocks to invest in, you don't have to do the research necessary for picking good stocks. And mutual funds give you a great level of diversification: With just one investment, you're buying shares in anywhere from 20 to 1,000 companies. If you choose a broad-based fund, meaning one that isn't too specialized but rather more representative of the larger market, you're not only getting quantity but your investment is spread across different industries as well— giving you another level of diversification and lessening the impact to your portfolio if one sector goes down. Buying each of those stocks individually would be costly and time-consuming, but a mutual fund lets you do it with one investment. All you have to do is choose the fund.

There are two very distinct kinds of mutual funds: actively managed funds and index funds. We'll discuss each in more detail later in Chapter 4, but briefly, if the fund is *actively managed,* an investing professional or a team of professionals chooses the stocks to buy and sell, based on the fund's objectives. *Index funds,* on the other hand, are passively managed, and are designed to track the returns of an underlying index such as the S&P 500 (an index of 500 of the most widely traded U.S. companies) or the Wilshire 5000 (just about the entire stock market). Although no index fund will exactly duplicate the results of the index it tracks, it will generally move in sync with it.

Once again, individual stocks, actively managed mutual funds, and index funds can each play an important role in a well-diversified portfolio. Including one doesn't preclude the others. The trick is figuring out the right mix for you.

Categories of Stocks and Stock Mutual Funds

When you set out to find that mix, you'll soon see that you have thousands of investments to choose from. So how do you decide what to buy?

Fortunately, stocks and stock mutual funds are categorized to help you narrow your search. Briefly, they're grouped according to four criteria, which are explained in detail below: domestic versus international, company size, investing style, and sector. Individual stocks are further grouped by industry. These categories help you to make sure you're adequately diversified. By choosing investments from each category, you'll know that you're spreading your investing dollars across many types of investments, rather than concentrating too heavily on one or two. You want that level of diversification because investments don't move in tandem. As the chart on the following page illustrates, in general one category of investments can go up while another goes down—and a category with the best performance one year can have the worst performance the next. If you're too heavily concentrated in the category that's going down, you're in trouble. Owning some of each helps manage the volatility of your overall portfolio.

Stocks and stock mutual funds are categorized according to the following criteria:

• **Domestic versus international**

Domestic stocks or funds include companies in the United States, while *international* stocks or funds include companies outside of the United States. International stock mutual funds are classified as *world* (or *global*) funds or *foreign* funds. World funds invest in securities issued throughout the world, including the United States, while foreign funds invest in markets outside of the United States.

• **Company size**

Domestic stocks and funds are grouped by *market capitalization,* which is the share price multiplied by the number of shares outstanding. *Large-cap* (for "large capitalization") stocks and funds include companies with market capitalizations in the top 5% of the largest 5,000 domestic companies, *mid-cap* (also called *medium-cap*) stocks and funds include companies with market capitalizations in the next 15%, and *small-cap* stocks and funds include companies with market capitalizations in the remaining 80%. Small-caps may have greater growth potential and higher possible returns, but they're also typically more volatile. Generally speaking, higher return potential involves higher risk.

• **Investing style**

Domestic stocks and funds are also grouped by investing style. *Growth* stocks and funds include companies that seek rapid growth

Asset Class Performance Varies from Year to Year

Highest Return ⟵⟶ **Lowest Return**

1993	1994	1995	1996	1997	1998	1999	2000	2001	2002
Intl 32.6	Intl 7.8	Large Value 38.3	Large Growth 23.1	Large Value 35.2	Large Growth 38.7	Small Growth 43.1	Small Value 22.8	Small Value 14.0	Bonds 12.9
Small Value 23.8	Cash 3.9	Large Cap 37.4	Large Cap 23.1	Large Cap 33.4	Large Cap 28.6	Large Growth 33.2	Bonds 12.6	Bonds 7.6	Cash 1.6
Small Cap 18.9	Large Growth 2.7	Large Growth 37.2	Large Value 21.6	Small Value 31.8	Intl 20.0	Intl 27.0	Large Value 7.0	Cash 3.8	Small Value -11.4
Large Value 18.1	Large Cap 1.3	Small Growth 31.0	Small Value 21.4	Large Growth 30.5	Large Value 15.6	Small Cap 21.3	Cash 5.9	Small Cap 2.5	Large Value -15.5
Small Growth 13.4	Small Value -1.5	Small Cap 28.4	Small Cap 16.5	Small Cap 22.4	Bonds 10.2	Large Cap 21.0	Small Cap -3.0	Large Value -5.6	Intl -15.9
Bonds 11.2	Small Cap -1.8	Small Value 25.8	Small Growth 11.3	Small Growth 12.9	Cash 4.9	Large Value 7.3	Large Cap -9.1	Small Growth -9.2	Small Cap -20.5
Large Cap 10.0	Large Value -2.0	Bonds 16.8	Intl 6.0	Bonds 8.4	Small Growth 1.2	Cash 4.7	Intl -14.2	Large Cap -11.9	Large Cap -22.1
Large Growth 2.9	Small Growth -2.4	Intl 11.2	Cash 5.2	Cash 5.3	Small Cap -2.5	Small Value -1.5	Large Growth -22.4	Large Growth -20.4	Large Growth -27.9
Cash 2.9	Bonds -5.1	Cash 5.6	Bonds 2.1	Intl 1.8	Small Value -6.5	Bonds -1.8	Small Growth -22.4	Intl -21.4	Small Growth -30.3

Source: Schwab Center for Investment Research with data from Ibbotson Associates, Inc. The indexes representing each asset class are the S&P 500 Index (large-cap); Russell 1000 Growth Index (large-cap growth); Russell 1000 Value Index (large-cap value); Russell 2000 Growth Index (small-cap growth); Russell 2000 Value Index (small-cap value); MSCI EAFE Net of Taxes (international stocks); Ibbotson Intermediate U.S. Government Bond Index (bonds); and 30-day Treasury bills (cash). Returns include reinvestment of all dividends and interest. Indexes are unmanaged, do not incur fees or expenses, and cannot be invested in directly. Past results are not indicative of future performance.

in earnings, sales, or return on equity. *Value* stocks and funds include companies whose assets are considered undervalued, or companies that have turnaround opportunities, with lower price-to-earnings ratios. For mutual funds, there's a third category: *Blend* funds generally include both growth and value stocks, or stocks that fall between the growth and value categories.

• *Sector and industry*

Finally, stocks and stock mutual funds are also grouped by sector and industry. The most commonly used classification system is the Standard & Poor's Global Industry Classification Standard (GICS), which categorizes companies around the world into ten sectors (energy, materials, industrials, consumer discretionary, consumer staples, health care, financials, information technology, telecommunication services, and utilities) and 59 industries (such as food and drug retailing, banks, building products, etc.) within these sectors.

A PENNY FOR YOUR STOCKS

Penny stocks are stocks that sell for five dollars or less. They sound like potential bargains, but there are drawbacks. First, when you buy penny stocks, you're seldom buying quality, something that's crucial in stocks. If you rank companies by quality, penny stocks will often be right down at the bottom. Second, penny stocks typically have very high potential for loss. In my experience, people usually get into penny stocks because they're acting on a hunch, and these stocks look like easy money—both bad reasons to invest. In short, it's so easy to buy quality stocks at incredibly efficient prices, why consider anything less? If you're really drawn to a penny stock, try a wait-and-see approach. If it's a fundamentally good company, let it prove itself a little before you jump in.

Building the Stock Portion of Your Portfolio with Core & Explore®

You now know the building blocks of the stock portion of your portfolio—individual stocks and stock mutual funds. How do you decide what and how much? The key factor is, once again, diversification. You need to own a wide range of companies, either by owning at least 20 to 40 individual stocks that represent all ten sectors and a wide range of industries, by owning shares of a mutual fund, or by combining the two. A good way to do this is by using an approach we call Core & Explore.®

Core & Explore is designed to help you choose the right mix of index funds, actively managed funds, and individual stocks. Developed by the Schwab Center for Investment Research, its goal is to minimize your risk of underperforming the market (with your Core holdings), while at the same time giving you the potential to beat it (with your Explore holdings). Viewed graphically, you can see the Core (at the center) and Explore (on the outside) in the following diagram:

Core & Explore®

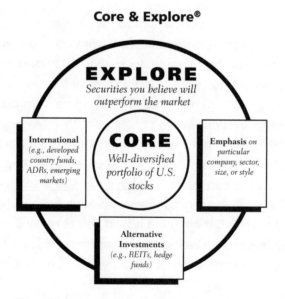

Source: Schwab Center for Investment Research.

The Core, or center, of Core & Explore is a well-diversified portfolio of U.S. stocks, representing 40% to 100% of your stock portfolio, depending on your time frame and risk tolerance. The more conservative you are, the higher percentage you'll use for your Core. (In fact, many investors find that Core holdings plus an international mutual fund are *all* they want to own for the equity portion of their portfolio.) Because you want your Core to be well diversified, one or more broad-based index funds or highly diversified active funds are a great choice for it. Individual stocks are fine, too, as long as they're well diversified across sectors, market capitalizations, and investing styles. You can also create your Core with a combination of funds and individual holdings.

The Explore portion, which makes up the balance of your stock portion, is more specialized, including investments such as international stocks, nontraditional asset classes such as REITs (real estate investment trusts) or hedge funds, or an emphasis on a specific company, sector, or style. Actively managed mutual funds and individual stocks (or a mix of the two) are good choices for Explore. Remember that in the Explore portion, you're trying to outperform the market and your Core holdings. Therefore, some of your Explore holdings might involve more risk than your Core investments. However, your overall goal is to create a well-diversified portfolio that works well as an integrated whole.

International Investing: A Whole New World

It's my feeling that international investing is a key part of asset allocation, and that all investors, regardless of what asset allocation model they're comfortable with (conservative or aggressive or somewhere in between), should own at least some international companies. Many American investors tend to shy away from international stocks, probably in part because they're less familiar with foreign companies and because it can be more difficult to analyze and purchase stocks. It's my belief that the benefits of including international stocks in your portfolio far outweigh the hurdles.

There are several strong reasons for international investing. First, it opens up a whole new world of opportunities. Our world is becoming more international and interdependent all the time, both in its thinking and in its business and trading; and international investing is no longer the exotic, only-for-the-pros endeavor it used to be. Despite the dominance of the U.S. market, if you include only domestic stocks in your portfolio you're bypassing nearly half of the world's stock market opportunities. Some of the largest and fastest-growing banks, auto manufacturers, and drug companies in the world are outside of the United States.

A second important reason for investing in foreign companies is diversification. You know how important diversification is in general; diversifying your investments across economies is simply diversification on another level, a global one, and it can reduce your portfolio's overall volatility *without* lowering your return; in fact, it may increase your return. This is because foreign economies don't necessarily mirror the U.S. economy, so when the U.S. market goes down, foreign markets can go up. It's often true—not always, but often enough—that the international market does well in years when the domestic market does not. Compared with a portfolio invested entirely in U.S. stocks, a portfolio composed of 75% U.S. stocks and 25% international stocks has historically produced slightly lower overall portfolio volatility (according to the Schwab Center for Investment Research, in a study of the 33-year period ending December 31, 2002).

WHERE DO YOU START?

While there are several ways to invest internationally, the vehicle that makes the most sense to me is international mutual funds, which offer the easiest way to diversify. You can also buy individual stocks (for the largest foreign companies you can buy ADRs, or American Depository Receipts, which are traded on the U.S. stock exchanges), but a mutual fund gives you professional management, which is more important than ever when you invest in foreign countries. If you have some in-depth knowledge about a particular security or a specific country or economy, you may be able to make sound choices about individual stocks. But if, like most of us, you aren't an expert in your own right, stick with mutual funds. It's hard enough to keep track of individual stocks in the United States. When those stocks are held in foreign countries, it gets even more complicated. And for the average investor, international bonds may not make sense because they're risky in terms of currency, as well as fluctuations in value.

In terms of overseas mutual funds, you have your choice of two kinds:

Foreign funds invest mainly in foreign companies; they do not normally hold stock in American companies. International funds often specialize by investing exclusively in companies in a specific region (such as Europe, the Pacific Rim, or Latin America) or a specific country (such as Japan), hoping to capitalize on the areas that will see the most growth. Other international funds invest only in the securities of emerging markets, or developing foreign countries.

World funds invest in both U.S. and non-U.S. companies, typically putting 20% to 50% of their money in American equities. That may not sound like much of a difference, but look closely. Say you want 20% of your asset allocation in foreign stocks. If you invest in a world fund without realizing that 50% of its holdings are in the United States and only 50% abroad, your foreign exposure will be far less than you wanted: 10% instead of 20%.

RISKY BUSINESS?

There are complications with foreign investing. One is the difficulty of obtaining reliable information; another is risk.

First, getting reliable information about potential foreign investments can be difficult because foreign countries don't require the kind of corporate disclosure to investors that U.S. companies are required to give. For the most part, in the financial literature of foreign companies, you'll find less of the information you need to make a judgment. Foreign taxes and regulations are another issue to consider. In short, the quantity and quality of information on specific investment policies and funds varies tremendously.

Second, your exposure to risk is greater when you deal with investments in foreign companies. In addition to the usual risks of investing, you have to consider political instability, illiquid markets, and currency risk. Currency risk is the potential for changes in currency exchange rates, which can decrease the value of your investments. If, for example, the U.S. dollar grows stronger relative to foreign currencies, the return for American investors in international stocks will be reduced. Conversely, if the dollar weakens relative to foreign currencies, the return to American investors will be enhanced. Some mutual funds do hedge their currency risk, but you'll need to consult the prospectus to make sure that's the case.

GUIDELINES

It's my feeling that despite the increase in risk, foreign investing is worthwhile. If you choose this path, keep the following points in mind:

• Invest about 20% to 30% of the equity portion of your portfolio in foreign mutual funds. If you're on the conservative side, you might start with 5% or 10%.

• Invest in a foreign (as opposed to a world) mutual fund.

• Invest in a fund that is well diversified, meaning one that isn't overly concentrated in any one economy, region, or country. If you examine performance tables when choosing a foreign fund, keep the information in perspective. For example, the performance of certain single-region or single-country funds may seem terrific. These very specialized funds invest in only one geographic area (say, the Pacific Rim) or in only one country (say, Japan or Singapore). But beginners beware: Funds restricted to a single region are riskier than diversified foreign funds because they're more volatile—and single-country funds are more volatile still. The reason is simple. If the region or country suffers a crisis or economic blow, many of its stocks are likely to suffer.

■ ■ ■

Those are the basics of individual stocks and stock mutual funds. Once you understand them, you can move on to the details and get more specific about which investments will be right for you and the best way to meet your goals.

The Bottom Line on the Basics of Investing in Stocks

• *There are two ways to invest in stocks: by investing in individual stocks, which means buying shares of stocks of one or more specific companies; and by investing in stock mutual funds, which allows you to invest in shares of 100, 500, or even 1,000 companies with one investment.*

• *You don't have to choose one method or the other; many investors will want to own both individual stocks and stock mutual funds. Each can play an important role in a well-diversified portfolio.*

• *When you buy stocks individually, you're buying shares of a company's stock, which means that you're essentially participating in company ownership. Whether you win or lose on your investment depends on the success or failure of that company over time.*

• *Stocks of established corporations are usually less risky than stocks of young, unproven firms.*

• *In my view, stock mutual funds are the investment of choice. They provide professional management and a great level of diversification.*

• *There are two kinds of mutual funds: actively managed funds, in which an investing professional or a team of professionals chooses the stocks to buy and sell; and index funds, which are passively managed and designed to track the returns of an underlying index such as the S&P 500.*

• *Stocks and stock mutual funds are grouped according to four criteria: domestic versus international, company size, investing style, and sector. Individual stocks are further grouped by industry.*

- *The key factor in deciding how many stocks and stock mutual funds to own is diversification. You need to own a wide range of companies, either by owning 20 to 40 individual stocks that represent all ten sectors and a wide range of industries, by owning shares of a mutual fund, or by combining the two.*
- *Core & Explore is a model that helps you choose the right mix of index funds, actively managed funds, and individual stocks. The Core is a well-diversified portfolio of U.S. stocks, representing 40% to 100% of your stock portfolio, while the Explore portion is more specialized, including riskier investments such as international stocks, alternative investments such as REITs or hedge funds, or an emphasis on a specific company, sector, or style.*
- *It's my belief that international investing is a key part of asset allocation, and that all investors, regardless of what asset allocation model they're comfortable with, should own at least some international companies.*
- *There are two kinds of overseas mutual funds. Foreign funds invest mainly in foreign companies; they do not normally hold stock in American companies. World funds invest in both U.S. and non-U.S. companies, typically putting 20% to 50% of their money in American equities.*
- *As a start, I suggest you consider investing 20% to 30% of the equity portion of your portfolio in foreign (as opposed to world) mutual funds that are well diversified. If you're on the conservative side, you might start with 5% or 10%.*

4

Investing in Individual Stocks and Stock Mutual Funds: The Details

Once you understand the basics of stocks and stock mutual funds, you can get more specific about choosing investments. As you look at each type of investment, start by narrowing your search and coming up with a list of potential investments. Then you can look at your potentials more carefully and do some research. Only then are you ready to invest. Remember that we're talking about your future here, so you don't want to just blithely choose whatever strikes your fancy. The time and energy you spend in researching your investments will pay off.

Choosing Individual Stocks

There are many approaches to choosing individual stocks. I start by first narrowing my search so that I have a list of potentials, then get more specific.

NARROWING YOUR SEARCH FOR STOCKS

To come up with a few potential stocks, I suggest that you do the following:

● *Pay attention.*

Simply paying attention to the world around you is a great way for beginning investors to get started. When I took my kids to Disneyland in 1963, I knew nothing about Disney as a company, but Disneyland was filled with more people than some towns I'd visited, and I didn't need a brokerage report to tell me what that meant. My kids talked me into trying McDonald's in 1968, and what caught my attention, more than the hamburger I ate, was the sign under the golden arches tallying the millions who'd been served. You don't have to be a wizard to figure what happens to stocks of companies that sell millions of their product. Toys 'R' Us was another one. The first time I walked in, the place was gaga with parents and kids, and clerks ringing sales as fast as they could run the registers.

Another way to discover good individual growth stocks is to observe how our culture's needs and tastes change, because change leads to new goods and services. For example, during the 1950s, the postwar boom unleashed a demand for housing, automobiles, and consumer goods. As a result, stocks of heavy industry, automakers, and manufacturers of consumer products performed well. In the 2000s, we can discern some clear trends. One is the rapid growth of the older population, which means that stocks of medical care services, nursing homes, and pharmaceutical companies could do well. This is also an age of heightened environmental awareness, so companies that clean up dump sites, restore ravaged ecologies, and engage in waste recycling may grow. Another area of opportunity is the newly democratized countries of Eastern Europe. These heavy centers of population lack many of the basic goods and services that we take for granted. High-tech, telecommunications, automotive, and other U.S. and multinational firms are moving fast to carve out a market share there.

You might spot a trend that's much more subtle. Maybe you see a way in which personal preferences are shifting, and then look for the issues that could cash in. One good place for trend-spotting is newspaper and magazine ads. By observing who's *selling* what, you're also observing who's *buying* what.

Also think about the economic environment. For example, now that we are in a period of very low inflation, companies that have "pricing power," or the ability to raise prices, are at an advantage. Therefore, companies whose products are perceived as higher quality than their competitors' (and therefore worth the extra price) would fall into this category. At the other extreme, companies that are extremely efficient—and therefore don't have to raise prices to remain profitable—may also have a leg up.

• *Watch for product stocks.*

You can also watch for "product stocks," or stocks of a company with a popular product or service, the sales of which drive revenues and stock price skyward. The product can be anything, even a service. Hundreds of stocks have been rocketed by a single product: personal computers, contact lenses, laparoscopes, cellular phones.

Product stocks are associated with technological advances, changing consumer tastes, and great marketing. But oddly enough, the same circumstances that encourage those stocks can also destroy them, and that's where you can run into problems. Product stocks have to sustain their magic to sustain their growth. If the product doesn't have legs, the stock's run will be short. Not only does the company have to keep the product going through refinements, improvements, and product-cycle extensions, but it is also always vulnerable to companies with new products that make the old ones obsolete.

• *Look at small companies.*

Finally, I like to watch the small companies, meaning firms with market capitalization (the number of shares outstanding multiplied by price per share) of less than approximately $1 billion. Sometimes small companies are defined as those with less than $200 million in sales. A big part of the appeal of a small and growing company is its higher potential for growth. Also, when a company has fewer shares, a relatively small increment of new revenue may add dramatically to its stock price and earnings per share (the total earnings for a period divided by the number of shares outstanding).

One place to spot promising small companies is *Fortune*'s annual issue highlighting America's 100 fastest-growing companies. Or you can subscribe to newsletters that follow small-company stocks. But with small companies, you have to be particular, and you have to be willing to tolerate giant price fluctuations. If investing in small companies appeals to you and suits your needs, you might also consider a small-cap mutual fund.

EVALUATING STOCKS WITH SCHWAB EQUITY RATINGS

Schwab has a tool that can greatly help your stock buying decisions. Called Schwab Equity Ratings (SER), it's an approach that rates over 3,000 of the largest U.S.-headquartered stocks, with letter grades ranging from A to F: A is approximately the top 10% of rated stocks, B the next 20%, C the next 40%, D the next 20%, and F is the bottom 10%. And while this system, like any other, isn't absolute, it can help you screen stocks from a list of candidates (for example, companies with above-average earnings growth or high dividend rates), or create an initial list of stocks for closer examination. To learn more about Schwab Equity Ratings, go to *www.schwab.com.*

GETTING MORE SPECIFIC

Once you've narrowed your search and found a few stocks you're interested in, you can get more specific. At this point, some people immediately feel pressured, as though this is a test and they have to come up with the right answers—and at the right time. Not so. Fortunately, because the overall long-term trend of the stock market has historically been up, weeding out the underperformers is more important than picking nothing but winners. Buying individual stocks is similar to making other important purchases, in that you're better off when you concentrate on quality and value. It's also similar in that you do some research before you buy. You don't just buy what looks good at the moment, whether that's a refrigerator or a car or a house—or a stock. In the case of stocks, the product you're looking at is the company—a company you believe in.

When you have a list of potential stocks, it's wise to follow them for a while and to consider the following factors, most of which are readily available on the Internet:

- *Get to know the company.*

If you're interested in a company, one of the first things to do is to find out as much as you can about it. (As a side note, there's a lot to be said for buying what you know; many investors wisely limit the individual stocks they invest in to industries that they're familiar with, and diversify in other areas with mutual funds.) Getting to know the company may sound obvious, but a lot of people either don't research at all or stop researching too early. Make sure this is a company you want to be part of; remember that when you buy stock, you're buying a portion of that company, albeit very small. Don't buy stock in a company you don't want to own, for any reason. As you learn about the company, learn about its stock as well. I look at factors such as how much of the company is owned by its management (in my opinion, the higher the percentage, the better, with 10% the minimum), and how the stock has performed relative to an index such as the Schwab 1000 or the S&P 500.

- *Look for quality: Earnings per share.*

My first criterion in looking at individual stocks is quality. Therefore, I look for a healthy, thriving company, meaning one that's doing well financially, with above-average earnings growth and reasonable debt. As we've said, a company is made to grow, so I always ask some questions: Is management quick and adaptable? Does the company create a product that more and more people will use? Is the product contemporary? Who's the competition? However, at the end of the day, all of these things need to show up in the numbers.

The quality of a stock can be measured in a number of ways, but probably the most popular is the company's earnings trend. A company's earnings are its net income or profit, often called its bottom line. Because company earnings are usually given in millions of dollars, it's handy to break that figure down to a smaller number, called earnings per share (EPS), which are the company's total earnings for a period divided by the number of shares outstanding. For example, a company with $50 million in earnings and 20 million shares outstanding would have earnings per share of $2.50.

That number has meaning only if you can compare it to earlier EPS numbers. A downturn in a year or a quarter due to special company problems or general economic change may be insignificant, but ideally you expect a company's EPS to increase over time. After all, you buy a stock today for a share in its future growth. In fact, when you look at long-term stock returns, it becomes clear that the companies with the strongest earnings growth also have the best long-term returns. In the short term, the stock market can be overly reactive and erratic, but in the long term, it's earnings that count.

Strong earnings momentum is likely to be shown by younger, growing companies. More established quality companies will make slight improvements over various quarters, but such a company is more likely to be branded as a company with "stable earnings." There's nothing wrong with stability.

As a young investor, I used to search for companies with accelerating earnings by circling earnings announcements in the *Wall Street Journal*. Today stocks are routinely ranked by comparing earnings to expectations and historical trends. The principle is the same: Buy stock in companies with accelerated earnings early, and continue to monitor their performance to see if the trend continues.

Stocks with improving earnings and accelerating prices are momentum stocks, and they're solid investments as long as earnings outpace price. William J. O'Neil popularized momentum investing through his newspaper, *Investor's Business Daily*. Its stock tables rank earnings per share growth, relative price strength, and other information for momentum investors.

• *Look for value: The P/E ratio.*

Buying stock at a good value is like buying anything else at a good price. Your overall return from a growth stock can improve significantly if you pay a price that's currently under historic levels for that stock.

It would be easy to think that the chief yardstick of a company's value is the price of its stock, but it's not. The price of the stock is more an indication of the public's current opinion of the company. On any given day, investors vote on a company, or they give it a performance appraisal, in a very tangible way: with their money. If they have faith in the company, they buy; if they don't, they sell.

The chief yardstick of a company's value is its price/earnings ratio (P/E). This ratio represents the relationship between the price of the stock and its earnings for the past year. To calculate it, you divide the current price by the earnings per share for that year. A $50 stock that earns $2 per share has a P/E of 25 (50 divided by 2). The P/E is also called the "multiple." At a 25 P/E, a company is selling at a multiple of 25 times its earnings.

When you look at stock listings (online or in the newspaper), you'll see a range of P/Es, some as low as 0.5 and others above 100. While there's no set rule on what's a good P/E, generally speaking, a lower P/E is a good sign because it often means that the price hasn't risen to reflect the company's earnings ability, so the stock may be undervalued and potentially a good buy. A high P/E, on the other hand, could be the result of either a runaway price or depressed earnings. Both are red flags, and should prompt you to understand the reasons for them. A high P/E can, however, also be a good sign, an indication that the market feels the company has high growth potential. This is particularly true of new companies, which typically pass through a development stage characterized by a high P/E. The company may have no earnings for years, and yet its stock may move higher as investors anticipate earnings. Then the company may enter the aggressive-growth stage, marked by strong year-to-year earnings gains. Earnings growth and P/E accelerate until the company exhausts its market or competition erodes market share.

Every successful company outlives its aggressive-growth stage. The company's earnings may continue to rise, but its P/E will decline as the market reevaluates an acceptable price for the company's future profits. Earnings growth also slows as the company grows; it's hard for larger companies to repeat big percentage earnings increases. A financially strong, mature company may become a blue chip stock, but it will sell at a lower P/E than companies likely to show accelerated growth.

• *Look at the big picture: Growth at a reasonable price.*

At the end of the day, a company's earnings growth and P/E are relative terms, and what matters most is finding the right combination of growth *and* value. The term *GARP* ("growth at a reasonable price") refers to the philosophy that neither growth nor value alone is sufficient—and that the best stocks will have both reasonable valuations and strong prospects for growth. Both an unproven high-flying growth stock and a low-priced laggard may seem attractive on one of these scales, but both also carry what I consider to be unacceptable risk.

• *Look at dividends.*

A dividend is an individual's share of any profits that a company distributes to its shareholders. Companies typically declare and pay dividends quarterly. Always look at a stock in terms of its total return: both growth (price per share) and income (dividends). The *dividend yield* is the annual dividend divided by the current price.

Historically, high-growth companies have paid either very low dividends or no dividends at all, reinvesting most of their profits back into the company for growth. In fact, in the past many investors shied away from dividend-paying stocks because dividends were taxed at the same rate as ordinary income. Now, however, that the tax rate on dividend income has been greatly reduced (see the sidebar on pages 99–100), dividends are no longer the exclusive domain of older, more established companies. In fact, it is my opinion that dividends are a great way for companies to reward both growth-oriented and income-oriented investors. Note, however, that the current legislation is scheduled to expire after 2008. Unless the law is extended, dividends will again be taxed at ordinary-income tax rates beginning in 2009.

And as always, be sure to keep the big picture in mind. When a stock's dividend yield gets very high—say, above 4% or 5% (the broad market average is about 1.5%)—ask yourself why. Perhaps the stock price is depressed (for a good reason), therefore giving the dividend yield a deceptive boost. In other words, you always have to evaluate companies not just on their ability to maintain and grow their dividend yield, but also on their overall health.

THE DIVIDEND TAX CUT: A BOON TO INVESTORS

As I prepared this manuscript in the summer of 2003, Congress had just passed exciting new tax legislation that I believe will go a long way toward helping all investors achieve their goals. Although I have long been a proponent of eliminating the dividend tax altogether, I believe that the new law, which among other things lowers the dividend tax rate from a maximum rate of 38.6% to 15% (and 5% for taxpayers in the 15% or 10% income bracket), is a huge step in the right direction.

Why was reducing this tax so important? In the short term, I have no doubt that this single move will promote a healthy rise in the stock market. In the long term, I am equally confident that it will help to restore investor confidence by allowing corporations to provide real value to their shareholders.

I say this because, at its most basic level, the dividend tax is unfair and skews corporate incentives away from the best interests of shareholders. The inequity stems from the fact that companies pay a corporate tax when they earn a profit, and then individuals are taxed again on that same money when they receive a dividend. As a result, companies have tended not to pay dividends at all, or to pay very low dividends, and to instead stockpile their cash.

By reducing this unfair double taxation, Congress is instead encouraging companies to reward their shareholders, providing them with real value. This, in turn, allows investors to focus on a company's financial fundamentals rather than on the rather capricious movements of the stock price.

There is an ancient proverb that says that if you give a man a fish, you feed him for a day, but if you teach a man to fish, he can feed himself for a lifetime. In my opinion, the dividend tax reduction effectively teaches a man to fish. It offers ordinary investors a better return on their investments, and it gives companies the right structure to attract investors, while growing their businesses and creating new jobs.

I applaud Congress for this significant step. I am confident that it will contribute to a long-overdue boost to the stock market, and to the economy.

• *Take your time.*

Finally, as you evaluate stocks, take your time. If a stock is fundamentally sound, you have plenty of time to buy it. The stock market is not a bargain basement, which means that just because a stock looks good this morning, you don't have to buy it this afternoon. If it's a good buy for the long term, you can wait a month or two, or even six, before investing in it. Be particularly wary of fads and trendy stocks. It's very easy for buyers to get excited over front-page news, and as buyers rush in, the prices of these stocks can leap far ahead of their earnings. Many of them eventually crash, so don't be in a hurry; finding quality and value can take time.

Choosing Mutual Funds

You know the advantages of buying stocks through a mutual fund: A lot of the work of choosing good stocks is done for you, so all you have to do is pick a good fund. But how do you do that?

Let's start by looking at the two types of funds: actively managed funds and index funds. (There are also mutual funds for bonds and cash-equivalent investments; we'll discuss these in Chapters 5 and 6.)

ACTIVELY MANAGED AND INDEX MUTUAL FUNDS

Actively managed mutual funds are those in which an investing professional or a team of professionals chooses the stocks to buy and sell, based on the fund's objectives. In choosing stocks to include in the fund, the fund manager (or group of managers) evaluates all of the characteristics of stocks mentioned earlier. The variety of actively managed funds is astounding; just about every sector of the economy and every type of investment strategy are represented. But that doesn't mean you have to consider all of them. Once again, you'll narrow your search and look at a small group of funds that meet your needs, then choose from that smaller group.

In contrast to actively managed funds, *index funds* are passively managed: They're engineered to track the returns of an underlying index, which is a group of stocks that together constitute a yardstick of market behavior. The fund moves in sync with its underlying index. Unlike actively managed funds, index funds don't try to outguess the market or pick only the top stocks. With an index fund, you don't play the odds; you play the averages, and you're not dependent on a manager's expertise. The objective of an index fund remains constant: to track the overall market returns, as measured by a specific index.

So why would you want to just track the market rather than try to beat it? Research tells us that to be a successful investor, you don't have to outperform the U.S. stock market. After reviewing the market's historical performance, you only have to track it. That's an important point, and one that a lot of investors miss. Far too many of them spend too much time and money trying to outperform the market.

Index funds have some advantages over actively managed funds. For example, while index funds don't try to outguess the market, actively managed funds do, and that's very hard to do, even if you spend every waking hour trying. If the manager has a good year, so does the fund, but the reverse is also true. In fact, in the ten-year period ending in 2002, only 23% of actively managed large-cap funds outperformed the market. Moreover, an actively managed fund can change managers at just about any time, and often you,

WHAT'S AN INDEX?

You probably already use indexes in other parts of your life, although you might not know it. We create them all the time to help ourselves compare different values. For example, let's say you are interested in buying a new Dodge Neon. If one of your main selection criteria is fuel economy, how do you know if the Neon performs well in that area? You compare its miles-per-gallon number to the average miles-per-gallon number of other mid-size passenger cars, such as the Ford Escort and the Honda Accord. After several comparisons, you know what is a good number, what is average, and what is below average. Notice that you don't compare the Neon's MPG to that of a Geo Metro or a Chevy Suburban. Those vehicles are in different classes and are irrelevant to your comparison. Thus, in this case, mid-size passenger cars make up your index.

Reprinted from *The Neatest Little Guide to Mutual Fund Investing* by Jason Kelly (Plume, 1997). Used with permission.

the investor, don't hear about the change for months afterward. This can be a problem because when managers change, the fund's style and performance can change as well.

Index funds also tend to keep their operating costs down, and they usually don't charge sales loads. They usually use a buy-and-hold strategy, which means they don't buy and sell the stocks on a frequent basis, and that means they keep their trading and research costs low. Index funds also keep their capital gains distributions low—which means they're tax-efficient, since capital gains are taxable. That's a big plus when you remember that taxes are the single largest drag on fund performance. Together, these factors help to raise your after-tax rate of return.

As you can see, I'm a big fan of index funds. It's my belief that investing in a broad-based index fund, which means one that includes a wide piece of the market rather than having a narrow focus, is one of the wisest and most efficient investments you can make. Remember, though, that index funds are long-term investments; you don't buy them for just a year or two. If you include index funds, you should do so as an ongoing part of your investment plan.

Also keep in mind that you'll want to include both index and actively managed funds in your portfolio, rather than only one type or the other. Remember the concept of Core & Explore? Index funds, which track the specific portion of the market represented by the fund's underlying index, are great Core holdings. Actively managed funds, on the other hand, especially those that pursue an eclectic style or invest in securities that benefit from active management (for example, international stocks and small-cap stocks), are great Explore holdings. The combination of the two gives you potentially higher returns than you'd have with index funds alone, and more protection from the risks of investing in actively managed funds alone.

HOW MANY OF EACH?

Like much of investing, deciding how many index funds and actively managed funds to include is a question of balance. As always, you need to diversify. But if you diversify too much—if, for example, you include ten funds from each category—your overall portfolio will resemble an index fund but at a much higher cost.

So what's the magic number? How many of each type of fund should you include?

For index funds, a good place to start is with one broad-based index fund that mirrors the entire stock market (for example, a fund based on the Wilshire 5000), as well as one large-cap, one small-cap, and one international index fund.

For actively managed funds, I suggest owning between three and eight. You want at least three in the interest of diversification, but

ANOTHER WAY TO INDEX: EXCHANGE TRADED FUNDS

Other indexing vehicles, first introduced in 1993 and rapidly gaining in popularity, are exchange traded funds, or ETFs. Like index funds, ETFs mirror certain indexes, such as the S&P 500 (among the best known ETFs are Spiders, with the ticker symbol SPY); the Dow Jones Industrial Average (or Diamonds, with the ticker symbol DIA); and the NASDAQ (or Cubes, because of its ticker symbol, QQQ).

Unlike an index fund, which can be bought only at the end-of-day price based on the fund's net asset value, exchange traded funds trade like stocks throughout the day on stock exchanges. Also, like stocks and unlike mutual funds, you'll have to pay a brokerage commission every time you buy or sell an ETF. Clearly this can be a significant drawback if you trade or invest new money frequently. However, ETFs carry other advantages, such as a low initial deposit (you can buy as little as one share of an ETF, although the commission may make that impractical), and they are designed to be even more tax-efficient than an index fund.

having more than eight can result in a sort of custom index fund, in which case you're better off with a real index fund. In addition, more than eight funds can lead to some fairly complicated tax considerations. Your choices might include a couple of growth funds, a couple of income funds, and a couple of international funds. Or you might include two large-caps, two small-caps, and two international.

NARROWING YOUR SEARCH FOR FUNDS

Scanning popular investment publications is a good way to become familiar with fund categories and to make a tentative shopping list of specific funds. But when you're just starting out, it's wise to be a little skeptical of these publications. By their nature, they tend to highlight the fund of the moment. Good performance generates publicity, publicity generates a sudden inflow of cash from investors, and lots of cash makes it that much more obvious when a stellar fund performs badly and goes into obscurity. I've seen too many investors buy into a fund at its high, only to find that the fund has already burned out. In fact, this is the reason, in 2002, *Morningstar* decided to change its rating system from only 4 broad asset classes to almost 50 categories. They believe that with the smaller categories, investors will have an easier time selecting the most appropriate, high-quality funds—and be less distracted by the hot streaks of the past.

The best source for current information on mutual funds is the Internet. It has the added advantage that you can easily sort the funds by various criteria. As a start to choosing the funds you'll invest in, consider the following as prerequisites for both actively managed and index funds:

1. Start with broad-based growth funds.

When you're starting out as an investor, look for funds that are specifically devoted to long-term capital growth without excessive risk. As you study the performance charts, remember that the funds with the best long-term records rarely appear among the top performers in any one short-term period. By the same token, the top performers in any one short-term period are rarely among those with the best long-term records. Don't try to excel by taking some exotic approach. Also, although sector funds, which invest solely in one industry, can be a great addition to the Explore portion of your portfolio, this is probably not the best way for a beginning investor to start.

For many investors, the funds available through large mutual fund families like American Century, Vanguard, and Schwab are good choices. These reputable investment firms offer an ample selection of funds and a customer service network that will make fund investing easier. Both selection and service are especially important if you intend to use switch privileges among the funds in the family. If you find yourself drawn to funds from several mutual fund companies, you can go through what's called a mutual fund supermarket. This is a sort of one-stop shopping for mutual funds, in which one brokerage firm makes available hundreds of funds from different fund families.

Finally, for index funds, I suggest those with a broad-based index, meaning one that includes a large portion of the market, rather than a narrow range. The Schwab 1000 Index® includes the 1,000 largest publicly traded U.S. companies as measured by market capitalization, representing around 90% of the market. That's pretty broad. The S&P 500 Index (Standard & Poor's Composite Index of 500 widely traded stocks) includes 500 companies, accounting for around 80% of the U.S. stock market value.

2. Consider only mutual funds with no-load and low fees.

A *load* is a commission or sales fee charged on the purchase or sale of mutual fund shares. A no-load fund is one in which you pay no such fees. With a load fund, on the other hand, you pay a sales charge when you buy shares (called a front-end load) or sell them (a back-end load). A low-load fund charges about 3%. A regular load is typically around 5% or 6%, but can go up to 8%. Whether the load is charged up front or on the back end, it's a significant chunk of your capital.

Most index funds are no-load; actively managed funds vary. In either case, I would suggest that you consider only no-load funds. It's easy to do: In mutual fund tables in the newspapers, the no-load funds have an "NL" in the offer price column. That means that the fund is bought and sold at the price listed in the NAV column (NAV stands for net asset value, which is the total value of the fund—less expenses—divided by the number of outstanding shares). All mutual funds are traded based on this value. A fund with an offer price that is identical to its NAV is either a no-load fund or a load fund carrying a contingent deferred sales charge. Some sector funds and emerging market funds that require a long-term investing horizon will demand a contingent deferred sales charge because they want to discourage investors from actively trading the fund. Often these charges decline for larger holding periods. Such funds are exceptions to my rule. If you're not sure if a particular fund is no-load or if there are other fees associated with it, ask your broker or consult the prospectus.

You should also look at the operating expense ratio, or OER, which is the ratio of the fund's annual operating expenses, management fees, and any 12b-1 fees relative to its average net assets. You should consider a fund's OER relative to the average OER for similar funds (see the chart below). For actively managed funds, I believe you should also rule out any fund whose OER tops 1.7. For index funds, the fees should reflect the diminished role that professional management plays in such funds. Somewhere around 0.7% of fund assets per year is the most you should expect to pay.

Average Annual OER

Investment Category OER

Domestic	
Small-Cap Growth	1.70
Small-Cap Value	1.50
Small-Cap Blend	1.56
Mid-Cap Growth	1.63
Mid-Cap Value	1.48
Mid-Cap Blend	1.44
Large-Cap Growth	1.58
Large-Cap Value	1.40
Large-Cap Blend	1.29
International	
Foreign Stock	1.73
World Stock	1.89

Source: *Morningstar*, Inc. (April 30, 2003).

A GREAT PLACE TO FIND NO-LOAD FUNDS: SCHWAB'S MUTUAL FUND SELECT LIST

One good way to begin your search for mutual funds is to refer to Schwab's Mutual Funds *Select List*™. Every quarter, the Schwab Center for Investment Research screens the thousands of funds available through Schwab's Mutual Fund Marketplace according to various performance, risk, and expense considerations, and then compiles the results into this handy list of no-load funds. Available both online at *www.schwab.com* and in print, the *Select List* is a convenient approach to finding funds from a wide variety of asset classes and categories. Whether you're looking for a stock fund, bond fund, or balanced fund, this can be a great place to start.

3. Read the fine print.

Once you spot a fund that you think might suit your purposes, contact the mutual fund company or your broker (online or by phone) and ask for the latest annual or quarterly report, which lists the investments the fund is holding and reviews the fund's performance during the past few years.

You'll also need to look at the fund's prospectus, which is a legal statement that lists the fund's goals, restrictions, advisers, and fees. Every mutual fund is required to publish a prospectus and to give investors a copy, free of charge. There are three key pieces of information you should look for: first, the detailed statement of the fund's investment policies, listed under "Key Features of the Fund," which tells you what investment objectives the fund is suited for; second, in the same section, an account of the kinds of transactions the fund may execute and the types of securities it can buy or sell; and third, a statement of the costs associated with buying the fund's shares and maintaining the investments, which are broken down by fee type under the heading "Summary of Expenses." The prospectus must also detail the fund's investment policies and it must say whether or not the fund has a sales load or charge.

Make sure you read both the annual report and the prospectus carefully before you invest; this is a time when it pays to read the fine print.

4. Examine the tax angles.

It's *extremely* important to be aware of the tax implications of mutual funds. Taxes can have a huge impact on mutual fund returns, particularly over the long term. An investment that's suitable for a tax-deferred account such as an IRA may not be as appropriate for a taxable account. When selecting mutual funds for a taxable account, it's crucial to consider the fund's potential after-tax returns. Two funds that have the same potential before-tax returns may not be equal when taxes are factored into the equation.

If your objective is to minimize taxes, the funds you select for your taxable account should have a way of minimizing capital gains and income distributions, through either low portfolio turnover or a tax-efficient investment strategy. The safest way to identify the tax efficiency of a fund is to check the investment philosophy or strategy defined in the fund's prospectus. If the fund has a strategy of attempting to minimize taxes, chances are that will be clearly stated.

See Chapter 8 for detailed information on how taxes affect your investments.

CHOOSING INDEX FUNDS

Once you've found a few broad-based funds that you're interested in, you're wise to do the following before investing:

1. Make sure that the index the fund is tied to is a good match for your investment goals.

Make sure you know what index the fund is tied to and what market the index covers. Most index fund investors want a fund that represents the general market, so they expect a fund's underlying index to represent "the market" or "broad stock market averages." But maybe you want to invest in a more specific group of stocks—for example, smaller companies with more aggressive growth potential.

A fund tied to the Wilshire 5000 wouldn't cover the right market for you, but a fund tied to the Russell 2000 might.

More indexes are being created all the time to address a larger variety of goals. For example, some blue chip indexes are based on stocks within the S&P 500 but not the whole 500. Other indexes track stocks with low price/earnings multiples, stocks of regional companies, or stocks of firms that purportedly operate with an elevated social conscience. The further a fund moves from a plain vanilla index, the more it resembles an actively managed mutual fund, and the greater will be its fees and the higher its risks.

2. Look at how closely the fund's performance correlates to its index.

If the fund is based on a broad-based index, the difference between the fund's returns and the index's performance shouldn't vary by more than the fund's expense ratio. An index fund based on the S&P 100 Index or the S&P 500 Index will probably own all 100 or 500 stocks in its portfolio. But funds based on the Wilshire 5000 might not own every stock in its index. Instead, it will create by computer a portfolio that tracks the intended index. There's nothing wrong with a synthetic index fund if it delivers what you pay for: results that track the behavior of the identified index. But a synthetic fund's performance should be 98+% correlated to its index.

THE MEASURING STICKS FOR INDEX FUNDS: STOCK INDEXES

An index fund is composed of a portfolio of stocks that attempts to mimic the performance of a specific index. An index can represent the whole market, or it can be a subset, such as utility stocks. The gains and losses of the index fund parallel the gains and losses of the index it's tied to (minus annual expenses). Most general market index funds are tied to one of the following indexes.

• The S&P 500 Index

The best-known index is Standard & Poor's Index of 500 Stocks—the S&P 500. It consists of 500 widely traded stocks chosen for market size, liquidity, and industry representation. It includes New York Stock Exchange (NYSE)–listed companies along with some NASDAQ-listed companies, and it accounts for about 80% of the market value of the U.S. stock market. An interesting aspect of the S&P 500 is that the companies are chosen by a committee, which uses subjective—as well as objective—measures to determine the index's composition. The purpose of the committee is to ensure that the index mirrors the performance of leading companies in leading industries.

• The Schwab 1000 Index

The Schwab 1000 Index includes common stock of the 1,000 largest publicly traded U.S. companies (excluding investment companies) as measured by market capitalization. It represents about 90% of the U.S. stock market's value. I believe that including those 500 additional companies gives the Schwab 1000 Index broader diversification than the S&P 500 since it better spans the market capitalization spectrum (large-cap, mid-cap, and small-cap). Including those additional companies means that the performance of the Schwab 1000 Index will vary slightly. Therefore, when small- and mid-cap stocks are doing well, the Schwab 1000 Index will generally outperform the S&P 500. Conversely, when small- and mid-cap stocks are underperforming, the Schwab 1000 Index will generally not do as well as the S&P 500.

• The Wilshire 5000® Equity Index

The Wilshire 5000 includes all U.S.-headquartered stocks (which in August of 2003 actually numbered just over 5,500) on the NYSE and AMEX, as well as over-the-counter stocks for which quotes are available. The Wilshire is a good proxy for the overall U.S. stock market. Many so-called total-market index funds use the Wilshire 5000 as their benchmark. If you subscribe to Schwab's Core & Explore philosophy for equity investing (see Chapter 3), the Wilshire 5000, the Schwab 1000, and the S&P 500 make good Core investments.

Other indexes focus on smaller companies, different markets, and foreign countries. For example:

• The NASDAQ 100® Index

The National Association of Securities Dealers (NASD) maintains indexes of stocks traded over-the-counter via its automated quotation system (NASDAQ). The NASDAQ 100 measures price changes in 100 of the largest NASDAQ-listed stocks, which can be domestic or international. It is important to note that the NASDAQ 100 Index is concentrated in technology stocks; as of August 2003, approximately 68% of the index was composed of technology or telecom stocks. Also, the top ten holdings make up a large portion (close to 50%) of this index; therefore, just a few stocks—or even one stock—can have a huge impact on this index.

• The Russell 2000® Index

The Russell 2000 Index is composed of the 2,000 smallest companies in the Russell 3000 Index. As such, it is a widely used measure of small-cap performance.

• The S&P Small-Cap 600® Index

The S&P Small-Cap 600 Index is another popular proxy for small-cap stocks. This index consists of 600 domestic stocks that make up approximately 3% of the U.S. stock market. Like the S&P 500, companies included are selected by committee rather than set rules.

• The Morgan Stanley Capital International MSCI® EAFE Index

The MSCI EAFE (Europe, Australasia, and Far East Index) is a market capitalization index that is designed to measure developed market equity performance, excluding the United States and Canada. As such, this index is typically used as a benchmark to measure international stock performance.

Note: All of the indexes mentioned above are market-value weighted indexes, meaning that companies with higher market values (shares outstanding multiplied by current market price) have a greater impact on the overall performance of the index than small-cap companies. Other types of indexes include price-weighted indexes, such as the DJIA, and equal-value weighted indexes (equal dollar value—they invest the same dollar amount in each stock) such as the Value Line Index. (And remember, an index is not an investment product available for purchase.)

CHOOSING ACTIVELY MANAGED FUNDS

Choosing an actively managed fund is like buying a new car. If you set out to find the right car by examining every car out there, the task could overwhelm you. Picture it: lot after lot of new cars, old cars, barely used cars. But when you're ready to buy a car, you don't consider every car available, new, used, foreign, American, sports car, sedan. You consider only the cars that fit certain criteria— criteria that are, for the most part, pretty obvious, at least to you— and that narrows the list of possibilities significantly.

So it is with actively managed funds. You already know to look for funds that are no-load broad-based capital appreciation funds. Now let's get more specific for actively managed funds. In addition to the considerations listed for both types of funds, keep these in mind:

1. Choose a fund with steady performance and a solid track record relative to its peer group.

You want a fund that has a good performance record, not only for this year but also for over the life of the fund. Consistent performance pays off in the long run. As you look at a fund's performance over time, make sure it holds steady during up and down markets. In the long run, those old plowhorses become thoroughbreds when they pull in a steady 10% or 12% instead of a volatile 35% one year and −7% the next. Look for the fund with a consistent record in good markets and bad.

Also, when you look at returns, make sure that you are comparing apples to apples. In other words, if you are evaluating a large-cap growth fund, make sure that you are comparing its performance to other like funds. As you saw in Chapter 3, different asset classes tend to perform very differently from each other. Comparing the record of a small-cap value fund to a large-cap growth fund would be meaningless.

Even though the media emphasize daily results, I pay attention to the previous three to five years because it seems to me that a cycle often lasts three years; there's usually been an up and a down market in that time. So by looking at three to five years of returns, you can see how the fund has performed in both kinds of markets. Of course, past performance is no guarantee of future results. (Note that performance records are less critical for index funds because we can calculate what that performance is for the last 100 years—it tracks whatever the index was designed to track.)

I believe there are good funds and bad funds generally, but even good funds have bad years. Bad funds are the ones that stay in the lowest quartile of performance rankings, meaning 75% of mutual funds do better, and they usually have high fees. Good funds fluctuate in the top two quartiles of performance rankings, taking only a rare dip below.

2. Don't buy a mutual fund in a regular account during the fourth quarter without doing some homework.

You may be hit with a distribution that you'll have to pay taxes on, even if you've owned the fund for only a few weeks or months. Mutual fund companies typically distribute any capital gains and dividends in December, and you pay taxes on those distributions even if you reinvest them, and even if you've owned the fund only for a short time. So find out what the fund's annual distribution date is (called the *ex-dividend date*) and hold off on investing until after that date. Note that this applies only to regular accounts. If you're buying the fund in a retirement account, any taxes will be deferred.

3. Avoid funds with a guru rather than a philosophy.

The smartest mutual fund investors, it seems to me, prefer funds ruled by a philosophy. Sometimes a market cycle doesn't reward the philosophy, but when the cycle returns, the philosophy will be rewarded because philosophies have staying power.

4. Avoid specialized, limited-purpose funds unless you specifically want and understand what they offer.

Highly focused funds are feast-or-famine performers, doing spectacularly when their restricted investment jurisdictions zoom and dismally when they don't.

A FEW RESEARCH BASICS

As you're evaluating specific stocks and mutual funds, investment research can be a great help. But not all research is created equal; don't act on it without considering the following.

Consider the Source

The first consideration is the source. All too often, those who call themselves researchers or analysts are really just salespeople—very good at selling, but not so great at providing solid research and advice that's free of conflict of interest. They may say that they have your best interest at heart, but meanwhile they're basing their recommendations on how much commission an investment provides, rather than on how well suited the investment is for your situation. Good research is objective, which means that the researcher's analysis, conclusions, and recommendations aren't influenced by personal factors. Independent sources are usually preferable to sources tied to the investment you're looking at.

Be Sure It's Good Research

In addition to being objective, good research is disciplined and unemotional. You want to be sure that your researcher hasn't fallen in love with the company he or she is researching, a not uncommon occurrence, since researchers and analysts spend a lot of time getting to know the companies they research. Some go overboard and lose their objectivity.

Remember the Big Picture

Remember that each investment in your portfolio is a piece of the puzzle. Don't lose sight of the big picture, and of how investments fit together. When you consider buying an investment, look not only at whether it's a good investment for you but also at how it will fit with your existing investments. The first question a piece of research should answer is: Is this a good investment? But the second question is equally important: Is this a good investment for me? Don't forget to look at potential investments in terms of the level of risk they entail.

■ ■ ■

When you start investing, you can feel overwhelmed. But don't worry; you'll get there. Remember that experience is a great teacher; the more experience you have, the better you get. As you gain experience, you'll learn to sense broad movements in the market. And you'll gain confidence. Remember that investing is a long-term affair. So be ready to learn from both your successes and mistakes, and you'll be better off in the long run.

The Bottom Line on the Details of Investing in Stocks

- *Because the overall long-term trend of the stock market has historically been up, it's more important to rule out the underperforming stocks than it is to pick only the winners. Concentrate on quality and value.*
- *Get to know a company and make sure you want to be part of it. Learn how much of the company is owned by its management, and how the stock has performed relative to an index such as the Schwab 1000 or the S&P 500.*
- *When considering stocks, look for growth, meaning a healthy, thriving company that's doing well financially, with consistent earnings (EPS) and reasonable debt.*
- *Look at value by looking at the company's P/E (price/earnings) ratio.*

• *Look at GARP (growth at a reasonable price) to find stocks that have both growth potential and intrinsic value.*

• *Always look at a stock in terms of its total return: both growth (price per share) and income (dividends). Although a healthy dividend yield can be a great source of income, don't let it blind you to the stock's potential problems.*

• *Actively managed mutual funds are those in which an investing professional or a team of professionals chooses the stocks to buy and sell, based on the fund's objectives. In choosing stocks to include in the fund, the management attempts to outperform the market.*

• *Index funds are passively managed: They are engineered to track the returns of an underlying index, which is a group of stocks that are considered yardsticks of market behavior. The fund moves in sync with its underlying index.*

• *Investing in a broad-based index fund can be one of the wisest and most efficient investments you can make. These are long-term investments that should be included as an ongoing part of your investment plan.*

• *Including both index and actively managed funds in your portfolio, rather than only one or the other, gives you potentially higher returns than you'd have with index funds alone, and more protection from the risks of investing in actively managed funds alone.*

• *As a start, you might invest in one large-cap, one small-cap, and one international index fund. You can then add additional actively managed funds, making sure you have both growth and value stocks represented.*

• *For any fund you're interested in, look at its most recent quarterly or annual report, and its prospectus. In the prospectus, look at the fund's investment policies, the kinds of transactions the fund can execute and the types of securities it can buy and sell, and the statement of the risks and costs associated with buying the fund's shares and maintaining the investments.*

• *It is extremely important to be aware of the tax implications of mutual funds. An investment that's suitable for a tax-deferred account such as an IRA may not be as appropriate for a taxable account.*

5

Choosing Bonds

Growth is what gives your portfolio steam and helps your money to outlive you. But growth is only part of the equation. As many investors have learned in the last few years, you also need to know how to handle the volatility associated with the stock market. One of the best ways to do that is to include bonds in your portfolio. Yes, you absolutely want to invest for growth, but you need to do so in a balanced way.

So even though bonds haven't provided the same historical long-term returns as stocks, they're still a valuable part of most portfolios, particularly as you age and near retirement. First, they provide diversification: By including bonds as well as stocks, you diversify across asset classes, thereby minimizing risk. This is because stocks and bonds often do well at different times, so by owning both asset classes you're somewhat buffered from downturns. In fact, research has shown that by adding bonds to an all-equities portfolio, you decrease your risk more than you reduce your anticipated return. This means a chance for better long-term results.

Safety of principal is another reason for investing in bonds. The likelihood of getting your money back at maturity can be a key consideration, especially as you near retirement, or when you know you'll need the money you're investing for a specific purpose at a specific time (especially if that happens to be relatively soon—for example, for college tuition). Bonds can also provide dependable income in the form of interest, another feature that makes them increasingly attractive as you approach retirement. Finally, some bonds offer tax advantages, making them attractive to investors in higher tax brackets.

All of that said, a word to the wise: The world of bonds is complex and not a do-it-yourself situation for many investors. It can be confusing, and you very definitely have to know what you're doing. The bond market is huge, much larger than the U.S. stock market, with several million fixed-income issues traded, and a market value of over $20.5 trillion. For all of those reasons, most investors will want professional advice when it comes to bonds. Your portfolio will probably benefit from the balance that comes from including bonds, but be prudent about how you go about it.

A Word of Caution for the Overly Cautious

The points discussed above are all valid and important reasons for including bonds in your portfolio. That said, I think it's important to talk about the mistake of going overboard on bonds. A lot of investors are drawn to bonds because they perceive them to be without risk. But it's my belief that some people operate with an unwarranted or exaggerated sense of caution about the stock market—along with a lack of understanding about the risks inherent in bonds. I say this despite the recent bear market, which I know has had a profound effect on people, just as the Depression did a few generations ago.

Remember: Every type of investment, including bonds, is exposed to some kind of risk; the question is what kind and how much. First, bonds carry varying degrees of *credit* risk (also known as *default* risk), or the chance that the issuer won't make its scheduled payments. Your money is just about as safe as it can get when you invest in Treasury bonds, but as soon as you buy a bond with a higher yield—for example, a corporate bond or an uninsured municipal bond—you also assume more risk. In addition, all bonds decline in value as interest rates rise (and this effect is most pronounced for long-term bonds). So if you sell a bond prior to maturity, you stand to lose money. And finally, even though bond yields generally will compensate you for expected inflation, if inflation rises unexpectedly, your yield may not keep up. The actual amount of money returned to you is the same, but in practical terms it has shrunk; it just doesn't have as much purchasing power as it did several years ago.

TRADE, OR BUY-AND-HOLD?

When you buy a bond, the issuer promises to repay your money at a specific date called the maturity date. But what if you need the money before that date? Can you get it back, or is buy-and-hold your only choice?

You can get the money back by selling the bond, which you do through a secondary market, but there are trade-offs. First, if you hold the bond until maturity, you're usually assured that you'll get your principal back. If you sell the bond before maturity, you do so at the bond's current market value, which may be higher or lower than what you paid for it. That's because bond prices are affected by current interest rates; when interest rates go down, bond prices go up, and vice versa.

So while you certainly can sell a bond before maturity, don't do it on impulse, and be wary about planning to do so in advance. Predicting what interest rates will do—and therefore bond prices—isn't a whole lot easier than predicting the weather.

The bottom line, then, is that bonds play a valuable role in a solid portfolio. Like anything in investing, just don't overdo it. Include them in moderation, and not out of fear. And remember that for your money to outlive you, you need growth. The task isn't choosing one investment over another; it's finding the right mix.

Narrowing Your Search

Bonds are similar to IOUs: Someone borrows your money (the money you invest) for a specific length of time, and in return they pay you interest for the use of your money. The bond states that you have loaned money to the borrower and that the borrower will repay you the full face amount (the amount borrowed) on a certain date, called the maturity date, at a certain rate of interest (the coupon rate), which is usually paid twice a year. The interest payments from the bond give you a steady stream of income, which is one of the main attractions of bonds. The interest rate is usually fixed when the investment is issued, and it stays the same until maturity. The borrower promises to repay you even if the market value of the bond fluctuates over time. The period of the loan can range from 1 to 30 years. The borrower, or issuer, can be the federal government, a state or local government, a corporation, or a bank. In each case, the issuer is borrowing money as a way to raise money.

People who follow bonds keep an eye on interest rates by watching the yield on the ten-year Treasury note, which tends to be fairly representative of the bond market, similar to the way the Dow or the NASDAQ is for the stock market. Institutional investors make up the majority of bond investors; these include insurance companies, mutual funds, pension funds, banks, corporations, and state and local governments.

Bonds are differentiated by who's borrowing the money: the federal government, a state or local government, or a corporation, which can also include a bank or savings and loan. Generally speaking, the attraction of government bonds is safety of principal. Bonds issued by a state or local government are called municipal bonds, or "munis," and their attraction is tax-free interest. The attraction of corporate bonds is higher yields; however, they also carry a higher risk of default.

Evaluating Bonds

To evaluate bonds, I start by categorizing them according to the risk they carry: those with minimal risk, those with a small amount of risk, and those with a greater level of risk than I'm comfortable with. All bonds are subject to interest-rate risk, or the chance that their value will decline when interest rates rise. In general, this risk tends to increase with time, so a bond with a 20-year maturity is considerably riskier than a bond that will mature in 3 years. To me, a maturity of two years or less is relatively risk-free; a maturity of two to five years has some risk, but it's acceptable. A bond with a maturity of more than ten years has more risk than I'm comfortable with.

The other aspect of risk concerns credit risk, or the chance that issuers may not be able to fully repay their obligations. In this regard, I view U.S. Treasury notes and insured muni bonds as having minimal risk, investment-grade corporate bonds as having a small amount of risk, and other bonds as having more risk than I'm comfortable with.

Based on these two criteria—risk and time—the bonds I prefer are five-year Treasury notes (which give you the advantages of bonds without the risk that long-term bonds entail), tax-exempt municipal bonds for investors in higher tax brackets, and zero-coupon bonds for investors who want to fund a specific future expense.

U.S. TREASURIES

Let's start with the minimal risk category, U.S. Treasuries. These are debt obligations issued by the U.S. government through the Department of the Treasury. They're backed by the full faith and credit of the U.S. government, which is why they're considered virtually free of the risk of default; in other words, your money is virtually safe. Treasuries also have tax advantages: The interest they pay is exempt from state and local taxes.

There are three kinds of Treasuries: Treasury bills, or T-bills, which are short-term, highly liquid investments with maturities of three months to a year; Treasury notes, which have maturities of 1 to 10 years; and Treasury bonds, which have maturities of 10 to 30 years. (Even though the Treasury stopped issuing new 30-year Treasuries in 2001, there are still a lot of them out there, and will be for quite some time.) T-bills are sold at a discount; your interest is the difference between your purchase price and the amount you receive at maturity (or when you sell the bond). Treasury notes and bonds pay a fixed rate of interest twice a year and return their face value at maturity. The minimum investment for each type of Treasury is $1,000.

LADDERING

Laddering, which means buying bonds or notes with staggered maturities, is a strategy that works well for long-term bond investors. It allows you to arrange your bonds so that they produce a steady income stream from the interest, and it moderates the effect of a change in interest rates.

Here's how laddering works. The first year, you buy a series of Treasury notes or munis with different maturities. You could buy, for example, five Treasury notes with maturities of one, two, three, four, and five years. As each note matures, you use the money if you need it, but preferably you keep the ladder going by reinvesting the money in another five-year note. It's wise to limit maturities to a maximum of five to ten years, because that both maximizes your yield and minimizes your potential risk.

TAX-EXEMPT MUNIS

Tax-exempt municipal bonds (munis) are debt securities issued by state and local governments and their agencies. Munis usually pay interest at a fixed rate twice a year, and the issuer promises to return your principal at maturity. The minimum investment is typically $10,000, and maturities range from 1 to 30 years, or even more.

The draw of munis is tax-free income, which makes them attractive to investors in high tax brackets. The interest is always free from federal tax, and if the muni is issued in your state of residence, the interest may be free from state and local taxes as well. For those in high tax brackets, the after-tax yields on munis can be better than those from other taxable bonds. But there can be drawbacks to munis. Some can trigger the Alternative Minimum Tax (AMT), a tax that applies to the interest on some state and local bonds, and tax-exempt interest can affect the taxable status of Social Security benefits. So make sure you check the tax angles thoroughly before you invest.

KEEPING UP WITH INFLATION WITH TIPS AND OTHER PRINCIPAL-PROTECTED NOTES

If you are concerned about rising inflation, one tactic to consider is buying a relatively new kind of fixed-income security known as TIPS, or Treasury Inflation-Protected Securities. (Note: The Treasury and Federal Reserve refer to TIPS as TIIS, or Treasury Inflation-Indexed Securities.) First introduced in 1997 and sold in multiples of $1,000, TIPS are special types of Treasury bonds and notes whose principal value is adjusted by the Consumer Price Index (CPI). As with other notes and bonds, when you own TIPS you receive interest payments every six months and a payment of principal when your security matures. The difference is that the amount of the interest and the size of the redemption payments are tied to inflation.

Here's how it works: The semiannual interest you receive is calculated as one-half of the interest rate (determined at auction) multiplied by the inflation-adjusted principal. This means that you will always receive a real rate of return above the inflation rate (but in the unlikely event of deflation, your interest payments will decrease). At maturity, the bond is redeemed at its inflation-adjusted principal amount or its par value, whichever is greater. Therefore, you will probably receive more at redemption than you paid at purchase. In fact, if you paid par value for the bond, you can't receive less.

Like other Treasury notes and bonds, TIPS are exempt from state and local income taxes, and subject to federal income tax. One caveat to keep in mind is that you have to pay income tax each year on the inflation adjustments you receive from TIPS, even though you won't get the actual cash until the bond matures. This makes TIPS most appropriate for tax-deferred accounts. In addition, the secondary market for TIPS is quite limited, so you should buy them only if you plan to hold them until maturity.

There are other variations of principal-protected notes that are available in the marketplace. Inflation-indexed savings bonds (I-Bonds), a variation of the tried-and-true U.S. government savings bonds, are also indexed to provide a hedge against inflation and are sold at face value in increments as small as $50. These bonds offer a guaranteed annual rate that remains in effect for the life of the bond, as well as an additional rate that is tied to the CPI and adjusted every six months. I-Bonds can be cashed out without a penalty if you own them for five years—but if you withdraw the money before that, you will lose three months' worth of interest, much as you do with a CD. In addition, other inflation-indexed notes are assembled by third-party suppliers, but be sure you check the issuers and the fees before investing in them.

ZERO-COUPON BONDS

Zero-coupon bonds, also known as "zeros," are another popular choice for bond investors. These bonds don't pay interest until maturity. You buy them at a discount from their face value, and that value increases as they near maturity. Your return comes from the bonds' appreciation. Zeros are a good choice when you need a specific amount at a specific time. The interest accumulates in the price; you can see a significant increase in your initial investment. For example, if you invested $1,000 in a 20-year zero with a 6% yield, you'd receive over $3,000 at maturity, more than three times your initial investment.

There are three types of zeros: corporate, municipal, and Treasuries. Treasury zeros, called STRIPs (separate trading of registered interest and principal), are the most popular and actively graded zeros, for good reason. First, they're backed by the U.S. government, so your risk of losing your money is minimal if you hold the bonds until maturity. Also, the income from them is exempt from state and local taxes. They are particularly attractive to investors who want to lock in a rate of return for an extended period of time, often for a specific date—for example, for making college tuition payments or paying off a mortgage. You could use a money market mutual fund (which we'll discuss in the next chapter) for these purposes, but STRIPs will often give you a better return. STRIPs are not available from the Federal Reserve; you buy them from your brokerage firm. Be aware that even though the interest from STRIPs isn't paid until maturity, a portion of the interest is subject to federal income tax each year you hold the bond, which means that STRIPs may work well in a tax-deferred account such as an IRA or 401(k).

The downside of zeros is their volatility. Because the interest isn't paid until maturity, the value of a zero fluctuates more than it does for other bonds of similar maturity. If interest rates rise, the value of a zero will drop more than the value of other bonds. But if interest rates drop, the zero's value will increase more than the value of other bonds, giving you a capital gain.

Bond Funds or Individual Bonds?

When you invest in bonds, you can do so by buying individual bonds or by buying shares of a bond fund. Generally speaking, if you have a need for a reliable income stream, are saving for a specific future expense (such as a child's education), or want to be actively involved in managing your bond portfolio, you may be best served by buying individual bonds. However, it is generally not cost-effective to buy or sell less than $5,000 of Treasury or corporate bonds, or less than $10,000 of municipals. Therefore, the minimum amount you will need to build a diversified portfolio of individual bonds is about $25,000 for Treasuries, $50,000 for corporates, and $100,000 for municipals.

BOND FUNDS

Like stock mutual funds, bond funds are operated by investment companies that pool money from many individual investors to purchase a variety of bonds and money market securities, and they're classified by the types of securities they purchase, such as U.S. government, corporate, or municipal bonds. You can purchase shares through a brokerage firm (some funds are offered only through brokers) or often directly from the fund itself.

Also like stock mutual funds, the chief advantage of bond funds is that they can provide the smaller investor with the diversification and professional management that would otherwise be possible only for a much larger portfolio. You do pay a management fee, but whether you're interested in buying Treasuries, munis, or corporates, you can get started with as little as $2,500 to $5,000. Bond funds are also a good choice if you think you'll need access to the money before maturity, because funds are more liquid than individual bonds. If you need the money, you simply sell shares in the fund at the current share price (which may be higher or lower than the price you paid for them). A disadvantage of bond funds is that they don't offer a fixed yield or repayment of principal at a fixed maturity date. If you want a fixed cash flow or are saving for a specific future event (for example, a child entering college), you won't get that from a bond fund. In addition, like all mutual funds, bond funds have some complicated tax issues. See Chapter 8 for more information.

INDIVIDUAL BONDS

If you're looking for regular income, buying individual bonds is probably the approach for you—provided, of course, that you have enough funds to build a diversified bond portfolio. Although most bonds pay interest twice a year, you can also use a laddering strategy (with six or more bonds) to create a monthly income flow. In addition, if you won't need access to your money before maturity, an individual bond has the advantage of providing you with a specific amount at a specific date in the future.

Finally, keep in mind that buying individual bonds and bond mutual funds doesn't have to be an either/or proposition. Your needs may be best met by investing in a combination.

These are the basics of investing in bonds. As you can see, bonds can be complicated, so you're wise to consult a bond specialist and your tax specialist about these investments. And doing so is worth your while. Bonds can give you the stability your portfolio needs to help you weather down markets, and the right balance for the growth you need.

The Bottom Line on Choosing Bonds

- *Even though bonds don't provide growth, they're still a valuable part of most portfolios. They can provide diversification, safety of principal, dependable income in the form of interest, and tax advantages.*
- *Because the world of bonds is large and complex, many investors looking at bonds will want professional advice.*
- *In terms of risk, bonds carry varying degrees of credit risk (also known as default risk), or the chance that the issuer won't make its scheduled payments.*

• *Bonds are similar to IOUs: Someone borrows the money you invest for a specific length of time, and in return he or she pays you interest.*

• *The coupon rate from the bond gives you a steady stream of income, which is one of the main attractions of bonds. The interest rate is usually fixed when the investment is issued, and it stays the same until maturity.*

• *Bonds are differentiated by who's borrowing the money: the federal government, a state or local government, or a corporation.*

• *The attraction of government bonds is safety of principal. Bonds issued by a state or local government are called municipal bonds, or munis, and their attraction is tax-free interest. The attraction of corporate bonds is higher yields, but they also carry a higher risk of default.*

• *Based on risk and time factors, the bonds I prefer are five-year Treasury notes, tax-exempt municipal bonds for investors in higher tax brackets, and zero-coupon bonds for investors who want to fund a specific future expense.*

• *When you invest in bonds, you can do so by buying individual bonds or by buying shares of a bond fund. This doesn't have to be an either/or proposition.*

6

Choosing Cash-Equivalent Investments

Cash-equivalent investments are those that give you easy access to your money because either they're easily converted to cash or they have less than one year to maturity. Their main purpose is liquidity, and they include money market funds, Treasury bills, and short-term certificates of deposit (CDs). Cash equivalents are appropriate if you think you might have a sudden need for your money, if you know you'll need it relatively soon, or as a place to keep ongoing emergency funds. Your return on cash-equivalent investments varies, depending on interest rates. If interest rates are low, your return will be, too. In fact, if interest rates are *very* low, you may not have any return at all. But return isn't what these investments are about; liquidity is their main function.

In contrast to stocks and bonds, diversification is not especially important when it comes to these savings-type investments. Most tend to minimize market risk and default risk. Conversely, they all expose you to some degree of inflation risk.

Oversaving

Apart from not having any liquid savings at all, the most critical savings mistake people make is to leave too much of their savings in cash equivalents. We've all known of someone who has most of his or her net worth in a passbook savings account. Or maybe you know someone who owns several nearly identical savings accounts earmarked for specific goals like kids' college and retirement.

These people know how to save. They just haven't taken the next step: to invest.

The problem is that these savers are using savings vehicles for investing. The primary purpose of savings is to build an appropriate emergency reserve, which means savings-type investments have to do only two things: preserve capital and provide a better inflation hedge than a safety deposit box (or the space between the mattress and the box springs). People who try to meet another investment objective—growth or income—by using savings-type investments face a different kind of risk: the risk of failing to meet their goals. After you have accumulated sufficient savings for emergency purposes, your excess cash needs to work much harder if you hope to reach your long-term goals.

What's an appropriate level of savings? I suggest that you consider limiting your cash to the money you *know* you will need in the next 12 months, plus whatever amount you think you need to cover any unexpected expenses (perhaps three to six months of living expenses). Money beyond that should be invested in either something that has the potential to grow over time, such as stocks, or, if your goal is current income, something that can potentially provide a better rate of return, such as high-quality notes and bonds.

The important point is to consider your savings in the total context of your financial situation. If your family has more than one income or you have access to reasonably priced credit, such as a home equity loan, or other assets you can borrow against, you might not need to hold as much emergency savings at low interest rates as someone with fewer resources.

Money Market Mutual Funds

This is the cash-equivalent investment that I prefer. Most money market mutual funds generally invest in high-quality, short-term obligations from corporations and from the federal, state, and local governments. With these funds it's usually easy to make deposits or withdrawals, and the rates of return fluctuate daily. People often use them as parking places for cash in between other longer-term investments. When choosing a money market fund, compare your own needs to the fund's particular objective (e.g., corporate or government, taxable or tax-free, etc.). Choose a fund from a substantial company. Be cautious about basing your decision solely on the highest yield; it may entail too much risk for what should be a low-risk investment.

Money market funds are available from brokerage firms and mutual fund families. Those from mutual fund families typically offer switching privileges with other funds in the family. Holding a money market fund with your broker enables you to use your account balance to pay for other investments.

An investment in a money market fund is not insured or guaranteed by the Federal Deposit Insurance Corporation or any other government agency. In exchange for this, you generally get a slightly higher rate of return than you would in a bank account. In addition, money market mutual funds generally don't charge a penalty for withdrawing your money, no matter when you do it.

Although money market funds seek to preserve the value of your investment at $1 per share, it is possible to lose money by investing in a money market fund. Prospectuses are available, and you should read them carefully before investing. But the flexibility and current income that money market funds can provide make them a good investment. The sweep feature that many such funds have will give you even greater flexibility and liquidity, since it makes your cash available to settle your other trades automatically, without your giving a specific order to sell your money market fund shares.

Municipal money market funds invest in short-term obligations from state and local governments, which may appeal to investors in higher tax brackets. Another type of fund invests exclusively in Treasury bills and short-term agency securities for maximum safety against default. Some Treasury-only funds pay dividends that are exempt from state and local income taxes.

All three types of money market funds have five features in common that make them good for *saving,* not investing:

1. You can open most money market funds with a relatively small initial investment and make subsequent investments in more modest amounts.

2. Money market funds are managed to minimize risk, and their securities are generally restricted to investment-grade quality. The SEC imposes stringent portfolio maturity, quality, and diversification restrictions on money market funds.

3. Money market funds are immediately liquid, often through check-writing privileges and a debit card. You can normally convert them to cash without delay or loss of value, which is important when you're depending on them for emergencies and sudden expenses. (CDs, on the other hand, often have early withdrawal penalties.)

4. Money market funds adjust fairly quickly to changes in market rates and continually compound the income they pay.

5. Money market funds are no-load. However, they do impose a fee to pay the manager and cover other expenses, which, while nominal, can vary widely from fund to fund.

Treasury Bills

Treasury bills, sometimes called T-bills, are short-term, highly liquid investments available in maturities from three months to one year. They are sold at a discount and return their full face value (minimum of $1,000) at maturity. Your interest, which is exempt from state tax, is the difference between the face value of the bill and the purchase price. In addition, unlike most cash-equivalent choices, T-bills are backed by the full faith and credit of the U.S. government.

If you decide to buy a T-bill, there are two ways to go. The first is to buy a newly issued T-bill directly from the government at *www.treasurydirect.gov* (without paying a commission). Alternatively, you can buy and sell existing T-bills through your broker—which gives you more flexibility but will also cost you a commission. The advantage of this method is that you get a choice of maturities and interest rates, and you can buy at any time, instead of exclusively at scheduled auctions.

Certificates of Deposit (CDs)

CDs are issued by banks, pay interest, and return your principal investment at maturity. They are short- and intermediate-term investments, with maturities of three months to five years, or longer. The most popular CDs have short maturities.

CDs have many apparently attractive features: They're guaranteed against default (subject to Federal Deposit Insurance Corporation, or FDIC, limits), they pay predictably, and there are no commissions. But it's my feeling that too many investors flock to them without considering other income securities. I'd consider other alternatives for several reasons. For one, CDs from your bank may offer only limited maturities, while bonds offer a range. CDs are not typically liquid; if you cash them before they mature, the bank usually requires you to forfeit interest. Also, interest on CDs is fully taxable; interest on Treasury bills and municipal bonds is not. CDs lock in a rate, which is a disadvantage in a rising-interest-rate environment. Money market funds help you keep up with rising interest rates; however, they are not insured. Depending on your risk tolerance and goals, there may be a place for CDs in your overall investment plan, but in my mind it's generally a far better idea to put your short-term or emergency savings in money market funds, which typically produce competitive income and can be easily converted into cash.

The Bottom Line on Choosing Cash-Equivalent Investments

• *Cash-equivalent investments, which give you easy access to your money, are appropriate if you think you might have a sudden need for your money, if you know you'll need it relatively soon, or as a place to keep ongoing emergency funds.*

• *The main purpose of these investments is liquidity. They include money market funds, Treasury bills, and short-term certificates of deposit (CDs).*

• *In contrast to stocks and bonds, diversification is not especially important when it comes to these savings-type investments.*

• *Apart from not having any liquid savings at all, the most critical savings mistake people make is to leave too much of their savings in cash equivalents. I suggest limiting your cash to the money you know you'll need in the next 12 months, plus whatever you would require to cover unexpected needs.*

• *The cash-equivalent investments I prefer are money market mutual funds, which invest in high-quality, short-term obligations from corporations and from the federal, state, and local governments.*

• *Treasury bills (or T-bills) are short-term, highly liquid investments available in maturities from three months to one year. They are sold at a discount and return their full face value (minimum of $1,000) at maturity.*

• *Certificates of deposit (or CDs) are issued by banks, pay interest, and return your principal investment at maturity. They are short- and intermediate-term investments, with maturities of three months to five years, or longer. The most popular CDs have short maturities.*

Part III

CREATING YOUR PLAN

7

Putting Your Plan into Action

It's time to take action. Now it is time to actually begin to invest your money. Sometimes people feel nervous about taking the first steps—opening a brokerage account, executing an actual order, and setting up a plan to invest regularly. But it's not difficult. It's just a matter of doing it.

Investing is a process in which you get more and more specific. In Part I, you did something very general: You looked at what kind of investor you are and you chose an asset allocation plan. In other words, based on your profile, you decided how you should divide your investment money among the three major types of investments—as well as possible alternative investments such as REITs (real estate investment trusts). In Part II, you got more specific: You learned about the advantages of each of those types of investments, and you got a clearer picture of which ones might best help you meet your goals.

Now it's time to get more specific still: to develop an investment plan, or a shopping list of specific investments. Which mutual funds? Which individual stocks? Which bonds? And then you'll put your plan into action by opening an account with a brokerage firm, beginning to build your portfolio by purchasing the investments you've chosen, and deciding how much you can invest each month.

Step 1. Turning Your Pie Chart into an Investment Plan

The first step is to turn the pie chart you chose in Chapter 2 into an investment plan. For example, say you want to end up with 95% of your portfolio in stocks. How much of that 95% should be in large company stocks? How much in small company stocks? How much in international stocks?

What follows are those pie charts again, this time with more detail on how you can implement them.

Aggressive Plan

If you want your asset allocation to be aggressive, I'd suggest you set up your portfolio this way:

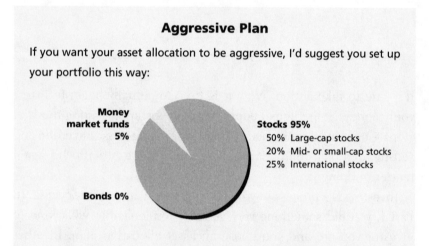

Money
market funds
5%

Stocks 95%
50% Large-cap stocks
20% Mid- or small-cap stocks
25% International stocks

Bonds 0%

Moderately Aggressive Plan

If you want your asset allocation to be moderately aggressive, I'd suggest you set up your portfolio this way:

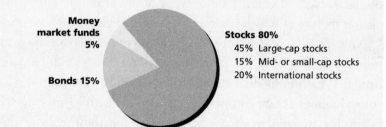

Money
market funds
5%

Stocks 80%
45% Large-cap stocks
15% Mid- or small-cap stocks
20% International stocks

Bonds 15%

Moderate Plan

If you want your asset allocation to be moderate, I'd suggest you set up your portfolio this way:

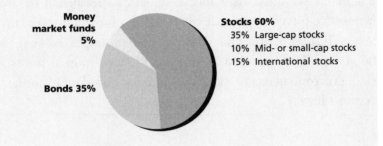

Money
market funds
5%

Bonds 35%

Stocks 60%
35% Large-cap stocks
10% Mid- or small-cap stocks
15% International stocks

Moderately Conservative Plan

If you want your asset allocation to be moderately conservative, I'd suggest you set up your portfolio this way:

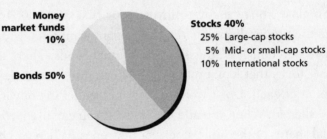

Money
market funds
10%

Bonds 50%

Stocks 40%
25% Large-cap stocks
5% Mid- or small-cap stocks
10% International stocks

Conservative Plan

If you want your asset allocation to be conservative, I'd suggest you set up your portfolio this way:

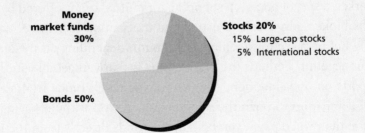

Money
market funds
30%

Bonds 50%

Stocks 20%
15% Large-cap stocks
5% International stocks

By now, you know I have a bias toward investing a higher portion of your investment dollars in stocks because they are investments that have the potential to grow. But as a rule of thumb, I believe that if you're over 60, you're probably going to veer toward a more conservative asset allocation, simply because if the market is negative for a few years, it will be harder for you to make up your losses. If, on the other hand, you're 45 or younger, I'd suggest you be at least 80% invested in stocks and stock mutual funds. That said, everyone needs to make the decision based on his or her own comfort level.

Step 2. Choosing Investments

Once you have an investment plan, you can get more specific: You decide on specific investments. The worksheet on the next page will help you organize what you want to buy.

Suppose you're ready to invest your first $50,000. In order to have the proper diversification, you might want to consider putting a good percentage of this in a few mutual funds. Then, if you find a few stocks that look promising, you can purchase an equal dollar amount of each. Don't worry if your money doesn't buy a round lot (100 shares). When you add new money, you can use it to buy additional shares of the same stocks or new ones. When you have 10 or 15 stocks, you'll be close to the number that most people can manage comfortably.

If you're planning on buying mutual funds from several different fund families, you may want to go through a mutual fund supermarket, a sort of one-stop shopping for mutual funds offered by various brokerages. There is usually no transaction fee; there may or may not be a fee for opening an account, depending on the size of your account. Perhaps the biggest plus is that you get all your fund reports on one statement. You can buy and sell funds from different companies through the same brokerage firm without paying any more than you'd pay if you bought the funds directly from the fund companies. If you use a fund supermarket offered by a broker, you can buy and sell individual stocks and bonds as well. At Schwab, where mutual fund supermarkets were invented, we call our mutual fund supermarket Mutual Fund OneSource®; other firms have followed suit, making everything far easier for the mutual fund investor.

You should be aware that, generally speaking, funds traded through a supermarket are subject to "short-term redemption fees." These fees are usually around 0.75% of the principal. They apply to redemptions made within 180 days of the time you purchased the fund.

YOUR PERSONAL ACTION PLAN

Investment Category	Asset Allocation Investment	Percentage	Example
Stocks	_____	_____%	Index funds,
	_____	_____%	actively
	_____	_____%	managed
	_____	_____%	mutual funds,
	_____	_____%	individual
	_____	_____%	stocks
Bonds	_____	_____%	Bond mutual
	_____	_____%	funds
	_____	_____%	
	_____	_____%	
	_____	_____%	
Cash Equivalents	_____	_____%	Money
	_____	_____%	market funds,
	_____	_____%	CDs, Treasury
	_____	_____%	bills

Step 3. Building Your Portfolio

Finally it's time to take action: by opening an account. That's very easy to do.

CHOOSE A BROKERAGE FIRM

As you consider various brokerage firms, keep in mind that you're not choosing a person; you're choosing a professional firm, the same way you would choose a bank or a real estate company. Don't base your decision solely on a specific broker (even if he or she is a friend or relative); you wouldn't pick a bank because you liked the teller. You'll be doing business with this firm for a long time, so keep factors such as reputation, location, and the breadth of services offered in mind. Now that many people are trading online, reliable technology and a secure system are important considerations as well.

OPEN AN ACCOUNT

Once you've chosen the brokerage firm you want to work with, you simply open an account. It's not all that different from opening a bank account. You'll need to provide personal information such as your Social Security number, and many firms require a minimum starting balance. But once you've opened the account and made your initial investment, you'll be able to buy and sell stocks, mutual funds, and bonds all from that one account. You can contact a brokerage firm in any of the following ways:

Contact them online through their Web site.
Call the brokerage firm on the phone.
Go into the brokerage firm's office.

Investing online is a great way to go. When you make your first contact online, all you have to do is request brochures describing the firm's various brokerage accounts, along with the appropriate application forms. That's it. Then you wait for the literature to come, look it over, and send in your application to get yourself on the brokerage firm's records. Or you may be able to download an application from the firm's Web site. Once you've opened an account, you should be able to trade securities as well as research them online, and you should be able to do it 24 hours a day.

MAKE YOUR INITIAL INVESTMENT

So far maybe all this has been a dry run. Maybe you've invested in a specific stock mentally and watched its ups and downs. But that's not enough anymore. As soon as you can, take $5,000—*something*, no matter how little—and actually invest it. You might invest in an index fund that you've watched and researched. If you have a lump sum, you may consider investing it in two or three mutual funds.

Investments other than mutual funds have different requirements concerning the minimum amount of money that you have to have in your account. If you buy a common stock, you'll have three business days to pay for it. For a mutual fund, you have to have your money in your account at the time of the order. Your brokerage firm can describe the specifics for buying and selling different kinds of investments.

Let's say you've decided you want to buy shares in a no-load mutual fund. You'll have to put enough money into your newly opened account to cover the cost of the shares you plan to buy. To do so, you either call, write, or go in personally to the brokerage's branch office. At Schwab, the great majority of investors place their orders by computer or phone.

When you place an order online or over the phone, you'll need to give the brokerage firm information for the transaction. They typically need to know:

- Your name and account number.
- The name of the mutual fund or stock you want to buy or sell.
- For buying shares in a mutual fund, the dollar amount you want to invest; for selling shares, the number of shares you are selling.
- For buying or selling stocks, the number of shares involved, and whether your order is "at the market" or a "limit order." A market order

is an order to buy or sell a security at the currently available price. A limit order is an order to buy or sell at a specified price or better (a limit order to sell sets a minimum and a limit order to buy sets a maximum). Most people place market orders, unless the stock is highly volatile.

• If a limit order, whether it's a "day order" or a "good-till-canceled" order. At the day's market close, if a "day" order has not been executed or canceled by the customer, it is canceled automatically. A "good-till-canceled," or GTC, order is an order that remains valid until executed or canceled by the customer. At Schwab, all GTC orders that are not executed or canceled by the customer will automatically expire 60 days after the date the order is taken. Unlike a day order, a GTC order can be executed over several days.

• Whether you want to reinvest your dividends. I suggest reinvestment, as discussed below.

For bonds, you'll need to provide some additional information, which a bond specialist at your brokerage firm can help you with. This information includes:

• The type of bond or issuer.

• The face amount (cash value at maturity) and average bond transaction size.

• The desired maturity. Bond maturity means the lifetime of a bond, concluding when the final payment of that obligation is due.

• Whether you want new securities ("at auction") or secondary market securities.

SPECIFY THAT YOU WANT YOUR DIVIDENDS REINVESTED

When you first open your account or when you place your initial order, you'll be asked whether you want your dividends to be reinvested—or in more formal language, how you want to handle "distributions of income." The better choice is almost always to reinvest your dividends and let them make more money for you before you even have the chance to spend it.

When a company you've invested in makes a profit and pays a dividend, you can look at that dividend in two ways: as income, a nice addition to your checking account; or as a vehicle for growth. Reinvesting your dividends, instead of using them as income, can add fuel to your portfolio growth engine, and it's a great way to systematically increase your investment. You can specify that your dividends are to be automatically reinvested in the same stock that generated them, in a sort of vote of confidence; or you can ask that the dividends be put into a separate account to purchase other stocks. Either of these is a productive use of your money. Even better, once you've specified that you want your dividends reinvested, it's effortless. And you get rid of the temptation to spend those dividends; it's a kind of forced savings. The power of compounding is another very compelling reason to reinvest your dividends.

CHOOSE A MONEY MARKET FUND FOR YOUR CASH BALANCES AND FOR SHORT-TERM INVESTING GOALS

Make sure your cash is earning income between long-term investments by signing up for a money market fund. This type of fund gives you the potential to earn income on your cash by automatically investing the cash balances held in your account while you're between other investments. While not insured or guaranteed by the FDIC, these funds are designed to offer relative stability of principal, competitive returns, and high liquidity. I recommend that you use a money market mutual fund or an asset management account if you might need the money relatively soon. They're good for short-term investing goals, as a savings vehicle (while you're accumulating enough for an investment requiring a larger minimum), and as a place for emergency funds.

CHECK THE WRITTEN CONFIRMATION OF YOUR ORDER

When you place an order over the phone, your order will often be executed (meaning completed) during the call itself. If you place your order online, you'll often receive confirmation very quickly as well. Your brokerage firm will send you written confirmation of your order by mail, usually within three business days. When you receive it, check it to make sure it reflects the information you were given on the phone or online. You should also make sure the transaction is listed on your next account statement from the brokerage firm. Your statement should give a comprehensive picture of the activity in your account during the previous period. It should list all of your securities and all of your transactions for that period. Make sure the transactions listed are consistent with your other confirmations. I know this sounds tedious, but remember it's your money, and mistakes can happen.

INVESTING ONLINE

Sometimes investing can seem more like an abstraction than a reality, which is why a lot of people put off doing it. What tangible difference does investing make? You look around your living room, and you see no evidence that you have or haven't done it.

But say you take some action. You open an account, and you set up a system to invest regularly, and it all begins to make sense, except that it can still feel distant. Sometimes when you put money into an IRA or some other kind of retirement account, it can feel like an act of faith, as though that money vaporizes, to return in 20 or 30 years. In the meantime, it's as though that money's locked up tight somewhere far away, in somebody else's care.

Investing online can change that perception dramatically. It's like going from black and white to color. Suddenly investing is real—it's all right there in front of you on your computer screen in your office or den or kitchen. And when it becomes more real, you become a more dedicated investor. You begin to feel more in control, both of your assets and of your life.

INVESTING A LUMP SUM

A lump sum is a large amount of cash, usually a onetime payout, that you might receive as retirement income, a year-end bonus, or from an inheritance or in the property settlement from a divorce or the sale of a house. Whatever the source, receiving a lump sum is both an opportunity and a challenge. It's an opportunity because it can open doors, or at least give you an idea of where the key is. And it's a challenge because you may feel a lot of pressure to do the right thing with that money. "Here's my chance," you think—"Don't make a mistake!"

You don't want to make a mistake, but it's wise to try to lessen that pressure. People deal with lump-sum distributions in a tremendous variety of ways, and this is most definitely a time to consult your tax adviser and perhaps a financial adviser as well. But take your time. What follows are some general considerations:

1. Understand the tax implications.

As always, examine the tax implications carefully. In very general terms, money received as a property settlement in the course of a divorce settlement is not taxable. Money received in an inheritance is the net or after-tax amount, meaning that it has already been taxed, and you keep what you receive. Money received from a retirement plan is taxable, which is why many people opt to open an IRA rollover account, where the money is not taxed until you take the distributions as income. (Another alternative is to receive retirement income in the form of an annuity, meaning that you receive a set amount for the rest of your life, with the amount being calculated based on life expectancy tables.) Capital gains distributions are taxed as well, though often at a much lower rate than income tax.

2. While you're considering your next move, put the money to work.

As Peter Lynch says, "Money is a great friend, once you send it off to work." And the larger the sum of money, the more work it can do. So while you're considering the best place to invest that money, don't let it languish in a low-interest savings account where, thanks to inflation, its purchasing power will diminish almost daily. Instead, put it someplace where it can compound a little more—a money market fund is a good "parking place" while you consider your next move.

3. Look carefully at how investing the sum will change your asset allocation.

How does this sum affect your portfolio? Is it a significant enough amount that you'll want to change your asset allocation? If so, you may want to reexamine your goals and your time frame. Or maybe you'll simply want to "add it to the pot"—in other words, to allocate it in the same way as you've allocated the rest of your portfolio, adding a portion to each of your investment classes.

4. Take your time.

A lot of people, when they receive a lump sum, feel as though they have to act tomorrow, to make an immediate decision about how and where to invest the money. If you're feeling this way, slow down. You don't have to decide how to invest it the week after you receive it. You don't even have to decide how to invest the whole thing. Maybe you'll want to invest half of it now by following the same asset allocation you've used for the rest of your portfolio, and think about the rest. Or perhaps you want to invest it even more gradually—perhaps the same amount every month for two to three years. This way you can ease your way, making adjustments as you go. The key is not to feel rushed or to make a rash decision.

Step 4. Deciding How Much to Invest Each Month

Investing isn't a onetime shot; opening an account and making an initial investment are only the start of a process, not an end in themselves. Once you've made your initial investment, you'll want to give some thought to how much you can invest each month, so that you'll meet your investing goals.

There are a few ways to decide how much to invest each month. In a way, the question is pretty easy; *invest as much as you can* is the best answer, and the one most people use. You might start with 5% to 10% of your gross earnings. Or choose a set amount that you think you can afford—$100 a month or $500 a quarter, for example. Think of it as another item on your budget—it's certainly as important as vacations or entertainment or dinners out. Remember that you don't have to stick with the amount you choose initially; just determine a starting amount and see how it goes. If, after several months, you find that you can comfortably increase that amount, that's great. As your income increases, you can increase your monthly or quarterly amount.

You may want to be more specific here, and figure out how much you'll need to invest each month to meet your specific goals. Some of those goals may be easy to estimate; for example, you can come up with an approximation of how much a four-year college education will cost, or the ballpark price of a first or second home. Retirement is harder, and we'll talk about estimating retirement expenses and goals in Chapter 9. (For now, to begin to get a rough estimate of how much you'll need to live on each year in retirement, you establish your current needs as a basis. You do this by using a percentage of your gross annual income. Most people use 80% to 100%, meaning that they'll need between 80% and 100% of their gross annual income per year in retirement to continue their current lifestyle.)

Once you have an idea of how much you'll need to meet your goals, you can use the tables on the next page to estimate how

Monthly Investment Estimates for Hypothetical 6%, 8%, and 10% Average Annual Return

6% Average Annual Return

Monthly Investment	5 years	10 years	15 years	20 years	25 years
$200	13,965	32,653	57,662	91,129	135,916
$300	20,947	48,979	86,493	136,694	203,874
$400	27,930	65,306	115,323	182,258	271,832
$500	34,912	81,632	144,154	227,823	339,790
$600	41,894	97,959	172,985	273,387	407,748
$700	48,877	114,285	201,816	318,952	475,707
$800	55,859	130,611	230,647	364,517	543,665
$900	62,842	146,938	259,478	410,081	611,623
$1000	69,824	163,264	288,308	455,646	679,581

8% Average Annual Return

Monthly Investment	5 years	10 years	15 years	20 years	25 years
$200	14,683	36,257	67,956	114,532	182,968
$300	22,024	54,385	101,934	171,798	274,452
$400	29,366	72,513	135,911	229,064	365,936
$500	36,707	90,642	169,889	286,330	457,420
$600	44,048	108,770	203,867	343,596	548,904
$700	51,390	126,898	237,845	400,862	640,388
$800	58,731	145,027	271,823	458,128	731,872
$900	66,073	163,155	305,801	515,394	823,355
$1000	73,414	181,283	339,778	572,660	914,839

10% Average Annual Return

Monthly Investment	5 years	10 years	15 years	20 years	25 years
$200	15,434	40,292	80,324	144,797	248,632
$300	23,152	60,437	120,486	217,196	372,948
$400	30,869	80,583	160,648	289,595	497,264
$500	38,586	100,729	200,811	361,993	621,580
$600	46,303	120,875	240,973	434,392	745,896
$700	54,020	141,020	281,135	506,791	870,212
$800	61,737	161,166	321,297	579,189	994,528
$900	69,445	181,312	361,459	651,588	1,118,844
$1000	77,172	201,458	401,621	723,987	1,243,160

Note: The above estimates are for illustration purposes and do not represent the performance of any particular security.

much you should invest each month to make that goal real. To use the tables, first choose the one that represents your pretax rate of return. It's wise to be conservative here; even though the market has achieved a 10% average return since 1926, you can't depend on that. Market returns vary widely, and the averages conceal long periods of both weak and strong performance. In addition, averages are based on past returns, and it's unlikely that the future will mirror the past in any precise way. So given the nature of averages, I think a 6% or 8% pretax average return is prudent; it may even build in some padding.

When you've decided on a projected rate of return, find the number of years you have to invest until you need the money. Then, in that column, find the amount closest to the estimate of your investing goal. The number in the left-hand column is your monthly investment.

Step 5. Making It Automatic and Systematic

Once you decide on the amount you can invest every month, there are several ways to make investing easy by setting up a system for regular investments. I encourage you to authorize a payroll deduction, so that a portion of your paycheck is deducted and automatically transferred to your brokerage account, to be used toward additional investments. Or you can authorize an electronic funds transfer (EFT), in which the money is automatically deducted from your checking or savings account. In either case, the amount of the deduction depends on you.

There are a couple of very good reasons for investing systematically. One of them is something that a lot of us were taught as we grew up: the idea of a self-tithe, or paying yourself first, meaning that you save some portion of each paycheck or income you receive, and you do it first, before the whole thing gets eaten up.

A second good reason has the complicated-sounding name *dollar cost averaging*, which simply means investing the same amount of money at regular intervals—for example, $100 a month or $500

FIGURING IN INFLATION

As you think about the cost of your goals, remember to include inflation. Ignoring it is a big mistake, one that can be a nasty surprise later on. You can't stop inflation, but you can do two things: First, you can invest with the goal of achieving a rate of return greater than the inflation rate; and second, you can be aware of the toll inflation takes, so that you're not caught off guard.

Suppose that your first child will be attending college in ten years, and you want to have $80,000 set aside for that education. But that's today's dollars; how much might it cost ten years from now? You can estimate that by doing the following:

	Example	You
1. Estimate the number of years to your goal	15	_____
2. Estimate the current cost of that goal	$80,000	_____
3. Enter your inflation factor from the table below, which assumes a 4% rate of inflation.	1.8	_____

Years to your goal	Inflation factor
5	1.22
10	1.48
15	1.80
20	2.19
25	2.67

4. Multiply item 2 by item 3 to find your inflation-adjusted investment goal	$144,000	_____

a quarter. By regularly investing the same dollar amount, rather than buying a specified number of shares, you automatically buy more shares when the stock price is low, and fewer when the price is up. As a result, you average out the highs and lows of the price.

While dollar cost averaging can't guarantee that your investment will gain or protect you from losses (and commission costs can make it impractical), it can help you buy *more* shares at a lower price, and *fewer* shares at a higher price. It's a natural way to participate in the market throughout its peaks and valleys, and to keep your emotions from short-circuiting your plan.

■ ■ ■

A thousand reasons can keep you out of the market, but I hope you don't let them. Every year for the past 30 years, some economic or political turmoil has made it seem intuitively illogical to invest, from the Cuban missile crisis to the S&L bailout to the recent bear market and the war in Iraq. But the market has always recovered. Compound growth can't work for you if you don't invest. So I urge you to start investing intelligently—and to stay with it.

The Bottom Line on Putting Your Plan into Action

• *If you want to buy mutual funds from several different fund families, consider a mutual fund supermarket, which gives you all your fund reports in one statement.*

• *The mechanics of opening a brokerage account are similar to opening a bank account.*

• *Once you've opened the account and made your initial investment, you can buy and sell stocks, mutual funds, and bonds from that account.*

• *Reinvesting your dividends, instead of using them as income, adds fuel to your portfolio growth engine and systematically increases your investment.*

• *Make sure your cash is earning income between making long-term investments by signing up for a money market fund.*

• *If you receive a lump sum, take your time. Put the money to work in a money market fund while you decide how to invest it. Make sure you understand the tax implications and how they will change your asset allocation.*

• *Once you decide on the amount you can invest every month, consider setting up a system for regular investments by authorizing a payroll deduction or an electronic funds transfer.*

• *Dollar cost averaging means investing the same amount of money at regular intervals. By doing so, you automatically buy more shares when the stock price is low, and fewer when the price is up, which averages out the highs and lows of the price.*

8

The Taxing Side of Investing

Taxes. A lot of people want to bury their heads in the sand at the mere mention of the word. But don't give up. Understanding the basics of how taxes affect your investing plan isn't that hard. You don't have to master the state and federal tax codes, or be a CPA. But because taxes can be a huge drag on your return, understanding the tax implications can make a big difference. Not only do you purchase almost all goods and services with after-tax dollars; the less money you pay in taxes, the more you can invest.

Fortunately, this is an area where a little information goes a long way. That said, although the information in this chapter will get you thinking along the right lines, you should consult your tax professional to review your particular situation.

A Few Tax Basics

Let's start with the basics—some general guidelines about how taxes affect investments:

• *As investors, there are two sides to us: the tax-advantaged side and the currently taxable side.*

While it's always wise to think of your portfolio as one entity, it can be helpful to think of yourself as two kinds of investors: On one hand, you're planning for your future by investing in a government-sanctioned tax-advantaged retirement plan—a traditional or Roth IRA, a SEP-IRA, a 401(k), or a 403(b)—whatever is available to you. Then there's the part of you that's investing outside the tax-advantaged accounts, where the money is currently taxable. This side of you invests money beyond what you can contribute to your retirement accounts and what you've earmarked for shorter-term goals (since you can be penalized if you withdraw your retirement money before you reach the age of 59½). When these investments produce income—interest, dividends, or capital gains—you're required to pay current federal and state taxes on that income now (unless you do some planning ahead).

• *Always take full advantage of tax-advantaged accounts that are available to you.*

Tax-advantaged accounts such as 401(k)s and IRAs are an investor's best friend, so much so that they should be at the heart of everyone's investment strategy. First, the earnings in these accounts grow tax-free (although they may be subject to tax when withdrawn). During your twenties, thirties, forties, and fifties—potentially four decades—the entire amount you invest in these accounts compounds free of taxation. The chunk of money that would otherwise go to the government is instead right there working for you, compounding over all those years. Over time, this makes a huge difference.

In addition, depending on the plan and on your circumstances, you may be able to *deduct* your contribution from your taxable income, leaving you that much more money to invest. Also, because many of us will be earning less in retirement, the money we withdraw from a 401(k) or traditional IRA may be taxed at a lower rate because we will be in a lower tax bracket. Withdrawals from Roth IRAs can be even better because they are often not taxed at all (because they are funded with *after-tax* dollars).

• *As you choose investments, consider whether you'll hold them in a tax-advantaged or a taxable account.*

Once you know your overall target asset allocation (the percentage of stocks and bonds you want to own), how do you decide where each investment should be? The answer to this question lies in a concept called *tax efficiency*. Although some people may advise you to put stocks in your taxable account and bonds in your retirement account, I think you need to dig deeper. Some investments—such as equity index mutual funds, individual stocks held for the long term, and municipal bonds—are by their very nature *tax-efficient*; that is, they allow you to keep a larger percentage of your pretax gains. It makes sense to use these in your taxable accounts when you have a choice. On the other hand, less tax-efficient investments, such as individual stocks that you buy and sell more frequently, actively managed mutual funds, and taxable bonds, could be good choices for your retirement accounts. By the way, now that stock dividends are taxed at the same favorable rate as long-term capital gains (at least until the end of 2008), it might make sense to consider holding dividend-paying stocks in taxable accounts as well.

So the important thing isn't whether you put stocks in your taxable account and bonds in your retirement account, or vice versa. What's important are the tax characteristics of the individual investments—how much of your return might be lost to current taxation. The following table provides a quick summary:

WHERE TAX-SMART INVESTORS PUT THEIR INVESTMENTS

Taxable Accounts	Tax-Advantaged Accounts
Individual stocks held over one year	Individual stocks held one year or less (when sold for a gain)
Tax-managed stock funds, index funds, low-turnover stock funds	Actively managed funds that generate significant short-term capital gains
Stocks or mutual funds that pay "qualified" dividends taxed at favorable rates	Taxable bond funds, zero-coupon bonds, or TIPS Treasury bond funds, high-yield bond funds
Municipal bonds	REITs (real estate investment trusts)

• *Index funds are a good choice for both tax-advantaged and taxable investing.*

Index funds have a sort of double personality in that they're a good choice for both tax-advantaged and taxable investing. They're a good choice for the taxable portion of your investments because they're tax-efficient. Since they are geared to track an index, they generally have a more stable portfolio and far less turnover than their equivalent managed funds—and that usually means far fewer taxable distributions. That's a good choice for a currently taxable account.

Some people feel you shouldn't include index funds in a tax-advantaged account because they produce lower realized gains, meaning that you're overdoing it on tax protection. I disagree. For reasons already discussed, if you own individual stocks and actively managed mutual funds, you might want to keep them in your retirement account where they'll potentially be taxed only when you withdraw your money. But I also buy my favorite index fund for my tax-advantaged accounts because it generally provides lower management fees and lower turnover costs, all of which can lead to better compounding effects and the most consistent returns.

In summary, if you want to own only index funds, they are suitable for both tax-advantaged and taxable accounts. If you own individual stocks and actively managed funds as well, it may make sense to keep those in a tax-advantaged account.

• *Tax-managed mutual funds are designed to be tax-efficient and are therefore a good choice for taxable accounts.*

Tax-managed mutual funds are a small but growing niche; as of 2003, there were around 75 such funds available to the public. These funds are designed to keep an eye on taxes, and they use several strategies to minimize the drag of taxes on their shareholders' returns. For example, they may minimize the taxable income they pay in the form of dividends and capital gains by buying low-yielding stocks or municipal bonds; they may reduce turnover; or they may offset realized capital gains with losses. While these funds share common goals, the funds themselves are diverse, ranging from index funds to actively managed stock funds to a mix of stocks and bonds.

• *Taxes are a great reason to buy-and-hold in your taxable accounts.*

This is a fairly obvious but often overlooked point: By not selling your appreciated investments in your taxable accounts, you save money simply because you don't pay taxes on capital gains (of course, you might want to sell to harvest capital losses). By buying and holding, you keep the money that would otherwise go to taxes. In addition, appreciated securities held long-term in taxable accounts receive a step-up in cost basis at death (something your heirs might appreciate) and could also provide significant advantages when gifted to your favorite charities. On the other hand, don't let a fear of taxes keep you from selling an investment that no longer holds promise for the future or that no longer fits your overall financial strategy.

• *Pretax return is relevant for tax-advantaged investments; after-tax return is what's important for taxable investments, particularly mutual funds.*

For many investors, the biggest problem with investing in mutual funds in taxable accounts is the large tax bite. After all, it's your after-tax return—or the money you get to keep—that's important.

Unfortunately, most published returns are pretax. In fact, it almost seems that a lot of mutual funds are managed as though taxes don't matter. That may be true, since the managers' compensation is often based on pretax return. In a study conducted at Stanford University, John Shoven and Joel Dickson concluded that "while it is not surprising that taxes lower the accumulations that one can achieve with mutual fund investments over all holding periods, our calculations show that the relative rankings of funds on a post-tax basis (and on our liquidation basis) differ quite dramatically from the published pre-tax rankings. That is, taxable investors cannot easily and reliably determine which of two funds would have offered them a better after-tax return with the publicly-available information."

What's an investor to do? First, be wary of advertised returns, unless they're the rare after-tax returns. Second, be careful and thorough when you research actively managed mutual funds. Fortunately, the SEC now requires mutual fund companies to disclose their after-tax returns in the funds' annual reports and prospectuses. Be sure to read this information carefully.

• *Think twice about investing in securities that produce tax-free income unless you're in a high enough tax bracket to justify it.*

Tax-free securities typically yield less return than equivalent taxable ones. So you have to be in a high enough federal tax bracket to benefit from tax-free investments. How high is high enough? If you're in a 25% or higher tax bracket, you're smart to at least consider tax-free income if the net yield (adjusted for tax savings) matches or exceeds that of a fully taxable investment. (Note: So-called private activity bonds may be subject to the Alternative Minimum Tax.) If your federal tax bracket is 15% or less, investments that produce taxable income are probably fine for you. You may end up with less return if you purchase investments that produce tax-free income.

• *Don't be caught off guard by year-end capital gains with actively managed mutual funds in your currently taxable accounts.*

Simply put, this rule often translates to "don't buy actively managed mutual funds at the end of the year," the reason being that mutual funds typically distribute capital gains in December. If you buy shares in a fund in October or November (in a currently taxable account), you could end up paying taxes on a capital gain from an investment that you've owned for only a couple of months. So you need to plan ahead. You can, on the other hand, invest in most index funds in December because their realized capital gains are generally low or nonexistent.

• *Understand the difference between long- and short-term gains.*

When you sell shares of a mutual fund at a higher price than your original purchase price in a taxable account, you recognize capital gains. Capital gains are first offset by capital losses. But assuming there's a net gain, the profits on shares that you hold for one year or less are short-term capital gains and are taxed at the same rate as ordinary income. Profits recognized on shares that you hold for more than one year are taxed at either 5% or 15%, depending on your income level. (However, the 5% rate goes to 0% for 2008 only, and then both rates revert back to 10% and 20%, respectively, for 2009 and beyond—unless Congress extends the lower capital gains and dividend rates enacted in 2003.)

• *Be aware of the record-keeping requirements for mutual funds.*

When you sell shares of a mutual fund, you have to figure out the true cost basis for tax purposes. That is, you have to add to your original purchase price all the dividends, and all the capital gains that you reinvested. Doing this yourself is a record-keeping nightmare. The good news is that your broker or mutual fund company may provide you with the information you need.

Generally speaking, all dividend and capital gains distributions paid by a mutual fund are currently taxable, whether reinvested or taken in cash (unless you're investing in a tax-advantaged account). Exceptions include dividends from municipal bond funds or municipal money market funds, which are usually exempt from federal income tax and sometimes from state and local income taxes as well. Each year your mutual fund company notifies you of the tax status of any distributions paid during the calendar year on IRS Form 1099-DIV. You must report this income on your federal income tax return.

• *Like all mutual funds, bond funds carry significant tax implications.*

In most cases, mutual fund investors are taxed on their dividends according to the kinds of securities in the fund's portfolio. For example, dividends passing on to you from a fund's corporate bond holdings are taxed at ordinary rates. Conversely, dividends passing to you from a fund's stock holding will potentially be taxed at favorable rates. The portion of your dividend subject to the varying tax rates will be reported to you on a Form 1099-DIV. As with any mutual fund, when you sell your bond fund shares in a taxable account, you end up with a capital gain or loss. The gain or loss is the difference between your sale proceeds and the original basis.

• *Taxes are important, but don't let them dictate your overall investment strategy.*

As an investor, your overriding goal is to maximize your *real* rate of return—that is, your return after taxes and inflation have done their damage. As we discussed in Chapter 2, your first and most important step is to choose an overall asset allocation that fits your goals, objectives, tolerance for risk, and time frame.

This big-picture perspective is what should drive your investment decisions, not taxes. Deciding which individual investments make sense for you, and where you should put them for maximum tax efficiency, should come only after you've determined how much of your portfolio belongs in stocks, bonds, and cash. Your focus should always be first and foremost on asset allocation and investment performance. That said, paying attention to tax efficiency could help you gain a significant advantage as you seek to build your wealth over time. Just remember that together your taxable and tax-advantaged side should make up one well-thought-out, cohesive portfolio.

Keeping Track of Your Mutual Fund Gains and Losses for Taxes

Figuring out the income tax on mutual funds in regular accounts is tedious at best—and that's if you keep accurate records. If you don't, it's a real pain, and a good reason for selling shares held in your retirement account, rather than your regular account. Also, when you sell an appreciated fund (or stock, for that matter) in a retirement account, the money isn't taxed until you withdraw it. With the exception of Roth IRAs, money you withdraw from a retirement account is usually taxed as ordinary income.

If you do sell shares in a regular account, you've got to have a system. Here are the basics:

- *Money you make in the form of dividends and capital gains from the fund is easy.*

Each January, your brokerage firm or mutual fund sends you (and the IRS) Form 1099-DIV telling you the amount and character of distributions you received during the last year. This includes income that you never saw—dividends that were immediately reinvested in a fund, for example. You enter the amounts on your tax return under the appropriate category, and it will be taxed at the applicable tax rate.

- *Selling is where things get interesting, to say the least.*

When you make a profit by selling shares of a mutual fund for more than they cost, you owe taxes on that profit. If you sell the shares for less than what they cost, you have a loss that can offset capital gains or, to a limited extent, offset other income. Sounds simple enough until you think it through. The cost is, of course, what you paid for those shares—but what did you pay? Over time, you bought shares at differing prices. When you sell part of those shares, which ones are they? Which cost do you use to calculate your gain or loss?

There are three ways to calculate your mutual fund cost basis: *First-in first-out* (FIFO) assumes that the first shares you purchased are the first shares redeemed. The IRS will presume that you are using the FIFO method unless you tell them otherwise. Another choice is the *average cost basis* (or *average cost per share*); to find this, simply add the total cost of all of the shares you have purchased (including reinvested dividends) and divide by the total number of shares you own. The third method is to identify the *specific shares* from all of your purchases as the ones you have sold. This is a bit more complicated, but it can save you money on taxes. However, if you choose this latter method you must, at the time of sale, identify with your broker which shares you are selling. Also, be very careful to keep records proving that you have sold those specific shares.

In general, the best advice I can give you in terms of calculating your gains and losses from the sale of mutual funds is to keep all of your brokerage statements, use a computer to simplify your calculations, and consult with a tax professional if you have any questions.

The Bottom Line on Taxes and Investing

• *Taxes can be a huge drag on your return, so understanding the tax implications of any investment decision you reach can make a big difference. The less you pay in taxes, the more you can invest.*

• *As investors, there are two sides to us: the tax-advantaged side and the currently taxable side.*

• *Take full advantage of tax-advantaged accounts that are available to you.*

• *As you choose investments, consider whether you'll hold them in a tax-advantaged or a taxable account. Some investments are by nature tax-efficient, so it makes sense to use them in your taxable accounts when you have a choice. Less tax-efficient investments could be good choices for your retirement accounts.*

• *Index funds are a good choice for both tax-advantaged and taxable investing.*

• *Because tax-managed mutual funds are designed to be tax-efficient, they can be a good choice for taxable accounts.*

• *Unless you have offsetting capital losses, taxes can be a great reason not to sell appreciated investments in your taxable accounts. By not selling in those accounts, you don't pay taxes on capital gains. You keep the money that would otherwise go to taxes. But don't hold on to a losing investment just for tax purposes unless you have reason to believe it will rebound.*

• *Pretax return is relevant for tax-advantaged investments; after-tax return is what's important for taxable investments, particularly mutual funds.*

• *Don't invest in securities that produce tax-free income unless you're in a high enough tax bracket to justify it.*

• *Don't be caught off guard by year-end capital gains with actively managed mutual funds in your currently taxable accounts.*

• *Taxes are important, but don't let them dictate your overall investment strategy. Your goal is to find an overall asset allocation and investment strategy that fits your goals, objectives, tolerance for risk, and time frame.*

9

Planning Ahead for Your Second Half

What do you see in your future? Traveling? A home at the beach? Leisure time with family and friends? There are a hundred answers to that question, but when you boil it down, we all want the same thing: We want to have enough to do the things we enjoy. That's what this chapter is all about—doing some planning now so that you'll have enough to do what you want once you stop working.

A lot of people rank planning for their future right up there with doing their taxes; it's about as interesting, only it somehow seems less relevant, and unlike taxes, it seems optional.

Planning for the future has a nagging quality to it, as though someone's pressing you to do something you know you should do but don't want to. You see yourself at the kitchen table late at night, papers everywhere, while the rest of the family sleeps. The questions seem unanswerable: How old will I be when I retire? What will I be doing? How much money will I need for the rest of my life? And anyway, how much is enough? In other words, if you want to retire in 2014, and your youngest kid has just started college and your spouse has cut back to part-time, *and* you're hoping to spend a little more time on the golf course or the tennis court, how much money will you need? It's as though you're being asked to solve an equation for x when you don't have the value of y or anything else remotely helpful.

But here's good news: Planning for your future doesn't have to be difficult. You don't have to know all the answers, and you don't have to stay up all night. And the result will be worth the effort. Doing some planning now can give you choices about what you want out of life. How do you want your life to look? *What do you want?* That's what this chapter is all about.

Redefining Retirement: The Second Half

The word we've traditionally used to talk about the time when we no longer work full-time is *retirement,* which meant working until you were 65, then retiring and having maybe ten years of leisure, during which you downsized and maybe took a trip now and then to see the grandkids. Retirement meant lower expenses and a quiet lifestyle, and if you were just a little careful, it wasn't that hard to prepare for financially.

But things have changed, and as a culture, we're redefining what that time of life means. Thanks to the fact that we're living longer and that some of us are retiring earlier, what we used to call retirement isn't just ten years or so; it's more like the second half of our lives.

There are several reasons for the transformation of retirement into the second half of life. First, statistics tell us that we're living longer, a trend that will probably continue. Because of dramatic advances in medicine, many of us can expect to live 15 or 20 years beyond our age at retirement. In fact, one anti-aging doctor tells me that if you're alive ten years from now, you can expect to live to be 100. And for people who are living longer, retirement lasts longer. We're fortunate that we may have another 20 years or more, except that it also means that we'll need more money.

Not only are we living longer; we're living healthier. Retirement doesn't mean just sitting around in front of the TV anymore; for more and more people, it means travel, sports, recreation, entertainment—an active lifestyle that clearly costs more than sitting on the couch. And a lot of people are retiring earlier—55 or even 50. If you retire at 55 and live to 85, that's 30 years! All of which is great news, but it does take some planning.

WHEN TO START PLANNING FOR YOUR SECOND HALF

Maybe that second half I'm talking about is a long way off for you. Maybe you're just starting out, you're in your late twenties, and you figure you don't have to worry about any of this yet. "I'm too young," you're thinking. "I'll never retire. There's plenty of time." Right?

Wrong, and it's a big wrong. Everyone, regardless of age, situation in life, or plans for the future, should be planning for that second half. Remember, we're talking about the second half of your life, not ten years. If you retire at 55 instead of 65, your retirement years could even equal your working years in number. Your approach to investing may change as you get closer to retirement age, but the key thing is to be doing it. And even if you're not so young, there's still time to do something.

So don't be fooled if you're in your prime and retirement seems as distant as the moon. Everyone should be planning for that second half, and the sooner you start, the better.

HOW MUCH IS ENOUGH?

That's the answer to the *when* question about investing for retirement. The answer to the other big question—*how much*—varies widely, thanks to the fact that it involves a lot of unknowns. Some of us have kids we want to help with a first home, or maybe we want to help with our grandkids' educations. Some of us want to travel around the world, while others want to stay put. And more and more of us are finding that we want to be able to help our parents in their later years, should they need or want the help. Your specific plans will play a big role in how you prepare for your future, but the quick answer is simple: You need more than you think.

HELPING OUT

When I was growing up in the Sacramento Valley, my dad's solid practice as an attorney gave us a comfortable lifestyle. He was always careful with money, but he was a good provider, and as a family, we had everything we needed. So he was somewhat caught off guard when, in his later years, he found that he was running short on money not only for himself and my mother but also for my dependent sister, whom he supported. The situation surprised him, for he had made a good income and he had always saved. The problem was that he lived longer than he expected to—and, in fact, longer than his money.

I would have gladly helped my parents out at any time, but he was a proud man who would never have approached me about his financial worries. Because of his pride, and because I knew he would not accept help, I was hesitant to bring up the subject of money. Finally it occurred to me to offer financial support not for him but for my sister—I asked if I could step in to be responsible for her care. Even then, it wasn't easy for my dad to say yes. His acceptance was gradual, not overnight, and the result of not one conversation but many.

I can't overemphasize the satisfaction I've received from being able to dramatically improve my dad's later years. In retrospect, I regret not bringing the subject up earlier than I did. But I'm grateful that I was, eventually, able to help, and for the lesson I learned: that perseverance and sensitivity to my father's perspective were what made the difference. And I'm extremely grateful that I was in a financial position to be of help, though it was not a "financial goal" that would ever have occurred to me.

There are several reasons for that. First, retirement means both less and more than it did in the past. It means less in terms of the financial support you will receive from the government. To be on the safe side, plan on receiving less Social Security, Medicare, and other government support. It's best to view Social Security as a help in your retirement, but only a help. It won't cover most of your expenses by any means. (See the sidebar on pages 172–173.)

But retirement means *more* in terms of time and possibilities. Because we're living longer, we have to plan for more years without a paycheck. And because we're living healthier, we'll want to plan for a more active second half than experienced by previous generations. Fewer and fewer retirees are just sitting around the house. They're traveling and doing things they've always dreamed of. And financing that takes some planning. Finally, as always, inflation will be nipping at your heels. The value of your money will dwindle if you're not careful.

So how much will you need? How much will be enough? Suppose your plans for retirement don't feature circling the world or dividing your time between two houses; suppose you're generally pretty happy with your current lifestyle, and you just want to maintain it. In that case, the ballpark figure most advisers use is 80% to 100% of your current annual income (less what you've been putting aside to save for your retirement) to maintain your present lifestyle.

The lower number, 80%, comes from the assumption that your retirement will cost slightly less than your current lifestyle because some of your expenses will decrease or even be eliminated. For example, you'll be earning less, so your income taxes will be lower, and you may not be paying employment taxes. If you own a home, perhaps you'll have paid off your mortgage or you'll move to a smaller home. Job-related expenses (such as commuting costs) will be eliminated or at least decrease. And if you've helped your kids with their college educations, they'll probably be out of school by the time you retire.

But because other expenses will most likely increase, that 80% estimate may be low. Statistics tell us that health-care costs and insurance are the big ones. Thanks to more leisure time, your recreation and entertainment costs may also rise. General living expenses such as food, fuel, and utilities can increase simply because you're spending more time at home. Home maintenance and property taxes will usually be higher as well. We'll look at how much you'll need for your second half in more detail later in this chapter.

SCOPING OUT SOCIAL SECURITY

When Social Security was developed in the early 1930s, its creators chose 65 as the retirement age because the life expectancy for the average American was 67—retirement was thought of as typically lasting about two years. In those days, Social Security payments went a long way toward financing that short retirement. Things have changed, to say the least, and we can no longer count on our Social Security payments to pay the bills in the second half. They will help; think of them as a windfall.

You'll have a choice about when you begin receiving your payments. You can retire early and start receiving checks as early as 62, but your payments will be smaller. Or you can wait until what the government calls "normal retirement age," which has traditionally been 65, and receive the full amount. "Normal retirement age" varies. For those born before 1938, it's still 65. But because so many Americans are living longer, delaying retirement, Social Security is gradually raising that age, based on your year of birth:

Your year of birth	Normal retirement age (year/months)
Before 1938	65
1938	65/2
1939	65/4
1940	65/6
1941	65/8
1942	65/10
1943–1954	66/0
1955	66/2
1956	66/4
1957	66/6
1958	66/8
1959	66/10
1960 and later	67/0

So you'll have a choice to make: whether to receive smaller checks earlier, or larger checks later. If you start receiving early, you can use that money in whatever way you choose, including investing it, which is a strong argument for receiving payments early. If you wait, you miss out on several years that you could have been investing. The flip side of the argument is that if you do receive payment early, your checks are reduced for the rest of your life. The amount of the reduction varies; it's calculated as five-ninths of 1% for each month (up to 36 months) that benefits start before normal retirement age. After that, it's reduced an additional five-twelfths of 1% per month. That seemingly small number adds up. For example, suppose someone who was born in 1960 had an annual benefit at normal retirement age of $10,000. By deciding to collect at 62, that person would receive only 70% of that amount (20% reduction for the first 36 months, and an additional 10% reduction for the next 24 months), or $7,000.

If you wait to collect beyond normal retirement age, your checks increase; the older you are when you start collecting (until the age of 70), the larger your checks. For those who choose to wait, their checks will increase by the percentage shown below. That percentage increases gradually to 8% in 2008 for each year you work past normal retirement age.

If you turn 65 in this year	Your benefits will increase by this percentage each year you delay receiving Social Security
2004–2005	7.0%
2006–2007	7.5%
2008 and later	8.0%

For more information, see *www.ssa.gov.*

Second-Half Investing at Its Most Efficient: Retirement Plans

Retirement plans, whether employer-sponsored or self-funded, are about the best deal going for investors because they give the money you invest the opportunity to grow tax-deferred until you withdraw it. That's a big plus for a couple of reasons. First, the tax deferral means that the money you invest in these plans can grow faster than it otherwise would. Second, although the money is taxed as ordinary income when you do finally withdraw it, you may be in a lower tax bracket at that time, and taxed at a lower rate—which means you keep more of your money. Retirement plans are such a great investing tool that perhaps the best piece of investing advice I can give you is this: *Every year, contribute the maximum amount allowed to every retirement plan you qualify for.* That's investing at its most efficient, and it's investing that's smart.

The variety of plans out there today is remarkable; there's something for everyone, and if you haven't already, it's well worth your time to do a little investigating and make sure you're taking full advantage of every plan available to you. In this section, we'll go over the basics so that you can see what you might qualify for. Remember, though, that the world of retirement plans can be fairly complex; you may want to talk to your financial adviser or accountant about what plan or combination of plans will work best for you.

Generally speaking, there are three types of retirement plans: Individual Retirement Accounts, or IRAs; employer-sponsored plans (such as 401(k)s and 403(b)s); and plans for those who are self-employed or who own a small business (SIMPLE IRAs, SEP-IRAs, and Keoghs). Remember that these aren't mutually exclusive; for example, having an employer-sponsored plan such as a 401(k) doesn't preclude you from having an IRA as well. For each type of plan, there are IRS regulations concerning eligibility, taxation, maximum contributions, and required withdrawals.

The rules regarding how much you can contribute to each type of retirement plan vary. The following table summarizes the regulations.

Maximum Contributions to Retirement Plans

IRAs (Traditional and Roth)					
	2004	**2005**	**2006**	**2007**	**2008**
Up to Age 50	$3,000	$4,000	$4,000	$4,000	$5,000
Age 50 +	$3,500	$4,500	$5,000	$5,000	$6,000
401(k), 403(b), and 457 Plans					
	2004	**2005**	**2006**	**2007**	**2008**
Up to Age 50	$13,000	$14,000	$15,000	$15,000	$15,000
Age 50 +	$16,000	$18,000	$20,000	$20,000	$20,000
SIMPLE IRAs					
	2004	**2005**	**2006**	**2007**	**2008**
Up to Age 50	$9,000	$10,000	$10,000	$10,000	$10,000
Age 50 +	$10,500	$12,000	$12,500	$12,500	$12,500

Source: Internal Revenue Service.

Individual Retirement Accounts (IRAs)

IRAs are, for many Americans, the heart of their investing plans, and for good reason. The money you invest in an IRA is tax-deferred, meaning that you don't pay taxes on it until you withdraw it during your retirement. Free of the yearly tax setback, the investment you make in an IRA has the potential to grow bigger and faster than it otherwise would. Simply put, I believe that investing regularly in an IRA is just too good a deal to pass up. It's long-term investing at its best, and investors who don't take full advantage of an IRA as an investment vehicle are, to my mind, making a huge mistake. I'd even go so far as to say that for a lot of people, most of their investing dollars should be in retirement accounts. I urge you to make contributions to your IRA (or other retirement account) central to your investing strategy. And if you're fortunate enough to qualify for an employer-sponsored retirement plan, you're still wise to contribute to an IRA. There are several types of IRAs. We'll talk about traditional, Roth, and rollover IRAs in this chapter. (There is a similar tax-advantaged account to help you save for your kids' education; we'll discuss this plan, formerly known as an Education IRA and now called a Coverdell Education Savings Account, in Chapter 10.)

Surprisingly, a lot of people seem to look the other way where IRAs are concerned. A 2002 Schwab survey of U.S. investors showed that only around one-third of households invest in an IRA. Many investors seem to have given up on IRAs as a result of the Tax Reform Act of 1986, which took away some of the IRA's tax deductibility for a lot of people. But the tax deduction associated with IRAs is only a minor benefit compared with the tremendous possibilities of tax-deferred and tax-free investment growth, and by focusing on the loss in terms of tax deductions, investors are essentially throwing the baby out with the bathwater.

There are other misconceptions about IRAs as well. Some people think they don't have to bother with an IRA because they're already investing in an employer-sponsored retirement plan, such as a 401(k) or 403(b), and they believe that investing solely in their company plan will see them through retirement. But if your goal is to have enough in the future, you'll want to be investing as much as you can right now.

The following are a few guidelines concerning both kinds of IRAs:

• *Whatever type of IRA you choose, make it an investment priority.*

In real estate, it's location, location, location. With IRAs, it's contribute, contribute, contribute. Make contributing the maximum amount allowed your top investment priority.

• *Whenever possible, contribute to your IRA early in the year.*

By making your annual IRA contribution on January 2 rather than waiting until the April 15 deadline of the following year, you give your IRA contribution the opportunity to grow and compound for an additional 15 months. This is a time when planning ahead can really pay off. Maybe a salary increase or bonus can give you an opportunity to make an early contribution to your IRA, or one you hadn't planned on making.

• *Remember that retirement accounts are intrinsically tax-efficient.*

Suppose you're walking downtown and it starts to rain. You run for cover and find it in a hotel lobby. All's well; you're warm and dry. Then you notice a guy walking around with an umbrella, inside, still worrying about the rain. That's what choosing tax-free investments for a tax-deferred retirement account is like: coming in from the rain and standing under your umbrella. The whole point of investing in retirement accounts is their tax advantage; when you invest in one, you're already out of the rain. To choose an investment for the retirement account based on its tax efficiency is redundant; you're doubling up, protecting yourself against something that's already taken care of. You'll be *paying* for it as well, because tax-free securities generally yield less than equivalent taxable ones. Specifically, tax-free bonds and annuities are not good investment choices for retirement accounts. They're redundant and costly. In general, the best idea is to put your most tax-efficient investments in your taxable accounts and less tax-efficient investments in your retirement accounts. See Chapter 8 for more details.

• *When you have a choice, consider using tax-efficient investments in taxable accounts and less tax-efficient investments in your IRA and other 401(k) accounts.*

With your total asset allocation in mind first and foremost, you might be able to maximize your after-tax return by holding individual stocks for the long term, and municipal bonds (when they make sense because of your tax bracket) and tax-managed or index mutual funds in taxable accounts. Put less tax-efficient investments—taxable bonds and/or taxable bond funds, stocks you hold for one year or less, and actively managed stock mutual funds—in tax-deferred accounts. The benefit can be especially significant for those in the highest tax brackets, since long-term capital gains in taxable accounts are taxed at 15% while distributions from retirement accounts could be taxed at ordinary rates as high as 35%. The one exception to this general rule of thumb is the Roth IRA, since qualified distributions come out tax-free anyway. Again, this presumes you have money in both types of accounts; if all your funds are in tax-deferred accounts, then forget about the tax-efficient placement idea. And always focus first on an appropriate overall asset allocation and individual securities that make sense from an investment standpoint for all your account types.

• *Contribute to a Roth or traditional IRA even if you don't qualify for full tax deductions.*

The tax deduction of an IRA is only part of the tax-saving benefit. As you put more money into an IRA year after year, the income can continue to grow and compound tax-free.

CASE IN POINT: HOW I'VE INVESTED IN MY IRA

In 1982, I decided to check firsthand the value of regular mutual fund investing. I especially wanted to see what I could do using information that's easily available in popular magazines and guides. I wanted to keep it simple, and I decided to test my approach using mutual funds in my IRA because tax deferral of income and capital gains makes tracking returns straightforward.

I set up my IRA at the end of 1982 by contributing $2,000 to a money market fund. Money funds were paying relatively high rates of interest at the time, and my next two contributions went there as well. That was a mistake. By being on the sidelines in the money fund, I missed a 50% advance in stocks over the next 12 months. Of course, mistakes like that can be rationalized. I had other things on my mind, and it wasn't until early 1984 that I again focused on my IRA. By then I had made three contributions totaling $6,000.

I wanted to select from mutual funds that reflected my philosophy of trying to ride along with the generally upward movement of the American economy. Therefore, I wanted funds that concentrated on companies with accelerating earnings that paid few dividends. Those preferences narrowed my focus to growth funds, small-company funds, and international funds. And I wanted good track records.

I found about 50 no-load funds that met those criteria. Then I looked at funds that had stayed in the top-performing 20% for the previous five years, three years, and one year. When I culled the number down to about ten, I compared how they had performed in down markets and I finally selected three growth funds for my IRA.

In the subsequent years, I put my contributions into additional growth funds, following a similar evaluation technique each time. Along the way, I bought and sold an international fund and added aggressive growth funds and small company funds. Generally I deleted a fund when its performance fell into the bottom half of all funds in its category two quarters in a row—and switched to a fund that I felt would have more potential going forward. This upgrading approach can help keep you from languishing in underperforming funds.

Traditional IRAs

Generally speaking, in a traditional IRA, you make annual contributions, which are tax-deductible for taxpayers without an employer-sponsored retirement plan, or who meet income limitations. As long as you have an earned annual income of $3,000, you can contribute up to $3,000 per year (up to 100% of earned income, whichever is less), plus $3,000 more in an IRA for a husband or wife who does not have earned income. There's even better news: The $3,000 you can invest in an IRA will increase to $5,000 by 2008, as shown in the table on page 175. You can then continue contributing until you reach the age of 70½. The earnings accumulated from those contributions, and the contributions themselves, are not taxed until you withdraw the money, and the contributions themselves are taxable only if they were tax-deductible at the time of contribution. There are penalties that apply if you withdraw money before the age of 59½, and if you do not begin withdrawing by the age of 70½.

Finally, there is some important fine print concerning traditional IRAs. If you or your spouse is covered by an employer-sponsored retirement plan (which the IRS calls being an "active participant"), and if in 2003 your adjusted gross income exceeds $64,000 for a couple ($44,000 for a single person), you cannot deduct your contribution from your income taxes. (Those amounts will gradually increase to $100,000 by 2007 for a couple and $60,000 for a single person by 2005.) If you aren't covered by an employer-sponsored plan, you can deduct your IRA contribution regardless of your income. And if only one spouse is an active participant, the income limit for deducting your contribution is $160,000. That said, even if you aren't eligible for the tax deduction, you're still wise to contribute the maximum allowed to your IRA every year to reap the potential rewards of tax-deferred growth.

ROTH IRAs

In August 1997, Congress enacted the Taxpayer Relief Act, which greatly improved Americans' retirement saving options. The most important part of that legislation was the creation of the Roth IRA (named after Senator William V. Roth Jr. of Delaware, the chair of the Senate Finance Committee), a type of investment plan that is structured to provide benefits to a broad segment of the population. The Roth IRA was first available for the 1998 tax year. (You can also establish a Roth IRA for a child with earned income; see the section "Investing for Your Children's Future" in Chapter 10.)

A Roth IRA differs from a traditional IRA in several key ways. First, although contributions to a Roth IRA are never deductible (as they are with a traditional IRA), once you've paid taxes on that contribution, you're done—you don't pay taxes on that money again when you withdraw it. No matter how much the contribution increases in value over the years it's invested, you don't pay taxes on it when you withdraw it. Maximum contributions are $3,000 ($3,500 if you're 50 or older in 2004), increasing to $5,000 ($6,000 if you're 50 or older in 2008), as shown in the table on page 175.

Second, you can withdraw your *contributions*—the money you contribute, not what you earn—at any time without penalty. (If you withdraw money from a traditional IRA before the age of 59½, you pay taxes and a 10% penalty on that amount.) Third, a Roth IRA does not require you to begin withdrawals at any age; with a traditional IRA, you incur penalties if you don't begin withdrawals by April 1 of the year after you turn 70½. Earnings in a Roth IRA can accumulate tax-free as long as the account is open. Earnings must remain invested until you're 59½, and they must have been held in the account for at least five years. If not, you'll have to pay taxes as well as a withdrawal penalty. The rules for inheriting a Roth IRA are basically the same as the rules for a traditional IRA. Assets in the Roth IRA are subject to estate tax, but when the beneficiary withdraws from the Roth IRA, he or she will receive the money free of federal income taxes. Special rules may apply to inherited Roth Conversion IRAs.

If you're eligible for both the Roth IRA and deductible contributions to a traditional IRA, the benefits of a Roth may be greater than those of a traditional IRA. More specifically, a Roth IRA is very probably the better choice if you believe your tax rate in retirement will be close to or higher than it is now. If, on the other hand, you think your tax rate in retirement will be lower than it is now, a traditional IRA is probably the wiser choice. (Because tax rules are complex, it's always a good idea to check with your tax adviser for information and advice based on your particular situation.)

Eligibility for a Roth IRA

Whether or not you are eligible to contribute to a Roth IRA depends largely on income; in very general terms, it's designed for single investors whose annual income is less than $95,000 and for married investors (filing jointly) whose combined annual income is less than $150,000. If, as a single person, your earned income is between $95,000 and $110,000 (for a couple, $150,000 to $160,000), you can make a partial contribution. If your income is beyond those amounts, you are not eligible for a Roth IRA. Income is determined by *modified adjusted gross income,* or MAGI, which refers to gross income including wages, salaries, tips, alimony, and other incomes, less certain deductions, not including itemized deductions.

Converting a Traditional IRA to a Roth IRA

If you already have a traditional IRA, you may be able to convert it to a Roth IRA. You can convert all or part of your current traditional IRA to a Roth IRA if your MAGI is $100,000 or less for the year in which the conversion occurs. This is the same whether you're single or married filing jointly. You may not convert if you are married filing separately. To decide whether or not to convert, you need to look at several factors. First, how long do you plan to keep your money invested? The longer that period of time, the stronger the argument for converting. Second, what do you think your tax bracket will be when you retire? A higher tax bracket is another strong argument for converting. If, on the other hand, you think you'll be in a lower tax bracket, converting probably isn't your best choice. Third, how many years do you have until retirement? The more time you have to accumulate earnings in your Roth IRA, the more you can take advantage of the tax-free benefit at withdrawal, as well as offset the impact of the tax you paid at conversion.

Lastly, think about the taxes. You'll need to pay taxes on the conversion amount in full at the time you convert. Converting makes sense only if you can pay those taxes from your taxable account (outside your IRA), since the government is likely to add an early withdrawal penalty if you withdraw money from your IRA to pay the taxes. How much will be taxed? If your earlier contributions were tax-deductible, you'll owe taxes on the entire amount. If you made only nondeductible contributions, you'll be taxed only on the interest, dividends, and capital gains.

> ## TRANSFERRING ASSETS FROM ONE PLAN TO ANOTHER: ROLLOVER IRAs
>
> A rollover IRA refers to a tax-free transfer of assets from one qualified plan to another. If you change jobs, retire, or receive a divorce settlement that includes a distribution from a company retirement plan, you can "roll it over" into an IRA to preserve your capital and protect it from current-year taxes. Your distribution will be subject to an automatic 20% withholding for income tax unless your old employer rolls it over directly from your current plan into the new plan. To roll your distribution over directly, your check or electronic transfer must be made payable to the sponsor of your IRA (or the trustee of your new employer's retirement plan for your benefit).
>
> If your old employer made your distribution directly to you, you must deposit the funds into a rollover IRA (or your new employer's retirement plan) within 60 days from the date of the distribution to avoid current-tax liabilities. If your assets are not transferred within the 60-day limit, they become current income for tax purposes, and in most cases carry a 10% additional penalty if you are under 59½ years old. Your employer will be required to withhold 20% of your payout, so you will get only 80%. In order to avoid paying taxes on the 20%, you will need to make it up out of other funds and roll over all the rest of your distribution into an IRA. You can then request a refund of the withheld taxes, but this is an undesirable approach.

Giving at the Office: Employer-Sponsored Plans

The traditional word for employer-sponsored plans is *pension*, but today the term *retirement plan* is used more widely, in part because *pension* has a more specific meaning. Statistics indicate that approximately two-thirds of American workers are covered by some kind of company-sponsored retirement plan (a 401(k) or 403(b), for example). Of that, an alarming number of people don't participate. In my mind, this is a tragedy because company-sponsored retirement plans are just about as good as it gets in terms of investing for your future, and those who don't take advantage of them are missing out on a great opportunity. The only problem is you have to enroll, and although it's not anything complicated or time-consuming—it usually amounts to filling out a form—it is something, and somehow it keeps a lot of people away. If you're in that category, don't wait any longer. It's never too late, and you can remedy this today by going to your benefits office and doing the paperwork to get things going. (If you're unclear about this, see the sidebar on page 188 for help on enrolling in a retirement plan.)

If you are fortunate enough to work for a company that grants stock options to employees, there is an important caveat: *Know and understand your stock option agreement well.* One of the intents of stock option offerings is to encourage employees to give their all and to remain with the company. If and when an employee retires, those are no longer valid considerations. As a result, in many companies, the time during which you can exercise your options after you retire is pretty limited. Worse, some companies even prevent you from exercising your options at all after you retire. This means that it's crucial that you know the details of your stock option plan—especially its stock option exercise dates. A publicized case in point involved an executive of Bally Manufacturing Company, which makes slot machines. The company offered this executive the option of buying one million shares of company stock. The option had a ten-year life as long as the executive still worked for Bally, and if he retired, he could exercise the option for one year after retirement.

The executive retired on January 8, 1993. On January 24, 1994, he tried to exercise his option, but the company refused. Those 16 days cost him millions.

Obviously, this is a time to pay close attention to the fine print. Be thoroughly familiar with your stock option agreement, and if you have questions, ask. Ignoring or breaking the rules can cost you substantially.

Within the realm of employer-sponsored retirement plans, there are qualified plans—those that the employer defines and contributes to, in return for which the company receives some tax breaks—and nonqualified plans, or those that the employer defines but doesn't contribute to, usually because, for one reason or another, the company doesn't qualify for the tax breaks mentioned above. Obviously, a qualified plan is the icing on the cake, but either plan is a great deal, one you shouldn't pass up; in each case, your money can grow tax-deferred until you withdraw it.

A *defined benefit plan* is one in which your employer alone funds your retirement plan—in other words, you don't contribute. The downside is that you don't have any choice in how or where the money is invested. The plan is open only to vested employees—those who've been employed for a certain number of years, typically somewhere between five and ten years. How much you receive when you retire is calculated according to a formula that considers your salary and the length of your employment. That amount is usually figured on a monthly basis, and you begin receiving checks in that amount when you retire. As a result of today's job-hopping, this vesting period can be a problem; if you leave a company before you're vested, you can wind up with nothing in terms of retirement.

A *defined contribution plan* is one in which you, your employer, or both of you contribute to your retirement account. These plans are popular to say the least; this category includes 401(k)s and 403(b)s. Unlike defined *benefit* plans, defined *contribution* plans do allow you, the employee, to have some say in how and where your money is invested. In some of these plans, the employee is responsible for *all* of those decisions. The big advantages are that you have control over your investments (of course with this control comes the responsibility to invest wisely) and that you don't have to be vested to benefit from the plan. If and when you change jobs, you keep your contributions and potentially those of your employer, as well. You can either roll your vested 401(k) balance into another retirement account, take it as a lump-sum distribution (usually with penalties unless you're 59½), or leave it where it is until you reach retirement age.

401(k) plan: Its cryptic name comes from the number of a paragraph in the Internal Revenue Code, but despite that dull name, a 401(k) is a wonderful retirement savings vehicle. Your employer takes money directly from your salary—which means you don't pay taxes on it now—and places it in a tax-deferred retirement account, which means that you don't pay taxes on that money until you retire (or withdraw it). The decisions about how and where the money is invested are usually yours. Employers often match your contributions, sometimes as high as 50 cents or more on the dollar.

403(b) plan: Another dull, tax-code name, but also another great vehicle. A 403(b) is basically a 401(k) in the world of charitable and nonprofit organizations, including educational institutions. Your contribution is deducted directly from your salary before taxes, and your employer can contribute.

ESOP: An acronym for Employee Stock Ownership Plan, a plan in which you acquire your company's stock. Its pluses and minuses are pretty obvious: If you not only like but also believe in your company, it's an appealing proposal. But if you have less than full confidence in your company, this is a worrisome plan. Another drawback is that you don't have much control; if an ESOP is your only retirement plan, you've put all your eggs in one basket—namely, your company. If you participate in an ESOP, be sure to participate in some other retirement plans as well (an IRA, for example), so that you're not overly dependent on the success of one company and diversify your holdings.

Retirement Plans for the Self-Employed

If you're self-employed or the owner of a small business, don't give up as you read about those great employer-sponsored retirement plans. Fortunately, there are plans designed specifically for you as well.

SIMPLE IRAs: A SIMPLE IRA (which stands for Savings

Incentive Matching Plan for Employees) is available to businesses that have fewer than one hundred employees, but it's typically very small businesses, meaning those with fewer than ten employees, who use them. These plans have low administrative costs, they are fairly simple, and the employees usually handle their investments themselves. Both the employer and employee can contribute to SIMPLE IRAs.

SEP-IRAs: Stands for Simplified Employee Pension IRA and is available to those who are self-employed or who own a small business with employees. You or the employer can fund a SEP-IRA each tax year, although annual contributions are not required. Contributions may be made until your tax filing deadline, including extensions. You can contribute up to 25% or $40,000 for each employee, whichever is less. There is a special contribution formula for self-employed employers. The withdrawal rules are the same as those for traditional IRAs.

A SEP-IRA is easy to administer and maintain, which makes it very popular with owners of small businesses because the employees manage their own accounts. The employer doesn't have to administer the program; he or she only has to contribute.

Keogh Plans: The Keogh plan, named for Eugene Keogh, the U.S. representative from Brooklyn who sponsored the legislation that established the plan in 1962, is for those who are self-employed. Strictly speaking, the Keogh plan doesn't exist anymore; rather, the term refers to retirement plans established by small businesses and self-employed individuals. Like employer-sponsored plans, Keoghs can be defined benefit or defined contribution. These plans can be complicated. If you establish a defined benefit Keogh, you're required by law to consult with an actuary each year to review your plan and calculate how much you have to contribute in the following year to meet your projected payout at the end of your employment. You're also required to submit a copy of the actuary's report with the plan's tax return. That said, if you're self-employed, it's worth looking at, particularly for older individuals, because it may permit you greater deductible contributions.

CHEAT SHEET FOR A VISIT TO THE BENEFITS OFFICE

If you find you're unclear about what is being offered or what you've signed up for in terms of an employer-sponsored retirement plan, go to your benefits office and learn the following:

1. The name of the plan being offered, and a simple description of it.

2. Whether or not you're required to pay fees to participate in the plan.

3. Whether or not you have a choice in terms of how and where your money is invested. If you do have a choice, find out (a) what those choices are (and see if there is printed information available); and (b) whether or not you can make changes, and, if so, if there is a charge.

4. The maximum you can invest in the program annually.

5. Whether the company contributes to the plan, and if so, how much.

6. Past performance of the plan's investments (although this is not a guarantee of future results).

7. If you leave the company, what happens to your money: whether you can take it with you, and whether there are penalties.

You might also find out whether or not that money can be automatically deducted from your paycheck. This is called an automatic investment plan, or AIP, and it's my method of choice. It falls in the category of paying yourself first, and it's one of the easiest and most efficient ways to invest regularly.

Doing the Numbers: Where Do You Stand for Your Second-Half Goals?

By following the steps explained below, you can estimate where you stand in terms of planning for your second half. It won't take long, and you don't need to know everything—mainly the current value of your retirement and other brokerage accounts. But by taking the time to see where you stand, you won't be caught off guard when it comes to your future.

HOW MUCH WILL YOU NEED?

To get a rough estimate of how much you'll need to live on in your second half, do the following:

	Your Information	Example
1. Current gross annual income	$_____	$100,000
2. Multiplied by the percentage of your gross annual income you estimate you'll need	× _____%	× 80%
3. Equals how much you'll need per year in the second half	= $_____	= $80,000

That's the first part of estimating how much you'll need: seeing how much you'll need each year. The second part is to come up with a rough idea of how much you'll need *to have invested* when you stop receiving a paycheck. To do that, you use what I call the guideline of 300K, which goes like this: *For every $1,000 you'll need each month, you should have at least $300,000 invested when you stop working.* When you look at your investments, be sure to use what's called a "total portfolio approach," which means including all of your investments—those in your regular brokerage account as well as any retirement plans you might have (IRAs and 401(k)s, for example). You should also be aware that this guideline assumes a conservative to moderate asset allocation and a 30-year retirement time horizon. The amount you actually need may be more or less if you invest differently or have a longer or shorter retirement.

To use this guideline, do the following:

	Your Information	Example
1. Start with the estimate of how much you'll need on an annual basis	$_____	$80,000
2. Subtract other sources of income (including Social Security)	$_____	$20,000
Subtotal	$_____	$60,000
3. Divide that annual income by 12 to get a monthly amount	$_____	$5,000
4. Divide the monthly amount by 1,000	_____	5
5. Multiply the result by 300,000 to get an estimate of how much you'll need to have invested for your second half	$_____	$1,500,000

How long will that last you? Again, the guideline of 300K assumes a second half of 30 years. Traditionally people estimate the length of retirement using an actuarial chart, but it's my feeling that we know ourselves better than the tables do, and this is a time when you don't want to underestimate. You want your money to outlive you, not the other way around. The last thing you want to worry about when you're 80 is money. So 30 years seems a generous and safe number to use for those retiring around the age of 60 or 65.

The guideline of 300K also takes inflation into account. Because that number is based on research that factors in volatility and a reasonably conservative rate of return, you should have a fairly high degree of confidence that you will be able to maintain your purchasing power along the way.

That's it: a way to come up with a rough estimate of how much you'll need to have invested for your second half. If you're already investing and on your way to that goal, congratulations. You're one step closer to making the future you hope for a reality. If not, the time to get started is now; the sooner you do, the sooner you'll be on your way.

HOW MUCH WILL YOU NEED TO INVEST?

Once you have an estimate of how much you'll need for your second half, you can look at the value of the investments in your retirement plans and estimate how much you'll need to invest to reach your second-half goal. To do this, you'll need the current value of your retirement plans and any other brokerage accounts, which you can find in your most recent printed statement, or online, through your brokerage.

To do this, follow the steps below:

1. What Are You Starting With?

	Your Information	Example
IRA accounts	$_____	$50,000
Employer-sponsored plans—401(k), 403(b), SEP-IRA, etc.	+ $_____	$75,000
Other investment accounts—regular brokerage accounts, money market accounts, etc.	+ $_____	$25,000
Total current balance	= $_____	$150,000

Note: This worksheet does not include personal assets such as your home, other real estate, life insurance policies, and personal property. For more detailed information on planning for your second half, you can review the retirement planning section of *www.schwab.com*.

2. What Will It Be Worth When You Start Your Second Half?

To estimate the value of your current investments when you begin your second half, find your compound growth factor from the table that follows. This number helps calculate the value of a dollar invested at a particular point in time and for a specific expected growth rate. It tells you how much you could have at the end of the selected time period if you invest $1 at the rate indicated. If you are in between years, I suggest using a shorter time frame, which will give you a more conservative estimate.

Compound Growth of Your Current Balance

Years Until Retirement	Expected Annual Investment Rate of Return Prior to Retirement							
	5%	6%	7%	8%	9%	10%	11%	12%
1	1.1	1.1	1.1	1.1	1.1	1.1	1.1	1.1
2	1.1	1.1	1.1	1.2	1.2	1.2	1.2	1.3
3	1.2	1.2	1.2	1.3	1.3	1.3	1.4	1.4
4	1.2	1.3	1.3	1.4	1.4	1.5	1.5	1.6
5	1.3	1.3	1.4	1.5	1.5	1.6	1.7	1.8
10	1.6	1.8	2.0	2.2	2.4	2.6	2.8	3.1
15	2.1	2.4	2.8	3.2	3.6	4.2	4.8	5.5
20	2.7	3.2	3.9	4.7	5.6	6.7	8.1	9.6
25	3.4	4.3	5.4	6.8	8.6	10.8	13.6	17.0
30	4.3	5.7	7.6	10.1	13.3	17.4	22.9	30.0
35	5.5	7.7	10.7	14.8	20.4	28.1	38.6	52.8

Note: This chart is a hypothetical illustration only, and not a projection of the future performance or value of a particular investment.

	Your Information	Example
The current balance of your investments from step 1	$_____	$150,000
Multiplied by your compound growth factor	× _____	4.7
Equals the estimated value of those investments when you begin your second half	= $_____	$705,000

(Does not include taxes or transaction costs)

3. Estimate the Additional Annual Contributions You Expect to Make Between Now and Your Second Half

To estimate the value of your additional contributions when you begin your second half, find your annual contributions compound growth factor from the table that follows. This number helps you estimate how much you could have if you invest $1 at the end of each year for a selected number of years and at a selected rate of return. Again, if you are in between years, I suggest using a shorter time frame, which will result in a more conservative estimate. This table assumes you invest the same amount each year.

Compound Growth of Your Annual Contributions

		Expected Annual Investment Rate of Return While You're Still Working							
		5%	6%	7%	8%	9%	10%	11%	12%
Years Until Retirement	1	1.0	1.0	1.0	1.0	1.0	1.0	1.0	1.0
	2	2.1	2.1	2.1	2.1	2.1	2.1	2.1	2.1
	3	3.2	3.2	3.2	3.2	3.3	3.3	3.3	3.4
	4	4.3	4.4	4.4	4.5	4.6	4.6	4.7	4.8
	5	5.5	5.6	5.8	5.9	6.0	6.1	6.2	6.4
	10	12.6	13.2	13.8	14.5	15.2	15.9	16.7	17.5
	15	21.6	23.3	25.1	27.2	29.4	31.8	34.4	37.3
	20	33.1	36.8	41.0	45.8	51.2	57.3	64.2	72.1
	25	47.7	54.9	63.2	73.1	84.7	98.3	114.4	133.3
	30	66.4	79.1	94.5	113.3	136.3	164.5	199.0	241.3
	35	90.3	111.4	138.2	172.3	215.7	271.0	341.6	431.7

Note: This chart is a hypothetical illustration only, and not a projection of the future performance or value of a particular investment.

	Your Information	Example
IRA	$_____	$3,000
Employer-sponsored plans—annual contributions made by you and your employer to a 401(k), 403(b), etc.	+ $_____	$13,000

Other accounts—annual investment amount in regular brokerage accounts and money market accounts, etc.	+ $_____	$2,000
Total annual contributions in today's dollars (add above amounts)	= $_____	$18,000
Multiplied by compound growth factor for annual contributions from the table on previous page	× _____	45.8
Equals the future estimated value of your contributions	= $_____	$824,400

4. See Where You Stand

First, find the estimated value of your portfolio when you begin your second half:

	Your Information	Example
The total from step 2	$_____	$705,000
Plus the total from step 3	+ $_____	$824,400
Equals the estimated value of your portfolio when you begin your second half	= $_____	$1,529,400

Then you can see how close you are to your goal by subtracting your second-half goal (the result of your 300K calculations on page 190) from the estimated value of your portfolio above:

	Your Information	Example
Estimated future value of your portfolio from above	$_____	$1,529,400
Minus your second-half goal based on the guideline of 300K	– $_____	$1,500,000
Equals your potential surplus (+) or shortfall (–)	= $_____	+$29,400

■ ■ ■

There, you've done it. You've gotten an idea of where you stand in terms of planning for your second half, and you know approximately how much you'll need to invest to meet that goal. Congratulations! You're one step closer to meeting that goal.

The Bottom Line on Planning Ahead for Your Second Half

• *Everyone, regardless of age, situation in life, or plans for the future, should be planning for his or her second half. Your specific plans will play a big role in how much you need for your second half, but chances are you'll need more than you think.*

• *To estimate how much income you'll need per year in your second half, a good ballpark figure is 80% to 100% of your current annual income (less what you've been putting aside to save for your retirement) to maintain your present lifestyle.*

• *We can no longer count on our Social Security payments to pay the bills in the second half. They will help; think of them as a windfall. You'll have a choice about when you begin receiving payments: smaller checks earlier or larger checks later.*

• *Retirement plans, whether employer-sponsored or self-funded, are about the best deal going for investors because they give the money you invest the opportunity to grow tax-deferred until you withdraw it.*

• *Every year, contribute the maximum amount allowed to every retirement plan you qualify for.*

• *If you're eligible for both the Roth IRA and deductible contributions to a traditional IRA, the benefits of a Roth may be greater than those of a traditional IRA.*

• *If your company grants stock options to employees, be sure you know and understand your stock option agreement well.*

• *The guideline of 300K gives you a rough estimate of how much you'll need to have invested when you stop receiving a paycheck. For every $1,000 you'll need each month, you should have at least $300,000 invested when you stop working. The guideline assumes a moderately aggressive asset allocation and a second half of 30 years, and it takes inflation into account.*

10

Families and Investing

Having children, as any parent knows, changes your life dramatically. It affects your investment plans as well, influencing everything from how you invest to the tax implications of the investments themselves. But our responsibilities as parents (and even grandparents) don't stop with the financial planning that comes with having kids; it's also our job to pass on our financial knowledge, and to teach our children to be responsible for the financial parts of their lives.

Teach Them Well

Strange as it seems, managing personal finances isn't something our kids learn in school. You'd think they would; they learn everything else, from algebra to cooking. But while some schools are beginning to address finances in at least a marginal way, the fact is our kids don't learn how to balance a checkbook or what investing is all about. Which means that as parents it's left to us.

In a way that makes sense because while teaching kids about money is a lot about the practical side of finances, it's also about teaching our kids what I'll call "financial values," and those can vary from family to family. So maybe it is appropriate that it's our job as parents, just as it's our responsibility to pass on our religious beliefs and moral values such as honesty and integrity and respect.

Teaching our kids well in terms of finances is a two-layered endeavor: It's both abstract, by teaching them financial values, and practical, by teaching them, as early as possible, how to manage money and to become financially responsible adults.

The abstract layer is something that goes on their whole lives. Kids are amazingly observant, and they tend to mimic what they observe, which means that they learn some of their financial values just by watching you. How you handle and view money—even how you talk about it in daily conversation—teaches them what you believe. If you have a healthy and clear relationship with money, all is probably well. If not, you may want to get your own house in order, so that your kids will be getting the right messages.

Then there's the practical level—the more explicit teaching, the stuff that really could be taught in schools (and probably should be), but isn't. So how do you teach money-handling skills? Do you sit your 6-year-old down and explain the bulls and the bears, individual stocks versus mutual funds? Of course not. Teaching your kids about money isn't done overnight; it's best accomplished a little at a time, in the same way you'd teach a sport or any other kind of skill. In this case, you're teaching them about one of the most crucial parts of their lives. What follows are some suggestions about that teaching.

- *Start them early.*

Exposing kids to some of the principles and practicalities of money management—from setting goals and saving to investing—helps get them off to a good start. We don't wait until our kids are in high school to start talking to them about morals or beliefs; neither should we wait till then to talk to them about monetary values. And by starting your kids early, you do them a big favor: You increase their chances of becoming committed investors themselves.

- *Start at their level.*

Remember to meet your kids where they are, just as you do when you're teaching them about any other endeavor, be it sports or chess or cooking. It's something of a balancing act; you don't want to talk down to them, but you don't want to go over their heads, either.

- *Make finances part of the conversation.*

Involving your kids in what's going on financially is a great learning tool. For example, you can explain, in very simple terms, the logic of refinancing your home or why you choose the stocks you do. You don't have to go into all the details; just give them the big picture. And you can teach them the basics of investing. If you do, you'll often find that kids make great investors. Give them a little cash, and they'll jump at the chance to invest it in something, if you've taught them how and why. It can be a good experience, and while it may be a little frustrating as well, the kids will learn far more by doing than they will by just listening.

- *Make it personal.*

Setting aside a small amount of money to buy stock in a company that means something to your kids is a great hands-on lesson. Maybe the company stands for something you believe in—it's environmentally or socially responsible, for example. Maybe you just like what it makes or does—its sneakers or snowboards or software. In any case, working with your kids to find a company you can all root for, a company for which you share affection or admiration, makes investing more personal. I'm not talking about following a hot tip; I'm talking about following your heart *with a very small percentage of your money.* Another way to make investing personal is to buy a no-load mutual fund in a family member's name, then persuade him or her to monitor its performance on the market pages. And then you can explain diversification.

Remember: Teaching your kids about money is a process, not a single conversation. Don't wait until they're teenagers to start explaining your values and views on money; it's something your kids should be learning as they grow. Also remember that actions speak louder than words where values are concerned, so be aware what your actions are saying about your values. Finally, be diligent about passing on what you know; teaching your kids to be financially responsible is one of the most valuable gifts you can give them.

PASSING IT ON

My father, though he was a lawyer, had a healthy interest in the stock market, and when I was about 13, he gave me my first glimpse at investing. He held out the stock page of the newspaper and said, "These things go up and down."

So I began to watch a couple of them. I'd choose one and ask him to buy some of it for me, and he'd nod and go back to his paper, meaning that I didn't really buy anything—we both understood that my investing was only mental. But it still counted, to me at least.

Often one of those mental investments would go up, and sometimes it would even double or triple in a relatively short time. I found all those ups and downs—all that movement in the market—fascinating from the start, and I began to watch for something I could really buy. I'd saved up about $100 from odd jobs, and I finally settled on a $1 stock and bought 100 shares. For a long time after that I faithfully and enthusiastically watched the market.

Years passed, and eventually I found myself in my father's place, teaching my children about the market. My eldest son—6 instead of 13—chose a few stocks, and they went up. I got him more interested by telling him about a couple of companies. Once again, he chose a few, and they went up.

Next I bought him some shares in two high-tech growth companies and told him he could pick a third. He chose Chrysler, even though, at that time, it was heading downhill. His choice wasn't based on any in-depth analysis—he just knew that the name was familiar and that because the price was low, he could buy a lot of shares. Sound familiar? It may—it's an approach a lot of beginning investors mistakenly adopt, confusing quantity with quality.

So, with $100 he had earned himself, he bought into Chrysler. And guess what? It went up. Lee Iacocca was in charge, the stock price climbed from $3 to $30, and my son's investment went up ten times. It did much better than the other stocks I'd suggested. And he learned the thrill of investing, something I suppose both he and my other children have come by honestly.

Investing for Your Children's Future

What do you want for your children? Maybe you have a daughter who has wanted to be a doctor from kindergarten on, and you want to be able to help her out with medical school. Maybe your son has talked about acting ever since the eighth-grade school play, and you're hoping to pitch in for acting lessons. Or maybe you just want to be able to support them in whatever way they need it, whether that means help in financing a small business or the down payment on a first home.

As parents, we enjoy helping our kids in all kinds of ways, and we usually know *what kind* of help we can offer. The trickier part is *how much*—the cost—which means you may have to use a ballpark figure rather than any exact number. The exception is college education, which is easier. In 2002–2003, a year at a public college cost an average of almost $13,000 for tuition, books, fees, and room and board. At a private college, the average price was over $27,500 a year, according to the College Board. (You can find more information at *www.collegeboard.com.*) Those numbers typically go up about 5% each year, so the estimate for kids starting college in 2020 is more than $110,000 for four years at a public school, and more than $240,000 for four years at a private school.

That's the bad news; fortunately, there's also some good news. First, financial aid is often a very real possibility. Millions of today's students receive government loans, grants, and scholarships. Most financial aid is based on need, but some is based on merit, and everyone can apply. Second, you can dramatically improve your chances of financing that education by making use of several tax-advantaged education savings plans, which we'll discuss in the following sections.

Whatever your kids' dreams, your best tactic is still to get started now and start investing wisely as early as possible. Begin by giving some thought to the financial goals you and your children may have, so that you can answer those "how much" and "how soon" questions we talked about in Chapter 2. And remember that investing for your children's future is no different from investing for other goals; the pie charts in Chapters 2 and 7 will still help you determine your investing plan.

Remember that your time horizon plays a crucial role here. The longer your time frame (the younger your child), the more risk you can take. If your son or daughter won't start college for five or ten years, it's my feeling that you're wise to consider investing at least a portion of your college fund in a well-diversified mix of stocks or stock mutual funds. The reason, of course, is growth: You'll make it possible for your money to grow at a faster rate. Then, as your child gets older and closer to college, you can gradually move the money into less volatile investments, such as CDs and money market funds. Zero-coupon bonds, which we discussed in Chapter 5, are also good investing vehicles for college funds, particularly when interest rates are high.

Investing for your kids' college educations can be daunting, I know. The costs can seem staggering, but don't let them overwhelm you. Remember that funding your kids' educations is one of the best things you can do for them. I speak as a parent and a grandparent here. My wife, Helen, and I have chosen to help with our grandkids' educations, and doing so has brought us a great deal of joy. We view our contributions to our children's and grandchildren's educations as sound investments in the future. And while we also plan to benefit our kids and grandkids through our wills, it's wonderful to help them out while we're alive.

There are several types of plans that can help you save for college. As you look at them, be aware that each has its pluses and minuses, and that you don't have to choose just one. Parents are often able to use them together to great advantage.

SAVING FOR COLLEGE: 529 PLANS

If you're investing solely for your child's college education, a 529 is often the best choice, thanks to its flexibility, its great tax advantages, and its generous contribution limits. These plans take their name from the IRS tax-code section that permits states to establish tuition programs. Though they vary from state to state in several ways, every state has one, and many have more than one. Most state plans are open to both state residents and out-of-state residents, although state tax benefits are offered only to state residents.

There are two kinds of 529 plans: One is an investment account, which, because it's more flexible, is the one used more often, and the one we'll discuss below. The other is the prepaid tuition plan, in which you buy units of tuition from a state university system, thereby locking in tuition costs. The university bases the price of the units on the year in which your child will enter.

529 plans combine tax breaks with high contribution limits. Your contribution grows free of federal tax, and your withdrawals for qualified expenses are also federal tax–free. Although the specifics vary from state to state, some plans allow you to contribute more than $300,000. In addition, most states won't tax a state resident's earnings, either, and many also let residents deduct their contributions.

I need to add a caution here, though: Contributing more than $11,000 per year to a 529 plan will trigger the federal gift tax. Families with the financial resources may give a onetime gift of $55,000 in one year as long as the gift is prorated as five separate gifts of $11,000 each, and there are no additional gifts for the next five years. Couples may give $110,000 in the same way—$22,000 per year over five years.

The flexibility of 529 plans is also attractive. They give you a little room to move in terms of the following:

- **Withdrawals.** You can withdraw funds for qualified expenses, which are defined as those made for educational purposes, including tuition, books, and necessary equipment, without paying federal tax (and usually state tax as well) on that money.
- **Financial aid eligibility.** Because the money invested in a 529 plan legally belongs to the donor, the money you invest in the plan is less likely to affect your child's financial aid eligibility than the money invested in your child's name.
- **Age limit.** There's no age limit regarding the student who will use the funds (called the beneficiary). The money can be used to pay for any kind of postsecondary education, as long as the school is accredited and in the United States. You could even establish a plan for yourself if you want to go back to school.

Because many aspects of 529 plans differ from state to state, you'll need to be thorough as you check them out. The easiest way to do that is to look at *www.savingforcollege.com*. For example, 529 plans can vary in terms of the following:

- **The total contribution limit over time.** This may change. As of this writing, the upper limit ranges from $100,000 to over $300,000.
- **How states administer the plans.** State plans vary in terms of initial investments, investment strategy, fees, performance, and state tax benefits. Unlike many other saving vehicles, with a 529 plan you choose among several established portfolios, rather than directing the day-to-day investments. Because you're allowed to switch to another plan only once a year, it's essential to be comfortable with all of the details before you invest.
- **State tax benefits.** Some states give you a tax credit for your contributions to a 529, while others offer a tax deduction.

If you have more than one child headed for college, you're smart to set up a 529 for each one. If your son or daughter decides not to go to college, you can transfer the plan's funds to someone else in the family, as long as you don't skip a generation (because of gift tax). You can even take back the money, though you'll pay a 10% penalty and regular income tax on the earnings.

Plans are available from many financial institutions, and some states sell directly to investors. In many states anyone can contribute to the account, although in some states only the person or persons owning the 529 account can contribute. You can have more than one 529 for a child, but the total contribution for one beneficiary can't be greater than the contribution limit for the plan with the highest limit.

FINANCING A CHILD'S EARLIER EDUCATION: THE COVERDELL EDUCATION SAVINGS ACCOUNT

A Coverdell Education Savings Account (or ESA) is a trust or custodial account established to help pay the education expenses of a child, grandchild, or other designated beneficiary. Formerly known as an Education IRA (or EIRA) and now named for the late Georgia senator who sponsored its legislation, the ESA is a great investing tool. While it may not offer all of the same benefits as the 529, it does have some advantages that the 529 lacks, chiefly the fact that you can use money in an ESA for primary and secondary education as well as postsecondary education (as opposed to the 529, which can be used only for postsecondary education). In addition, unlike 529 plans, with an ESA you can direct your investments.

Here's how an ESA works: The person establishing the account (the parent or guardian, for example) controls the account. You must open a separate account for each child, and if you're eligible, you can contribute up to $2,000 a year on behalf of a child until the child reaches the age of 18.

The money must be used by the time the beneficiary is 30 (unless there are special factors such as a disability or other special needs). The contributions aren't deductible, but earnings are free from federal income tax and you can withdraw money tax-free as long as it's used for qualified expenses. Whether or not you're eligible for an ESA depends on your income. If you're single, you're eligible if you earn $95,000 or less (contribution limit fully phased out at $110,000); if you're married and filing jointly, you're eligible if you earn $190,000 or less (phased out at $220,000).

One final detail to note with ESAs: Because the account is technically owned by the child, the assets in the account can influence the child's eligibility for need-based financial aid.

UNLIMITED CONTRIBUTIONS: CUSTODIAL ACCOUNTS

Custodial accounts offer a great deal of flexibility in terms of how much you can contribute. Basically, you can contribute as much as you want, although amounts over $11,000 per year ($22,000 for couples) would be subject to gift tax (which means you would use up some of your individual lifetime $1 million gift tax credit— check with your tax adviser). Like ESAs, with custodial accounts you can choose the investments. And you can use the money for anything—tuition, a car, acting lessons—as long as the withdrawals are for the sole benefit of the child.

The tax advantages for custodial accounts aren't as great as they are for 529s or ESAs, but they're still significant. Until your child reaches the age of 14 (13 or younger), the first $750 of investment income is tax-free; the next $750 is taxed at your child's income tax rate. Investment income beyond that is taxed at your marginal income tax rate. When your child reaches 14, all earnings are taxed at his or her income tax rate. One potential investment strategy in this tax situation might be to develop a mixed portfolio with enough high-income-producing securities to generate taxable earnings up to the $1,500 ceiling, with the balance invested in tax-free securities or high-growth, low-dividend stocks.

Perhaps the most important factor to be aware of with a custodial account is that when your child reaches the age of majority (18, 21, or 25, depending on your state), the money is your child's to use as he or she wants. Also, because a custodial account is owned by your child, it can play a significant role in eligibility for need-based financial aid.

Some rules regarding custodial accounts depend on whether the account is governed by the Uniform Gifts to Minors Act (UGMA) or the Uniform Transfers to Minors Act (UTMA). While the basics are the same, a few things vary from state to state. For example, in some states the account terminates when the child reaches 18, while in other states the account doesn't terminate until the child reaches 21. UGMA, the stricter of the two, allows you to give minors gifts in the form of money and securities. UTMA is the more common of the two—it has been adopted by almost every state—and it's more flexible, allowing you to give real estate, royalties, patents, and art, in addition to money and securities.

THE ROTH IRA

You can also establish a Roth IRA for a child, as long as the child has earned income. It's particularly advantageous for children because any earnings have the opportunity to compound for many years. Once the child earns income—from anything from a paper route to a restaurant job—the parent can make a contribution to the child's Roth IRA equal to the child's earned income or $2,000, whichever is less. Individuals can take withdrawals from their IRAs to pay qualified higher-education expenses (tuition, books, fees, supplies, and equipment) without paying the 10% federal penalty that usually applies to pre–age $59\frac{1}{2}$ distributions. Traditional IRA withdrawals would still be subject to income tax. Contribution amounts withdrawn from a Roth IRA for qualified higher-education expenses will generally be free of both penalty and income taxes, while earnings will still be subject to income tax. For more information, see the section on Roth IRAs in Chapter 9.

SOME TAX CONSIDERATIONS

The tax considerations for investing for your children are significant, in terms of both income tax and gift tax. As we all know only too well, tax laws and regulations are complex and they change frequently, so be sure to consult your tax professional to review the tax consequences of any plans you make. What follows are some general guidelines and suggestions.

Tax Deductions Versus Tax Credits

The government offers tax relief to those financing their kids' educations in two ways: through tax deductions and tax credits. Tax deductions reduce the amount of income that's taxed, giving you a lower tax bill. Tax credits are taken from the amount of taxes you owe. You're allowed one or the other, not both, so be thorough when you look at which will benefit you more.

• *Tuition deductions.* Single filers earning less than $65,000 per year ($130,000 for couples filing jointly) can deduct up to $4,000 in college expenses. Single filers earning between $65,000 and $80,000 ($130,000 to $160,000 for couples) can deduct $2,000 for college tuition costs. The good news is that this is an "above-the-line" deduction, which makes it better than an itemized deduction. The bad news, at least for now, is that this special deduction is set to expire in 2005. For now, this deduction applies only to you and your legal dependents, is not available if you are married filing separately, is not available in a year when you use a HOPE Scholarship or Lifetime Learning credit, and excludes tuition paid for with 529 earnings or ESA funds.

• *Tuition credits.* There are several types of tax credits. First, there's the HOPE Scholarship tax credit, in which single filers earning less than $41,000 ($82,000 for couples) are allowed to subtract the following amounts from their tax bill: 100% of the first $1,000 spent on qualifying tuition and fees, and 50% of the second $1,000, for a total of $1,500 *per student.* If you earn up to $51,000 as an individual or $102,000 as a couple, this benefit is gradually phased out. Also, the credit is available only during the first two years of postsecondary education (not for graduate or professional programs). There's also the Lifetime Learning tax credit, which lets you subtract 20% of the first $10,000 you spend on tuition and fees, but this limit applies *per tax return,* no matter how many dependent students you have. Qualifying income levels are the same as for HOPE. You may receive HOPE or Lifetime Learning credit in addition to using 529 or ESA withdrawals to pay for other college expenses.

Income Tax

The Tax Reform Act of 1986 introduced a new set of rules called the "kiddie tax" for children under 14 with investment income. It changed tax rules for each of the kinds of accounts you might use for a child's funds: an account in your name (intended for your kids), a custodial account (which we discussed earlier), and an irrevocable trust. The tax implications for the first two are fairly straightforward. If you hold an account in your own name, even though it's intended for your kids, you get no special tax breaks. The investment income is taxed in the usual way, at your own tax rate. The tax implications for a custodial account were discussed earlier.

With a properly drafted *irrevocable trust,* a different set of tax rules applies. An irrevocable trust is a legal agreement that, as its name implies, is designed to be a permanent arrangement. In it, you relinquish ownership of whatever assets you place in the trust, which means they're no longer part of your estate. Properly and carefully drawn, such a trust should not be subject to estate tax (the gift tax rules would apply at the time assets are transferred into the trust, however). Potential estate tax savings aside, one of the main attractions of such trusts is that although you relinquish ownership of the gifted assets, the trust vehicle allows you to maintain a degree of control over the management of the assets, as well as how and when distributions from the trust might take place. This is complicated stuff, to say the least; you'll very definitely need the advice of an attorney to prepare the trust documents. You should also consult a tax adviser to prepare your tax returns.

Gift Tax

There's good news where the gift tax is concerned—news that provides you with a good opportunity to help your kids meet their financial goals. You can currently give up to $11,000 a year per individual in cash, securities, or other property without owing any gift tax or even filing a gift tax return. A couple can give $22,000 to an unlimited number of individuals, free of gift tax.

Looking Ahead: Some Thoughts on Kids and Estate Planning

It's wonderful to help our kids while we're around, but most of us want to leave something behind for them as well. The questions of what to leave and how much are complicated and very personal, though; and they depend a great deal on the individuals involved, for what seems right for one child may not seem right for another. You can find people who run the gamut from wanting to leave everything to their kids to wanting to leave very little, and all with sound reasons. Sage investor Warren Buffett says that the right amount to leave children is "enough money so that they would feel they could do anything but not so much they could do nothing." It's his belief that it's unwise to leave more than a few thousand dollars to a college graduate.

All of which is to say that deciding what and how much to leave your kids and grandkids demands a good deal of careful thought. On one hand, a large inheritance can demand a lot of a kid. You run the risk of taking away some of his or her initiative—something I've been very cautious about with my own children. And not every child is prepared to manage a large chunk of money responsibly. It's important to remember that it's just that—a big responsibility—and to ask yourself if a young person is ready for that. If the idea of leaving a large amount of money gives you anxiety rather than joy, that may be a sign that it's not the right thing to do. And the amount you leave isn't the only consideration: You'll also need to give some thought to when your heirs will have total control over what they inherit.

It's complicated stuff, and I have no easy answers. I have five grown children, and I continue to wrestle with the question of how to help them along the way. Each one is different; their skills and needs vary as much as their personalities, and what's right for one isn't always right for another. Being fair on top of all that makes the whole thing even trickier.

But it can be done. Give yourself time and you'll find the right balance between the kind of overabundance that can steal initiative and a level of generous support that can give a foundation for future success.

The Bottom Line on Families and Investing

• *It's crucial that we, as parents, teach our kids to be financially responsible. It's one of the most valuable gifts we can give them.*

• *Teaching your kids about money is a process, not a single conversation. Start them early and at their level, and make finances personal and part of the daily conversation.*

• *While college costs are rising at around 5% per year, the good news is that financial aid is often a very real possibility. Millions of today's students receive government loans, grants, and scholarships.*

• *Whatever your kids' goals, your best tactic is to invest wisely as early as possible. Your time horizon plays a crucial role: The longer your time frame (the younger your child), the more risk you can take.*

• *Thanks to its flexibility, its great tax advantages, and its generous contribution limits, the 529 plan is a great way to save for college. There are two kinds: the investment account type and the prepaid tuition plan. If you have more than one child headed for college, consider setting up a 529 for each one.*

• *Like a 529 plan, a Coverdell Education Savings Account provides tax-free earnings for qualified education expenses. Unlike a 529 plan, you can use the money for primary and secondary education as well as postsecondary education. However, the contribution limits are much lower (no more than $2,000 per year per beneficiary).*

• *Custodial accounts offer a great deal of flexibility in terms of how much you can contribute. You can choose the investments, and you can use the money for anything, as long as the withdrawals are for the sole benefit of the child.*

• *The government offers tax relief to those financing their kids' educations in two ways: through tax deductions or tax credits. Tax deductions reduce the amount of income that's taxed, giving you a lower tax bill. Tax credits are taken from the amount of taxes you owe. You're allowed one or the other, not both.*

Part IV

STAYING INVOLVED

11

Monitoring Your Results

So far we've talked a lot about knowing yourself as an investor, and building a portfolio to fit your risk tolerance, time frame, and goals. Those are important steps, and if you've completed them, as I hope you have, congratulations! You're definitely on the right track. It's important to realize, though, that investing doesn't stop there, and that you also need to monitor your progress so that your plans really do become reality.

In a way, staying on top of your investments is a lot like taking care of your health. Even if you pass your physical with flying colors, you don't just ignore everything from then on. You continue to get regular checkups, and if you notice that something doesn't feel quite right, you pay attention and investigate further. Taking care of your portfolio is the same: You don't ignore it just because it's fine. Professional money managers know this well. They don't simply invest their clients' money and then *hope* they meet their goals. They look at *measurable outcomes,* continually monitor their progress, and make adjustments as needed.

I'm not suggesting that you need an advanced degree or that you turn this into a full-time job. Monitoring your performance doesn't have to be complex or time-consuming. But it *is* essential to stay engaged, periodically review your progress, and make changes if you're off track. So every once in a while—typically once or twice a year, at tax time or year-end, for example—it's vital to take a good, hard look at your portfolio's performance.

How do you do that? Before you can answer the question "How am I doing?" you have to know the answer to a second question: "Compared to what?" The answer to that question lies in consulting the appropriate *benchmarks*. Remember, different investments carry different levels of risk and perform differently at different times. You can't expect a bond to behave in the same way a stock does, or even a tech stock to behave as a utility stock does. Only by comparing your results to the *appropriate* benchmarks will you know where you've hit your mark and where you've fallen short.

In this chapter we'll talk about how to do this. First, you look at the performance of your individual holdings; then you look at your entire portfolio to get a big-picture view. You don't have to crunch a lot of numbers to get a good feel for how you are doing, but if you enjoy that kind of in-depth analysis—as some of us do—you can learn how in Appendix A. Or, if you're working with a financial adviser, he or she may already be providing you with a detailed performance report. In that case, just make sure that you understand the numbers, as well as how your performance measures up on a relative basis.

I have to add that in a down market, taking a close look at the performance of your investments can be tough psychologically. But not doing so can cause real damage to your portfolio, in much the same way that ignoring a leaky roof will only make things worse. The sooner you face where you are and do what you can to improve your situation today, the better off you'll be tomorrow.

Think of this chapter as a kind of reality check for your portfolio. If you're confident that you're on track to meet your goals, that's great—keep up the good work. But if you even *suspect* that your performance has been below par, now is the time to take a closer look and find out why. And if at any time you feel unsure of yourself, that could be a good sign that it's time to consult a pro. Or if you're currently working with a broker or a financial adviser and think that you may be off track, talk to the individual! If your adviser or broker doesn't want to discuss performance, or if you don't feel you are getting an adequate explanation of your performance, it may be time to find a new adviser. We'll talk about the qualities of good advice at the end of the chapter.

Finding the Right Benchmarks

In Chapter 4, we talked about the value of using index funds as your core investments. This strategy works because, to be a successful long-term investor, you don't have to outperform the stock market, you simply have to track it. Index funds are a simple, inexpensive way to do just that (minus fund fees, of course). For the same reason, using market indexes as benchmarks is the best way to evaluate your performance. Once you've put together a portfolio that fits your risk tolerance, time frame, and goals, your continuing objective is to perform in line with your target indexes. (Of course, during a bear market you may not *feel* very successful if you are matching declining benchmarks. However, even the most successful long-term investor experiences poor performance in down markets.)

As you can see in the figure on the following page, which covers the 20-year period from 1983 to 2003, different asset classes perform very differently at different times—and very differently from each other—which is why we diversify our holdings in the first place. That's also why, in order to accurately evaluate the performance of any of your investments—whether domestic stocks, international stocks, bonds, or anything else—it's essential to start by using an *appropriate* market index as your benchmark. That's the only way to make an apples-to-apples comparison between your performance and that of the market.

Historical Asset Class Benchmark Performance

20-Year Performance Ending June 2003

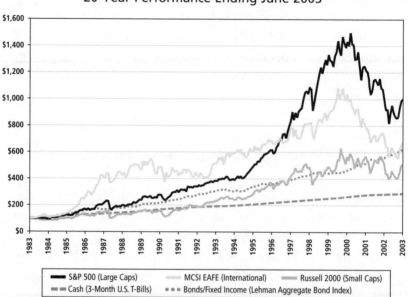

Legend:
- ━━ S&P 500 (Large Caps)
- ▬ MCSI EAFE (International)
- ▬ Russell 2000 (Small Caps)
- ▬ ▬ Cash (3-Month U.S. T-Bills)
- ▪ ▪ ▪ Bonds/Fixed Income (Lehman Aggregate Bond Index)

Note: This chart illustrates the growth in value of $100 invested in various financial instruments on June 30, 1983, through June 30, 2003. Results assume reinvestment of dividends and capital gains on stocks and coupons on bonds, and no taxes or transaction costs. **Source:** Schwab Center for Investment Research with data from Ibbotson Associates, Inc. Indexes are unmanaged, do not incur fees or expenses, and cannot be invested in directly. Past performance is no guarantee of future results.

So how do you choose the correct indexes to use as your benchmarks? When the media report on the stock market, they often focus on the performance of the Dow Jones Industrial Average, the NASDAQ, or the S&P 500. But because the Dow includes only 30 stocks, it's not a good comparison for most investments. Similarly, the NASDAQ may be a good benchmark for technology stocks, but certainly not for stocks traded on other exchanges or the market as a whole. The S&P 500 Index, which includes 500 widely traded stocks on U.S. exchanges—and represents about 80% of the market value of the U.S. stock market—is a great benchmark for large-cap stocks, but not for small companies. (See Chapter 4 for more information on various stock indexes.)

The table on the next page lists some of the most widely used indexes for a variety of investments, many of which are available in the financial press. For example, every day the *Wall Street Journal* and the *New York Times* publish both year-to-date and 12-month returns for a wide variety of stock and bond indexes, as well as interest rates. Another approach is to go directly to the vendors' Web sites (see the table below for addresses); although not all of the data are free, a lot are available without charge. In addition, many brokers, including Schwab, provide a substantial amount of free data on their Web sites.

FINDING THE APPROPRIATE BENCHMARKS

Asset Class	Benchmark Index	Web Site
Domestic Equities	Wilshire 5000 or Russell 3000	*wilshire.com* *russell.com*
Large-cap Equities	S&P 500 or Russell 1000	*standard-poors.com* *russell.com*
Large-cap Growth	S&P 500/BARRA Growth or Russell 1000 Growth	*barra.com* *russell.com*
Large-cap Value	S&P 500/BARRA Value or Russell 1000 Value	*barra.com* *russell.com*
Small-cap Equities	S&P 600 or Russell 2000	*standard-poors.com* *russell.com*
Small-cap Growth	S&P 600/BARRA Growth or Russell 2000 Growth	*barra.com* *russell.com*
Small-cap Value	S&P 600/BARRA Value or Russell 2000 Value	*barra.com* *russell.com*
International Equities	Morgan Stanley Capital International EAFE	*msci.com*
Domestic Bonds	Lehman Brothers Aggregate Bond	*lehman.com*
Cash Equivalents	3-Month U.S. T-Bill Yield	*treasurydirect.gov*

Note: *Cap,* which is short for *capitalization,* refers to the market value of a stock at a given moment in time. It is determined by multiplying a company's current market price by the number of shares outstanding. Growth stocks seek rapid growth in earnings, sales, or return on equity, and generally have higher price/earnings multiples than *value* stocks.

As you can see, if you want to evaluate your entire stock portfolio, the best place to start is with a broad index such as the Russell 3000 Index or the Wilshire 5000 Index, which include large- and small-cap stocks, as well as growth and value stocks. If you want to evaluate your entire bond portfolio, the Lehman Brothers Aggregate Bond Index is a good choice because it contains corporates, governments, and munis, as well as other bond segments. From there, you can get more specific. For example, you can use the S&P 500 for large-cap stocks, the Russell 2000 for small-cap stocks, and the Morgan Stanley Capital International (MSCI) EAFE Index for your international stocks. If you want to get more detailed still, there are indexes for different stock sectors, styles, and size. In the bond world, you can also look at indexes tied to specific categories such as investment-grade corporates, governments, munis, high-yields, and so on.

Checking Out Your Funds and Other Large Holdings

Just about the easiest way to quickly "take the pulse" of your portfolio is to look at some of your largest mutual fund holdings. Many financial Web sites, including *schwab.com*, have great charting tools for their clients. In my opinion, this is one of those times when a picture is worth a thousand words. For example, let's take a look at hypothetical Fund A, a stock fund:

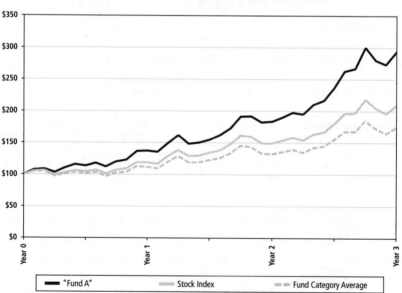

Fund A vs. Index and Peer Benchmarks

Note: This chart is for illustrative purposes only and does not represent the performance of any particular mutual fund or index.

You can immediately see how Fund A has performed over a three-year period, and you can also see how its performance compares to both the benchmark index and other comparable funds. In this case, not only has Fund A outperformed its benchmark; it has also consistently outperformed other funds in its category. Personally, I would continue to hold Fund A because of its consistently excellent performance relative to the index.

On the other hand, let's take a look at hypothetical Fund B, which is a bond fund:

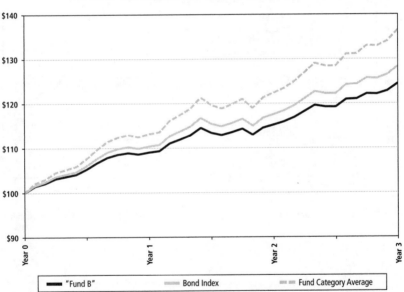

Fund B vs. Index and Peer Benchmarks

Note: This chart is for illustrative purposes only and does not represent the performance of any particular mutual fund or index.

In this case, you can see that Fund B has lagged behind both the bond index and similar funds. In this case, I would recommend digging deeper to see why the fund has underperformed. If I were reassured that things would turn around, I might continue to hold the fund. But if not, I would swap out of Fund B into another fund that has a better track record.

And finally, let's take a look at how hypothetical stock Fund C performed during a bear market.

Fund C vs. Index and Peer Benchmarks

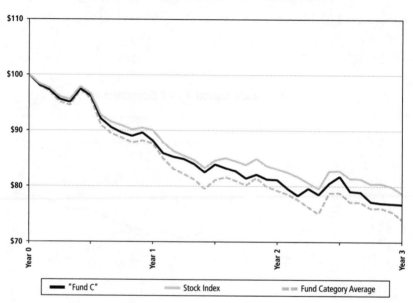

Note: This chart is for illustrative purposes only and does not represent the performance of any particular mutual fund or index.

In this case, you can see that Fund C's performance is almost identical to the index. I would continue to hold this fund—provided, of course, that it still suits my asset allocation.

Looking at your portfolio in this way—fund by fund—can be a useful exercise. And if most of your portfolio is made up of mutual funds—whether they're stock funds, bond funds, or blended funds—this type of simple check may be all you need to get a good sense of how you're doing. It can also be interesting to look at individual stocks in this way; but because putting too many of your investing dollars into any one stock is very risky, the performance of one holding shouldn't be an accurate indicator for your overall portfolio. If it is, you need to diversify your stock holdings more.

The bottom line is that comparing your largest holdings to the appropriate benchmarks is a good way to do an initial assessment. But if you want to get a better sense of whether you are on track to meet your long-term goals, it's best to investigate a bit further, and look at your portfolio as a whole.

Taking a Look at Your Whole Portfolio

Now it's time to take a big-picture view. After all, your ultimate success as an investor is tied to having a well-diversified portfolio that fits your tolerance for risk, time frame, and specific goals. In fact, the main reason for diversifying in the first place is that we expect some holdings to underperform at the same time that others outperform. So while it's instructive to keep an eye on how your individual holdings are performing, a total portfolio approach is the best way to make sure you're on track to realize your long-term goals.

For most investors, an annual—or, at most, semiannual—review is fine. Anything more than that is probably unnecessary. Remember, portfolio returns can and will fluctuate a lot over short-time horizons. Your objective is to review your progress toward your long-term goals, not to get sidetracked by the short-term ups and downs.

To start simply, let's begin by looking at a hypothetical all-stock portfolio. Suppose you start with $100,000, and three years later you have $113,000. You may think that this is a positive result, but when you compare your results to a benchmark such as the S&P 500, you can see that you underperformed on a relative basis, as illustrated in the figure on the following page.

Investor Portfolio vs. Benchmark in a Bull Market

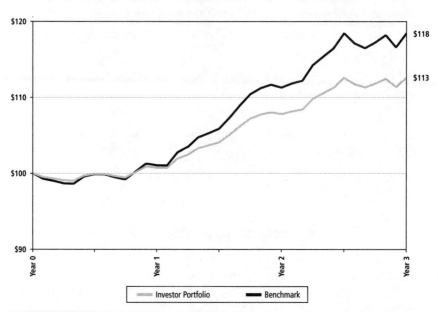

Note: This chart is for illustrative purposes only and does not represent the performance of any particular mutual fund or index.

Even though you closely tracked the benchmark for the first year, after that you began to slip. In other words, after year 1, you would have done better simply to invest your money in a fund that tracks the index (in which case you would have had approximately $118,000 at the end of three years—minus some amount for portfolio expenses—instead of $113,000). So even though your portfolio increased in value, it *underperformed* on a benchmark-relative basis.

On the other hand, let's take a look at a hypothetical portfolio during a bear market, as illustrated in the figure on the next page.

In this case, you may feel discouraged because you lost money— in fact, this is how many investors felt during the bear market of 2000–2003, the time period with the worst equity performance in my lifetime. However, on closer examination you can see that you outperformed the benchmark—so this is actually a positive outcome. In this case, I would encourage you to hang in there; if you keep this up when the market rebounds, you will be in a very favorable position.

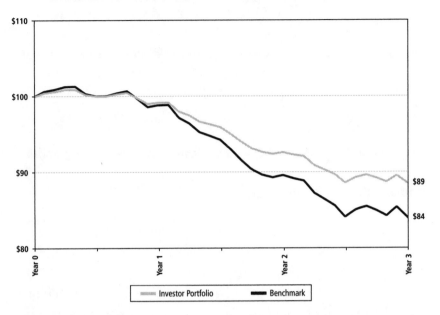

Investor Portfolio vs. Benchmark in a Bear Market

Note: This chart is for illustrative purposes only and does not represent the performance of any particular mutual fund or index.

Now let's look at a more typical portfolio—one that includes bonds and cash as well as stocks—and walk through a more in-depth, three-step process of first calculating your total portfolio return, then finding the appropriate benchmark return—or combination of benchmark returns—and finally comparing the results.

Step 1. Calculate Your Return

If you haven't deposited or withdrawn money from your account, calculating your percentage gain (or loss) is a simple process:

(ending value – beginning value) ÷ beginning value.

Using this formula, if you started with $100,000 and now have $110,000, you have achieved a 10% return:

(110,000 – 100,000) ÷ 100,000 = 10%.

Things are more complicated when you've deposited or withdrawn money. To get a general sense of how you did, you can simply subtract the money you added (subtract a positive value) or withdrew (subtract a negative value) from your ending value, and see how your original investment performed. For example, say you started with $100,000, deposited $5,000 some time during the period, and ended up with $110,000. In this case, you can use the following formula:

(ending value − beginning value − cash flow) ÷ beginning value.

Substituting your numbers, this becomes:

(110,000 − 100,000 − 5,000) ÷ 100,000 = 5%.

That is, you had a 5% return.

(Note: In this example we sacrifice a certain degree of accuracy in order to keep the math simple. If you want to be more precise and take the timing of your deposits and withdrawals into consideration, you'll find the steps for calculating a more accurate "time-weighted" return in Appendix A. This method isn't hard, but it does require going back to your monthly statements, calculating month-by-month portfolio returns, and then linking them in a quarterly or annual compounded return. There is no question that this takes some time, but it is the most accurate way to assess your performance.)

Step 2. Find an Appropriate Benchmark
Once you have a numerical figure for your portfolio's return, the next step is to find an appropriate benchmark return to compare it to. Assuming that you have a broadly diversified portfolio, your goal is to create a "blended" benchmark that has approximately the same percentages of asset classes as your portfolio so you can make an apples-to-apples comparison between your performance and the performance of such a blended benchmark. To keep things simple, you can use the Wilshire 5000 Index for your stocks, the Lehman

Brothers Aggregate Bond Index for your bonds, and the 90-day T-bill rate for your cash. Here's the formula for calculating the weighted average return of your blended benchmark:

(% in stocks × Wilshire 5000 return)
+ (% in bonds × Lehman Brothers Aggregate Bond Index return)
+ (% in cash × 90-day T-bill return)
= blended benchmark return.

For example, suppose you are a moderate investor with 60% of your portfolio in stocks, 35% in bonds, and 5% in cash. If the Wilshire 5000 were up 8%, the Lehman Brothers Aggregate Bond Index up 4%, and 90-day T-bills up 1%, here's how the formula would look:

(60% × 8%) + (35% × 4%) + (5% × 1%)
= 0.048 + 0.014 + 0.0005
= 0.0625, or 6.25%.

That 6.25% would be your customized blended benchmark return—a benchmark that mirrors the percentages of stocks, bonds, and cash in your specific portfolio, but uses the individual asset-class benchmark returns instead of the actual returns experienced in your own portfolio. Essentially, this customized blended benchmark approximates the return you could have realized for the period if you had simply invested in index funds rather than in the actual securities you owned in your portfolio (minus fund fees, of course).

If you want an even more precise comparison, you can break down your stock portfolio further into more distinct asset classes. For example, you could break up your stock holdings into smaller groups by using the S&P 500 for large caps, the Russell 2000 for small caps, and the MSCI EAFE for international stocks.

Step 3. Compare Your Results
Now you can directly compare your return to the blended benchmark return to really understand how you're *entire* portfolio is doing on a relative basis. As you compare your results, remember—and

this is important—that to be a successful investor, you don't have to outperform the benchmarks; tracking them is fine (minus fees, of course). There are no hard-and-fast rules, but if your return is more than five or ten percentage points off the benchmarks on an annual basis, or if you're consistently off by a smaller amount year after year, you owe it to yourself to understand why. If you're too far off, it may be a symptom of a bigger problem that requires you to take action. It's always better to fix these problems sooner rather than later.

USING THE SCHWAB MODEL PORTFOLIOS AS COMPARISONS

You can also use the Schwab model portfolios (the pie charts from Chapter 2) as comparisons, or as another type of blended benchmark. Although your portfolio probably doesn't exactly mirror any of these portfolios, you can see the types of cumulative results you might have achieved in the last one, three, five, and ten years (ending in 2002), depending on whether you are a conservative, moderate, or aggressive investor:

As you can see, the bear market of 2000–2002 was very tough on the short-term performance of the more aggressive portfolios. During these three years, the aggressive portfolio, which is composed of 95% stocks and 5% cash,

	Conservative Portfolio	Moderate Portfolio	Aggressive Portfolio
1-year return (2002)	1.3%	–9.25%	–20.4%
3-year return (2000–2002)	11%	–13%	–34%
5-year return (1998–2002)	29%	16%	–2%
10-year return (1993–2002)	100%	129%	132%

Note: The 3-, 5-, and 10-year returns are cumulative, not annual. Also, these returns do not include expenses, which would lower the real-world returns by anywhere between 0.5% and 2.0% per year. Past performance is no indication of future results.

was down 34%; the moderate portfolio, which is composed of 60% stocks, 35% bonds, and 5% cash, was down 13%. (And don't forget, when we talk about either stocks or bonds in this portfolio context, we are referring to well-diversified holdings in each category.)

You can also see that after ten years, the conservative portfolio lagged significantly behind the moderate and aggressive portfolios—even after one of the worst bear markets in history. Remember, though, that the conservative portfolio carried much less risk along the way. Even though some investors think of performance strictly in the context of returns, performance is always about both return and risk.

Viewed graphically, the chart following this sidebar shows the historical returns for the three model portfolio.

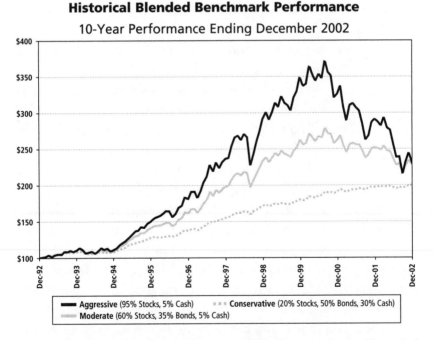

Historical Blended Benchmark Performance
10-Year Performance Ending December 2002

Legend:
- **Aggressive** (95% Stocks, 5% Cash)
- **Conservative** (20% Stocks, 50% Bonds, 30% Cash)
- **Moderate** (60% Stocks, 35% Bonds, 5% Cash)

Source: Schwab Center for Investment Research with data provided by Ibbotson Associates, Inc. The growth of $100 for the time period displayed represents three hypothetical asset allocation plans. Each asset allocation plan is a weighted average of the total returns of the indexes used to represent each asset class in the plan and is rebalanced annually. The indexes representing each asset class are the S&P 500 Index (large-cap stocks); Russell 2000 Index (small-cap stocks); MSCI EAFE Net of Taxes (international stocks); Ibbotson Intermediate U.S. Government Bond Index (bonds); and 30-day Treasury bills (cash). Past performance is no indication of future results.

What Does It All Mean?

In this chapter, you've learned about the tools that can help you "look under the hood" of your portfolio, and get a good feel for how things are going. If your initial look tells you that something might be off, these are some things to think about:

• The most common reason for significantly underperforming a benchmark is a lack of adequate diversification across and within asset classes (i.e., owning fewer than 20 to 40 different stocks that represent a wide range of sectors and industries), giving you an over-concentration in one asset class (such as stocks), or an overconcentration within a specific sector (for example, technology, airlines, or utilities), style (growth versus value), or size (large-cap, mid-cap, or small-cap). As explained in Chapter 3, the easiest way to build a well-diversified Core stock portfolio is to buy one or more broad-based index funds.

• Another common reason for underperforming the benchmarks is that you're paying too much in portfolio expenses. These expenses can come from trade commissions, operating expenses charged by mutual fund companies, or an advisory fee you might pay to a personal portfolio manager. Portfolio expenses are to be expected, but if you're paying a significant amount in total fees on your portfolio and you're not at least tracking the benchmarks less those fees, you could probably be doing better.

• Underperforming isn't the only warning sign; significantly over-performing can also be a red flag because it's often an indication that you've taken on more risk than you realize or than is appropriate given your goals and time horizon. Although significantly out-performing the benchmark this period is a good thing, your results could easily swing in the other direction in the next time period.

• If you performed on a par with the benchmarks (your bench-mark-relative return was near zero), but you had an uncomfortable absolute loss (both your portfolio and the benchmark were down more than you're comfortable with), it could indicate that your portfolio construction was adequate, but that you've chosen a portfolio with more inherent risk than is appropriate given your tolerance for risk. In other words, you could have the wrong asset mix in your portfolio, and it may be time to reassess your asset allocation and rebalance your portfolio accordingly, which we'll discuss in Chapter 12.

• Finally, never forget that thanks to index funds, which are engineered to track the returns of market indexes with low expense ratios, there's simply no reason to accept significantly below-benchmark results.

A Little Advice on Good Advice

If your return is significantly below the benchmarks, the next thing to look at is the quality of the advice you're receiving. If you're not receiving professional advice, now may be the time to do so, even if that just means a one-time consultation. If you are receiving advice for a fee (from a brokerage firm or an independent financial adviser), you should discuss any significant below-benchmark performance with the advice provider. If he or she won't discuss the issue with you, or the response is not satisfactory to you, it may mean that it's time to reevaluate that advice and go elsewhere. That's one of the most important reasons for looking at performance: How you're doing is a direct reflection of the advice you're getting.

Seeking professional investment advice can be one of the wisest moves you make; in fact, there comes a time when it's a good move for just about every serious investor. People seek professional investment advice for a lot of reasons besides poor performance. Time is a big factor; maybe you just don't feel you have the time necessary to devote to monitoring your investments. Interest is also important; maybe this just isn't your thing. Expertise can figure in; maybe your portfolio and overall circumstances have become complex enough that you simply can't handle it yourself. And just as a bull market encourages investors to think that they can manage their own portfolios, a tough market can send a lot of investors looking for help.

WHAT IS GOOD ADVICE?

If and when you do decide to get help, remember that you're not just seeking advice; you're looking for *good* advice. Let's talk about what that means.

First and foremost, you're looking for integrity and objectivity. You want advice that's based on experience and expertise, and—this is key—that is truly *unbiased,* which means that your adviser has your best interests at heart, not his or her own.

Second, good advice should start with your specific investing objectives, situation, and even your personality. A good adviser should talk with you about your risk tolerance, time horizon, and your goals. Based on this information, he or she should then help you develop an asset allocation that's appropriate for you. If you don't think your adviser understands you as an investor, it's time to look for another adviser. Any recommendations you receive should be based not on the adviser's personal bias but on an in-depth analysis of your situation. Remember that your success as an investor depends on how well the parts of your portfolio work together. Good advice has to be based on your big picture; buying an investment just because it looks good on its own is dangerous stuff. The question to ask is this: What role will this investment play in the bigger picture?

Third, your performance speaks volumes. If you're paying a fee to a financial adviser, you should expect to receive performance reports based on calculations similar to those in Appendix A. You should also be achieving results that consistently match or exceed the market benchmarks. Remember, the ultimate measurement for the quality and consistency of the advice you're getting is the outcome.

SOME GUIDELINES ON FINDING GOOD ADVICE

There are several things to know up front about getting professional investing help. The most obvious is this: Generally speaking, it doesn't make financial sense to hire someone to manage your money if you have less than $100,000 to invest—and in most cases, financial advisers won't be interested in taking on accounts for less than that amount, either.

In addition, consider the following:

• *Be clear about what kind of help you want.*

There are quite a few kinds of professional help available out there. Know what's available, and be clear about what kind of help will best meet your needs. Maybe you just want a session or two with an expert, during which you go over your portfolio and get some buy or sell suggestions for a one-time consulting fee. Or maybe you're at the other extreme, where, because of time or interest or expertise, you're ready to hand over the day-to-day management of your portfolio to a professional for a recurring asset-based fee. Just about every level of professional help is available, so give some thought to the level of involvement you want.

• *Take some time to find the right adviser.*

It's crucial to check around and find the right person—someone reputable and without conflict of interest. Word of mouth is one of the best ways to do this, so asking around is a good first step. Check with friends and with other professionals such as your lawyer or accountant. The National Association of Personal Financial Advisors (888-333-6659 or *www.napfa.org*) is another good resource.

• *Understand how independent advisers are compensated.*

Some advisers charge on an hourly basis, which works well if you want to meet with someone on a short-term basis. For ongoing management, compensation is typically fee-based: You're charged a percentage of the assets under the adviser's control on a recurring basis, typically 1% to 2% per year. I feel that fee-based compensation tends to be more unbiased than commission-based compensation: The adviser is not directly receiving a commission on investments you buy or sell. And it's in the adviser's best interest for your portfolio to grow: The greater the value of your portfolio, the greater the adviser's earnings.

■ ▨ ▧

Investing is a process; I'm sure you're becoming more aware of that with every chapter you read. It's an important concept because once you realize that, you're no longer tempted to sit back and stop taking care of business. You have to be vigilant; the stakes are high. That doesn't mean you worry about your investments constantly; it just means you give your portfolio the attention necessary for it to thrive. The biggest mistake isn't a bad stock pick or even under-performing your benchmark. The biggest mistake is neglecting the maintenance part of investing and failing to plan for your future. But keep your eye on the ball—watch your performance, get good advice, and make changes when necessary—and chances are good that you'll end up just where you want to be.

The Bottom Line on Monitoring Your Results

• *Investing doesn't stop with building your portfolio; it's crucial to monitor your progress by looking at measurable outcomes and making any necessary adjustments along the way.*

• *Before you look at performance, you have to know which benchmarks to use. Only by comparing your results to the appropriate benchmarks will you know where you've hit your mark and where you've fallen short. You do this by looking at the performance of both your individual holdings and your entire portfolio.*

• *Looking at performance during a down market can be tough psychologically, but the sooner you face where you are and do what you can to improve your situation, the better off you'll be.*

• *If most of your portfolio is made up of mutual funds— whether they're stock funds, bond funds, or blended funds— looking at your portfolio on a fund-by-fund basis may be all you need to get a good sense of how you're doing.*

• *While it's instructive to keep an eye on how your individual holdings are performing, a total portfolio approach is the best way to make sure you're on track to realize your long-term goals. For most investors, an annual or semiannual review is probably fine.*

• *The most common reason for significantly underperforming a benchmark is a lack of adequate diversification across and within asset classes. Paying too much in portfolio expenses is also a common reason for underperformance.*

• *If your return is significantly below the benchmarks, look at the quality of the advice you're receiving. That's one of the most important reasons for looking at performance: How you're doing is a direct reflection of the advice you're getting.*

• *Seeking professional investment advice can be one of the wisest moves you make. Good advice has integrity and objectivity, and it starts with your specific investing objectives, situation, and even your personality. Any recommendations you receive should be based not on the adviser's personal bias but on an in-depth analysis of your situation.*

• *Generally speaking, it doesn't make financial sense to hire someone to manage your money if you have less than $100,000 to invest—and in most cases, financial advisers won't be interested in taking on accounts for less than that, either.*

• *Investing is a process, which means you have to be vigilant. The biggest mistake isn't picking a bad stock or underperforming your benchmark. The biggest mistake is neglecting the ongoing maintenance part of investing and failing to plan for your future.*

12

Staying on Track

Once you've followed the steps in Chapter 11 to get a good idea of your portfolio's performance, you may find you want to make some changes. Maybe you want to sell some investments that no longer meet your goals or are consistently and significantly underperforming, for while buy-and-hold is certainly a wise and time-tested investing philosophy, there are times when selling is even wiser. Or maybe you want to rebalance your portfolio, meaning you wish to take some action to change your asset allocation. Investors do this for several reasons. For example, perhaps you find yourself unhappy with the level of risk you've taken on—whether it's too much or too little—so you want to change your original asset allocation. Or you might find that, as a result of the fluctuations of the market, your portfolio no longer reflects the asset allocation percentages you so carefully chose and you want to do what it takes to return to those percentages.

Let's start by looking at when to consider selling stocks and stock mutual funds. Then we'll talk about rebalancing.

THE ARGUMENT FOR A BUY-AND-HOLD STRATEGY

While there certainly are times when selling an investment is the wise choice, it's important not to overdo it where selling is concerned. Some people seem to think of investing as a constant buy-and-sell endeavor: You buy and sell based on what the market does day to day. But there are very compelling reasons for staying in the market—in other words, buying and holding—rather than getting in and out. First, taxes are a very strong argument for not selling. Quite simply, if you don't sell, you don't pay taxes on the sale. And if you don't pay taxes on the sale, that percentage of the profit that would otherwise go to the government stays in your portfolio and continues to work for you.

Second, the fact is that the longer you're in the market, the more you're exposed to its potential rewards. And the largest gains often come when conditions look darkest—and that's when someone who's constantly buying and selling is least likely to be invested. Instead of trying to sell at the right time, invest for the long term and be very picky about when you even consider selling. Consider it only in the situations listed later in this chapter.

When to Consider Selling Stocks and Mutual Funds

Deciding whether it's time to sell a stock or mutual fund can be difficult. It's hard to be objective and to know if selling is the right thing, especially if you've held the investment for a long time and are, in a way, attached to it. It's important to be objective and clear about the kinds of situations that warrant selling.

Let's start with two situations that apply to both stocks and stock mutual funds. First, a change in your personal situation can be a reason to sell. Things change, and if your personal life changes, chances are that your investing life will be affected. Your time frame, risk tolerance, and goals could all be altered. Second, rebalancing your portfolio, which means making some adjustments to change your asset allocation, is a common reason to sell. There are several reasons for rebalancing, which we'll discuss later in this chapter.

WHEN TO SELL A STOCK

In addition to those two general situations, there are three more specific situations that warrant selling a stock: if you made a bad choice in the first place; if the stock's fundamentals have deteriorated; or if you find you're overconcentrated in that stock or in the sector it represents.

Notice that that list doesn't include a drop in stock price. That's because if you're thorough in your evaluation of stocks before you buy, a drop in stock price isn't, by itself, reason to sell. Stock prices fluctuate, so don't let those drops put you in a selling panic. Any number of factors can drive a stock price down, such as legal issues, competition, or corporate misjudgment. The important factor isn't the drop in price; it's the reason for the drop.

Let's look at the situations in which selling is the right thing to do.

1. You made a bad investment choice.

We all make mistakes, and if you find, over time and after doing some research, that you made a bad investment choice, it's not the end of the world. The important thing isn't the mistake; it's how you react to it. The best thing to do is to cut your losses and sell the bad investment, reinvest the money in a better place, and move on. If you find yourself stalling, remember that there's no guarantee that this is the end of your losses; things could get worse. Generally, the sooner you cut your losses, the smaller your losses—and the smaller losses are a lot easier for your portfolio to bear than the big ones.

And don't forget the tax write-off. When you realize a capital loss, you can use it to offset any capital gains you realize in the same year. You can also claim net capital losses of up to $3,000 in any given tax year, and you can use them against your ordinary income. If your capital losses exceed $3,000, you can carry them forward into the next tax year.

2. *The fundamentals have changed.*

A drop in stock price may mean you've made a mistake, but it can also mean that your buy decision was good but that something has changed since then. If you're wondering about a specific stock, your first move should be to take a good look at the company to see if there have been any major changes. Bad signs include basic problems with the company itself, its products, or its business prospects, such as a significant drop in earnings, weak management, or outdated technology. A drop in market share is also serious. If a company begins to lose some of its share of the market, it may be losing some of its competitive edge—and that can mean more trouble ahead. One possible indication of a loss of market share is a drop in one company's stock while the stocks of similar companies are headed up. Then you go up a level: Entire industries can become outdated or simply erode, and that's a problem. If the company's competitive position is eroding, or if its industry is evaporating in what looks like a permanent way, that can be serious.

To help you in your sell/not-sell decision, start by asking yourself this: "Knowing what I now know about the company and the stock, would I still buy this stock?" Then research the stock as though you were buying it for the first time. Look at the company's P/E ratio and management, and at the industry as a whole. Check out the annual and quarterly reports and the company's balance sheet. If, after your research, you wouldn't want to buy the stock, it may be time to sell. If you're still on the fence, it may be time to get help from a pro. Having a financial adviser go through your portfolio on an investment-by-investment basis can be a tremendous help.

3. You're overconcentrated in the stock or sector.

Too much of a good thing is always a possibility in investing, and it can lead to increased risk. If you see that one stock or sector is starting to take over your portfolio, you may need to cut back on it, in the interests of proportion and risk.

EVALUATING STOCKS WITH SCHWAB EQUITY RATINGS

When you're considering selling a specific stock, Schwab's Equity Ratings can be a great tool. This online tool rates over 3,000 stocks with a letter grade (A, B, C, D, or F) that gives you quick and clear information about the stock's fundamentals and valuation. To learn more about Schwab Equity Ratings, go to *www.schwab.com*. You'll also find more information on the system in Chapter 4.

WHEN TO SELL A MUTUAL FUND

Because mutual funds are core investments, constituting the heart of your portfolio, I feel that a buy-and-hold strategy is even more crucial with these investments. I tend to hold mutual funds for at least three years; I hold most of them for much longer than that. In my experience, three years is a fairly typical cycle, and it usually includes a down market and an up market. I like to see how the managers of a fund perform through the test of a down market. Basically, the longer I can hold the fund, the better, and I don't trade a fund unless circumstances really warrant it. A drop in a fund's performance isn't in itself reason to sell. At times a fund will underperform its peer group; managers have good years and bad. If the fund's objectives and philosophy are the same, hang in there.

In addition to the general situations mentioned above—a change in your personal situation or the need to rebalance your portfolio—

WHEN *NOT* TO SELL: SURVIVING A DOWN MARKET

With investing, it's hard enough to hold your emotions at bay during the normal downturns, but chances are that sometime in your life you'll face a formidable down market. Eventually stocks recover to new highs, but many investors lose faith before the recovery and flee to "safe" cash equivalents and fixed-income investments. As a result, it's virtually impossible for them to catch up when the market does turn around. After a 30%, 40%, or 50% loss, you would need a 60%, 80%, or 100% gain to break even. But if you've sold your stocks, you will have a very hard time ever making up your loss.

Since 1926 we've had 24 bear markets. Some were worse than others, but the typical bear prowled around for about ten months and took the market down 25 to 30 percent. Every single one of them was followed by a bull market. Remember that record. It tells me that I'm investing in something that has always come back, and I believe it always will. When the market falls to panicky lows, it's tempting to believe the doomsayers. But when your fears are at their peak, that's the time to make the extra effort to resist them. If you do some research and decide that now really is the time to sell, that's one thing; but don't give in and sell out of fear or panic. Know that history has shown that American financial markets come back from every apparent abyss and sit tight.

the following are more specific situations in which you would be wise to consider selling a mutual fund:

1. *It exhibits low performance over time.*

The first thing to understand about performance is that it is only meaningful in context. The only way to know if a particular fund has performed well (or poorly) is to compare it to its peers. In other words, it means little to compare a large-cap growth fund to a small-cap value fund, or even a large-cap growth fund to a total stock market fund. So the first step is to make sure that you are comparing an apple to another apple. If one of your mutual funds performs worse than its peers or benchmarks for two or three years, I think that's reason to sell, as is performing in the bottom quartile for even one year. If the fund performs as well (or close to as well) as its benchmark, you should be okay; you might even add to it.

2. *The fund's management changes.*

If the manager of an actively managed fund leaves, that isn't reason enough to change in and of itself, but it can definitely be a warning. It may not be bad news for certain—it's possible that the new manager may do as well as or better than the previous one—but it's more likely that the new manager will significantly change the fund's holdings.

3. *The fund's objectives change.*

A change in investment style or objectives is another red flag. Any major change—for example, from large-cap stocks to small-cap stocks, or from domestic stocks to international stocks—is a warning. To stay current, you can, once a year, check the writeups for your funds in *Morningstar.* If you see a change, keep an eye on that fund's performance for the next year or so. If it goes down, you may want to sell.

SOME ADVICE FROM THE PROS

Research from the Schwab Center for Investment Research about when to sell a fund tells us the following:

• On average, funds with lower expenses tend to perform better than those with higher expenses.

• Selling funds that underperform their peer groups can lead to slight improvements in portfolio returns (without considering tax and transaction cost implications).

• The best returns in this study typically came from selling funds that had fallen into the bottom quartile for performance (i.e., the lowest 25%—funds that were outperformed by 75% of their relevant peer groups) on an annual basis.

• The difference in annualized returns, however, was slight—only 0.42%—suggesting that you consider the above strategy more of a guideline than a mandate.

• Evaluating your fund's performance—along with your financial situation—every year is a critical step in your decision-making process.

• When evaluating fund performance, make sure you compare your fund to the most appropriate peer group. Comparing apples to apples is the only accurate way to see how a fund is doing.

(Note: This study is a hypothetical representation, and the results are not necessarily indicative of the results you may experience in the future.)

The Balancing Act Called Rebalancing

If, over time, you suspect that your portfolio no longer reflects the percentages of the asset allocation you once chose, don't be surprised. Given the movements that are inherent in the stock market, change is inevitable. For example, suppose you start out with an asset allocation plan of 60% stocks and 40% bonds. After several years, you find that because stock prices have increased, 70% of your investing dollars are now in stocks, and only 30% in bonds.

When you chose your original asset allocation, your decision was based on the level of risk you were willing to accept, and the potential rewards a specific allocation might offer. Given that, it follows that if your stock holdings rise above your original allocation, your exposure to risk increases, while if your stock holdings fall below that original allocation, your future growth potential is probably lower. So the first question is whether or not you want to return to that 60/40 model.

That change isn't a bad thing; the important thing is to keep an eye on things, to periodically take a look at what your current percentages are, and to make sure they're what you want. Looking at your asset allocation and rebalancing when necessary are crucial steps in successful investing, for the simple reason that so much of your success as an investor depends on your asset allocation. Remember that when you chose your original asset allocation, you did so based on the level of risk you were comfortable with and the potential rewards from a certain mix of investments. That means that if, for example, the stock percentage of your portfolio rises above your original percentage, your exposure to risk increases, just as if your stock percentage goes down, your potential for growth probably decreases as well. That's why it's important to look at your current asset allocation: It may have drifted from an allocation that meets your needs. No matter how carefully and wisely you chose those original percentages, if you don't keep an eye on them and do something to keep them where you want, your portfolio may suffer. The good news is that evaluating and rebalancing aren't hard; once you've done it a couple of times, the process will become routine.

LOOKING AT YOUR CURRENT ASSET ALLOCATION

Before you can know whether or not you need to rebalance, you need to know where you stand: what your current asset allocation is. As you examine this, remember to look at your asset allocation for your entire portfolio—all of your money and investments—not just your IRA or your regular brokerage account. Remember to include cash in bank checking and savings accounts as well.

The easiest way to determine your current asset allocation is to go online; your brokerage firm's Web site should give you this information in a few minutes. You can also figure it out yourself by following these steps:

1. Find out what the current market value of each of your investments is. You can use the value shown in your most recent brokerage statement, or you can go online.

2. Determine the total value for each class of investment—stocks, fixed income, and cash equivalents. Be sure to consider all of your money—investments in tax-deferred accounts and regular accounts, in 401(k)s or 403(b)s, and in your savings and checking accounts. The money in retirement accounts can seem as though it's separate from the rest of your investments, but it's not. It's all your money—all part of your nest egg—and you have to think of all those parts as a whole. If you're married or part of a domestic partnership, you should look at both portfolios. The second half should be, after all, a joint venture.

3. Once you have the market value for each investment class, calculate the percentage of your portfolio that each class represents. For example, suppose your portfolio contains stocks and stock mutual funds worth $150,000, and bonds and bond mutual funds worth $50,000, and that your portfolio is worth a total of $200,000. You can then calculate percentages:

Investment Class	Current Value	% of Whole
Stocks and stock mutual funds	$150,000	75%
Bonds and bond mutual funds	$50,000	25%
Total value of portfolio	$200,000	100%

Those percentages tell you your current asset allocation.

▦ ▦ ▦

Once you know what your current percentages are, you can decide what you want to do next. To start, take another look at the pie charts in Chapter 2. Are you still comfortable with the one you chose as a starting point? Or do you want to make a change, toward either a more conservative or a more aggressive approach? If you're happy with the new percentages, all is well and you don't need to do anything for now. If you want to change those percentages by either returning to your original percentages or altering your asset allocation in some other way, then you'll need to rebalance.

CHANGING YOUR ASSET ALLOCATION

If your current percentages aren't what you want, it's time to think about rebalancing. Deciding to rebalance should be something to which you give some careful and logical study. It's not an emotional decision, or something you decide on a whim or out of fear.

First, if you want to stay with your original asset allocation, see how your current asset allocation compares. If one asset class is off (plus or minus) by more than 5%, rebalancing is probably in order. A nice side effect of doing so is that it's possible to realize the gains from your best-performing investments while at the same time adding to assets that have underperformed. This can help reduce your risk or loss during down markets. And it keeps your risk in line with your original strategy.

There are also times when you'll find you want to depart from the asset allocation you chose and to adopt a new one. Maybe you've changed since you adopted your original plan. Investors often do; with time and experience, many people become more comfortable with a more aggressive approach. Don't be afraid to change your asset allocation plan—to choose a different pie chart—if you're so inclined. Just go slow and make sure you think everything through.

Whether you're rebalancing to return to your original asset allocation or to change your current allocation, you need to start by giving some thought to *where* and *how*.

First, the *where* part of the equation: Will you rebalance in your retirement account or your regular account? I think you're wise to consider rebalancing in your retirement account, if possible, for the simple reason that, thanks to the fact that these accounts are tax-deferred, they have fewer tax considerations. That said, if you have substantial investments outside of a retirement account, you may need to trade in your regular account. If you do so, be sure you thoroughly understand the tax consequences of any trade you consider. To my mind, selling an investment in a regular account is a last resort, for the simple reason that if you sell at a profit and realize capital gains, that money will be taxed (even the new long-term capital gains rate of 15% can affect your bottom line). This is an important time to consult your tax adviser. You've worked hard for this money, and you don't want it eaten away by taxes.

Next, the *how*: Regardless of which account you're using, there are two ways to rebalance:

• *Buy what's low.*

Buying more of the asset class that's low is a great way to rebalance. To me, it's the easiest and the most beneficial, mostly because if you buy more of what's low, you may not have to sell any of what's high, thereby avoiding possible capital gains taxes. This approach can be a little harder to fine-tune, and you may sacrifice some accuracy, but you avoid the taxes you'd pay if you sold and incurred capital gains tax.

If you're investing regularly, you can redirect what you're buying each month or quarter so that you're buying investments in the class that's low. You can also instruct your brokerage firm to direct dividends away from the high investment and into the low one.

• *Sell what's high.*

Selling off some of the investment class that's over the target percentage is another obvious fix. Clearly, in this case you will want to sell the securities that you believe have the least potential going forward. Just a couple of caveats, though: First, selling what's high can trigger capital gains taxes. Second, because I'm a long-term investor, I'm very cautious about when I even consider selling.

REBALANCING IN THE SECOND HALF OF LIFE

One of the most common times to adopt a new asset allocation and do some rebalancing is during the second half of life. At that point—somewhere around the age of 50—you're wise to rebalance every five years or so, gradually decreasing the stock portions of your portfolio and increasing your fixed-income and cash portions. At this stage of life, factors such as how you handle risk, how much money you have invested, and how much money you'll be withdrawing to live on will influence your asset allocation decisions. In general, I think that each five years after you turn 50, you're wise to reduce the stock portion of your portfolio by 10% and add that portion to the bond and cash-equivalent portions. (This assumes you're starting with a fairly aggressive portfolio, with somewhere around 90% invested in stocks.) I also feel strongly that it's crucial to stay invested for growth—meaning stocks or stock mutual funds. For that reason, I encourage most people not to go lower than about 40% of their portfolios in stocks for as long as they live.

In addition to selling what's high and buying what's low, there's another way to rebalance in the second half: by using your retirement withdrawals to change your asset allocation. Once you begin to withdraw from your retirement accounts in your second half, you can use your annual withdrawals to rebalance by selling from the asset group you want to decrease. Or you can spread out your withdrawal amount among types of assets to bring them to the percentages you want.

TOO MUCH OF A GOOD THING: CONCENTRATED EQUITY PORTFOLIOS

A *concentrated equity portfolio* is one that includes a large amount of one company's stock. This usually happens as a result of company stock options, but it can also be the result of inherited stock. People use different percentages to define concentrated equity; I think that once one company's stock represents 20% or more of your total portfolio, you need to start thinking about whether this is a wise position.

As I hope you see, holding that much of one company is risky business, plain and simple, even if that company is a great company—even if it's *your* company, the place you've worked forever. Don't be swayed by company loyalty. The risks of concentrated equity are significant, including the potential for underperformance and increased volatility. At the very least, concentrated equity can hold you back and make it harder to reach your investing goals. As you age and approach your second half, concentrated equity becomes even riskier because you don't have as much time to recoup your losses. A drop in the stock of even 20% could mean real trouble.

If you suspect you may be in a concentrated equity position, the first task is to do the math and figure out exactly where you stand. Just what percentage of your total portfolio does that company occupy? Remember to look at your total portfolio—all of your investments, including retirement accounts.

If you find that you are in a concentrated equity position, the first thing you should do is try not to increase it even more. For example, many people automatically add company stock to their 401(k) plans every month. If you have the choice, think about redirecting that money.

Another tactic is to cut back on risk in other areas of your portfolio because a concentrated equity position increases your exposure to risk. You might, for example, minimize investments in higher-risk investments such as emerging markets.

If and when you reach the point at which you want to cut back on your ownership of that stock, be thorough about finding out what your choices are. Selling some company stock is obviously a possibility, but it isn't the only one. Just as in other kinds of rebalancing, you can also add money to your portfolio and invest it in ways that will help to balance things out, such as in fixed-income choices. You could also consider using some of the company stock in a charitable giving plan.

If you do decide to sell, know the tax implications. To be thorough, you'll need to know your cost basis and holding period. And remember that if you decide to sell a large amount of stock, you don't have to do it overnight. You can do so gradually, in six months to a year, to average out the variability in the market.

The Ever-Present Tax Considerations

As I said earlier, if you sell investments in a retirement account, you don't have to worry about taxes for now. If you sell in a regular account, there are some important tax considerations, the most important of which is the potential capital gains tax. And if you're rebalancing at the end of the year, there may be additional tax factors to take into account. For example, if you've realized significant gains during the year, a loss could help offset those gains.

In addition, the following considerations apply to selling shares of a mutual fund in a regular account:

• If you want to sell shares of a fund that has gone down during the year, do so before the fund makes its year-end distribution. By doing so, you're not taxed on the dividend in addition to a tax loss, if you bought the shares at a higher price. Many, if not most, funds make their capital gains payouts in December, and some funds issue an estimate of payouts in November—a nicety, since fund companies aren't required to provide any advance warning of payouts.

• Figuring out the income tax on mutual funds in regular accounts is tedious at best—and that's if you keep accurate records, which can be critical, as explained below. If you don't keep good records, examining your tax angles is like climbing Mount Everest, and it's one of the main reasons for selling shares held in your retirement account rather than in your regular account. That said, it is easy to know how much you've made from a fund's dividends and capital gains: In January of each year, your brokerage firm or mutual fund sends you (and the IRS) IRS Form 1099-DIV, which tells you the amount and character of distributions you received during the previous year. This includes income that you never saw—dividends that were immediately reinvested in a fund, for example. For funds in regular accounts, that amount will be taxed as ordinary income or capital gains.

• If you're selling only a portion of the shares you own in a particular fund or stock, it's possible to control the amount of gain or loss you report. Your profit or loss in the sale is the difference between what you paid for the shares plus any dividends that were reinvested (your cost basis) and the price you sold at (the sale price). If you bought shares over a period of time, some shares cost more than others. If you sell 100 shares of a fund, the IRS assumes that you're selling the shares you bought first. The IRS calls this the *first-in first-out* (FIFO) rule. If the shares you bought first cost the least, the FIFO rule would give you the largest gain, and therefore work against you.

There is a way around this. Fortunately, you are allowed to specify which shares you want to sell, which means that you can, by doing a little homework, find the highest price you paid and sell those shares, thereby lessening the amount of your gain. You do this by referring to the date and price of the sale—for example, you might say that you want to sell the 100 shares you bought on August 2, 1999, at $50 a share, rather than shares you bought two years earlier for $30 a share. By selling the shares with the highest price, you minimize your taxes on that profit. You can also reverse this. If, for example, you wanted a large gain because you had losses to offset it, you could sell the $30 shares. If you place the order online or by phone, make sure you receive written confirmation of the sale of the shares you specified. And as you can see, to sell specific shares, you have to know the price you paid for the different shares, which means you need to keep thorough and accurate records of your mutual fund transactions. One caveat: If you've already been using an average-cost method for previous sales of a particular mutual fund holding (most fund companies and brokerages will supply you with the average-cost information), then you must continue using that method unless you get permission from the IRS to switch to the specific identification method. Again, this is an important time to be in close communication with your tax adviser.

■ ■ ■

Staying on track is as important in investing as it is in any other part of life. It's crucial, in good times and bad, to stay focused on where you want to go in terms of your investing goals. It won't take you long, and once you get into the habit, you'll reap the rewards: the peace of mind that comes from knowing you're doing the right thing for your future.

The Bottom Line on Staying on Track

• *Two situations in which you might consider selling a stock or mutual fund are a change in your personal situation and the need to rebalance your portfolio, which means taking action to change your asset allocation.*

• *In addition, you should consider selling a stock if you made a bad choice in the first place; if the stock's fundamentals have changed; or if you find you're overconcentrated in that stock or in the sector it represents.*

• *A drop in a stock's price is not, in and of itself, reason to sell. Any number of factors can drive a stock price down. What's important is the reason for the drop.*

• *If, over time, you find you've chosen a bad investment, in general the sooner you cut your losses, the smaller your losses.*

• *Don't sell out of panic during market lows. Although we can never predict the future, since 1926 we've had 24 bear markets, each one followed by a bull market that attained new highs.*

• *Because mutual funds are core investments, a buy-and-hold strategy is crucial. I tend to hold mutual funds for at least three years, most of them much longer.*

• *In addition to the general situations I've just mentioned, consider selling a mutual fund if it exhibits low performance over time (it performs worse than its peers or benchmarks for two or three years or at the bottom quartile for even one year), or if there is a change in the fund's management or objectives.*

• *Because so much of your success as an investor depends on your asset allocation, looking at your asset allocation and rebalancing when necessary are crucial steps in successful investing.*

• *If possible, you're wise to rebalance in your retirement account because there are fewer tax considerations.*

• *Regardless of which account you use, there are three ways to rebalance. You can buy more of what's low, sell some of what's high, or redirect dividends or investing money.*

• *Starting at around the age of 50, you're wise to rebalance every five years or so, gradually decreasing the stock portion of your portfolio and increasing your fixed-income and cash portions.*

• *As always, taxes are a crucial part of sell and rebalancing decisions. Be sure you know the tax implications of any move you consider.*

APPENDIXES

The Mathematics of Performance Measurement

In Chapter 11, I showed you how to get a ballpark sense of your performance as compared to a benchmark or combination of benchmarks. However, as we mentioned, this comparison becomes more complicated when you deposit or withdraw funds. In this appendix I'll walk you through the steps of calculating what is known as a *time-weighted return,* which provides the best comparison to industry benchmarks.

TIME-WEIGHTED VERSUS DOLLAR-WEIGHTED RETURNS

Let's work through an example. Suppose on January 1, Investor A buys 500 shares of a mutual fund at $10 a share, and by the end of the month the fund has climbed to $12. He then buys 250 additional shares on February 1, and by March 1 the fund value returns to $10. The $8,000 he invested is now worth $7,500—a $500 loss. Compare that to Investor B, who bought 800 shares on January 1 and just held on, resulting in no gain or loss. So, Investors A and B bought the same fund, held it over the same time period, and invested the same total amount of dollars, but one had a loss and the other did not. This is because Investor A bought his shares at two different points in time (the second purchase at a higher price that subsequently fell), while Investor B bought all of her shares at the beginning of the period.

To complete our example, let's say the benchmark for this fund turned in a 1% loss during the same period. Clearly, the fund's performance was acceptable in this case. After all, the fund experienced a 0% return for the whole period, while the benchmark had a −1% return for the same period, resulting in a +1% relative return for the fund—a positive result that suggests holding on to the fund. Investor A may not agree, given that he actually lost $500 over the period. However, it was his decision to buy more of the fund at exactly the wrong time. This decision led to the loss, not something the fund manager did when making portfolio-management decisions.

This example highlights the major differences between the two most common types of return calculations: time-weighted returns and dollar-weighted returns. Both provide valuable but different information. A dollar-weighted return, which measures the average return per dollar invested (including the dollars invested or withdrawn during the holding period), will answer the question "Taking into account all of my investing decisions—including which securities I chose and when I chose to buy them—how have I done?" A time-weighted return, on the other hand, which removes the timing effects of cash flows, is better for answering the question "How has my fund or portfolio manager performed compared to the benchmarks?"

Time-weighted returns are best suited to answer the second question for two reasons: (1) Typically, the fund or portfolio manager does not control when cash is deposited or withdrawn, and therefore should not be judged on decisions he or she did not make; and (2) because benchmark returns never have cash flows associated with them, time-weighted returns provide the best way to compare a fund's or manager's performance directly against that of a benchmark index. Therefore, although dollar-weighted returns can convey information about certain aspects of portfolio performance, we focus on time-weighted returns in this appendix. They offer the best way to make a direct apples-to-apples comparison of your portfolio returns to industry benchmark returns.

CALCULATING YOUR TIME-WEIGHTED RETURN

You can calculate your time-weighted return in several different ways, some more complicated and precise than others. The most practical is what is commonly called the "simple Dietz method," which provides a fair degree of accuracy with a minimum amount of complexity by assuming that all cash flows occur mid-month. Although it is possible to use this technique over longer periods of time, it is most appropriate to use *monthly* account data, which you can get from your monthly brokerage statements. In other words, you need only to calculate your performance once or twice a year, but when you do, you must build your performance up from your monthly portfolio activity. In addition, calculating your results either for a calendar year or on a year-to-date basis will make it easier to compare your return to standard benchmarks, since these time periods tend to be more readily available in the *Wall Street Journal* and other financial publications.

To find your time-weighted return, start by plugging each month's data into the equation below. Then it's just a matter of linking the monthly data in one compounded result for the whole period. Note that "cash flow" refers to the money you've deposited or withdrawn. Deposits are expressed as a positive number, and withdrawals as a negative number.

(Month end value − month beginning value − cash flows)
+ [Month beginning value + (cash flow + 2)]
= your return, stated as a percentage.

Let's look at a three-month example and calculate a quarterly return: Suppose you started the first month of the quarter with $100,000 and end up with $105,000; and that during the month, you deposited a total of $5,000 and withdrew a total of $7,500. This means that your net cash flow was −$2,500 ($5,000 of deposits minus $7,500 of withdrawals). Using those numbers with the equation gives you:

$$[105,000 - 100,000 - (-2,500)] \div [100,000 + (-2,500 \div 2)]$$
$$= (105,000 - 100,000 + 2,500) \div (100,000 - 1,250)$$
$$= 7,500 \div 98,750$$
$$= +7.6\%.$$

This means your return was +7.6% for the first month.

Now let's calculate the return for the second month. If you started the month with $105,000 (where you left off the month before) and ended with $115,000, deposited a total of $5,000 and withdrew $1,000 during the second month, the equation looks like this:

$$[115,000 - 105,000 - (+4,000)] \div [105,000 + (4,000 \div 2)]$$
$$= 6,000 \div 107,000$$
$$= +5.6\%.$$

In this case, you had a +5.6% return for the second month.

Finally, you need to determine the return for the third month using the same technique. Let's say you started the month with $115,000 (the ending value of the prior month) and ended with $103,500, with no deposits or withdrawals; the formula would look like this:

$$(103,500 - 115,000 - 0) \div (115,000 + 0)$$
$$= -11,500 \div 115,000$$
$$= -10\%.$$

To complete your calculation, you need to link each month's data into a quarterly compounded return by using the following formula:

$$[(1 + \text{Month 1 return}) (1 + \text{Month 2 return})$$
$$(1 + \text{Month 3 return})] - 1$$
$$= \text{quarterly return}.$$

Or, alternatively, if you had 12 months of data, you could calculate your annual compounded return in the same way:

$$[(1 + \text{Month 1 return}) (1 + \text{Month 2 return})$$
$$(1 + \text{Month 3 return}) \ldots (1 + \text{Month 12 return})] - 1$$
$$= \text{annual return.}$$

Plugging the monthly numbers from our example into our quarterly compound return formula gives you:

$$(1 + 7.6\%) (1 + 5.6\%) [1 + (-10\%)] - 1$$
$$= (1 + .076) (1 + .056) [1 + (-.1)] - 1$$
$$= (1.076) (1.056) (.9) - 1$$
$$= +2.3\%.$$

Your portfolio's compounded return for the quarter is 2.3%.

A WORD OF CAUTION: THE EFFECT OF LARGE CASH FLOWS ON YOUR CALCULATION

Monthly cash flows (dollars invested or withdrawn) exceeding 10% of your portfolio's value in any given month can significantly skew the estimate of time-weighted returns as calculated by the simple Dietz method used here. To accommodate for this, divide the month into two distinct subperiods, and then use exactly the same formulas and linking (compounding) techniques described for monthly returns. For example, if your portfolio has a value of $100,000, and in any given month the net of your deposits and withdrawals exceeds $10,000, you are better off splitting the month into two subperiods, one subperiod from the start of the month to the date of the cash flow, and another subperiod from the date of the cash flow to the end of the month. At this point, you would treat both subperiods the exact same way as you treated a whole month. The ending value for the first subperiod, and the beginning value for the second subperiod, would be the portfolio value on the day of the cash flow in that month. Then, instead of linking three monthly returns to get the quarterly return, you would have four periods.

Now that you have calculated your portfolio's quarterly time-weighted return, you can directly compare it to an appropriate benchmark using the methods described in Chapter 11. And remember, if you are comparing the time-weighted return of your entire portfolio, as opposed to a specific security or holding, the most appropriate benchmark is typically a "blended benchmark" constructed from several different market indexes weighted with the same asset allocation as that of your portfolio.

Appendix B

The Language of Investing

1099-DIV form. The IRS form from your brokerage or mutual fund company that tells you how much income you received during the year.

12(b)-1 fees. Annual fees assessed by some mutual funds to cover the costs of marketing and distribution, as a percentage of the fund's total assets. For a fund to be considered no-load, its 12(b)-1 fee must be .25% or lower.

401(k) plan. A defined contribution plan in which your employer takes money directly from your salary and places it in a tax-deferred retirement account, which means that you don't pay taxes on this money until you retire or withdraw it. The decision about how and where the money is invested is usually yours. Employers often match your contributions, sometimes as much as 50 cents or more on the dollar.

403(b) plan. Basically a 401(k) plan in the world of charitable and non-profit organizations, including educational institutions. Your contribution is deducted directly from your salary before taxes, and your employer can contribute.

529 plan. A state-sponsored education savings program that allows parents, relatives, and friends to plan and invest for a child's college education. An adult sets up the account for the student. While contributions aren't tax-deductible, earnings in the account grow tax-deferred until withdrawn to pay for college fees and expenses. In addition, qualified withdrawals are exempt from federal tax.

actively managed mutual fund. A type of mutual fund in which the fund manager actively attempts to outperform the market by making decisions to buy or sell individual securities. For comparison, see INDEX FUND.

active market. A market in which there is a great deal of trading. Because of the large number of transactions, active markets are characterized by liquidity. They tend to have narrower spreads between the bid and the ask price than do less active markets.

after-tax rate of return. A rate of return that takes taxes into account, a key factor since taxes are the largest single drag on your investment return. See also PRETAX RATE OF RETURN.

aggressive growth fund. A mutual fund that seeks rapid capital growth, often from small or emerging growth companies.

Alternative Minimum Tax (AMT). A tax system that works to make sure that at least a minimum amount of tax is paid by high-income individuals and corporations.

American Depository Receipt (ADR). A receipt for shares of foreign-based companies that entitles the shareholder to all dividends and capital gains. ADRs allow Americans to buy shares of foreign-based corporations' securities at American exchanges instead of having to go to overseas exchanges.

annual report. A financial statement issued each year by a corporation or mutual fund. It lists assets, liabilities, and earnings, as well as some historical information. Each shareholder receives a copy of the annual report.

ask price. The price at which you can buy shares of a security.

asset. A property that has monetary value, including personal possessions such as a house, car, or jewelry, and financial properties such as savings and investments.

asset allocation. The process of deciding how to divide your money among various asset classes such as stocks, bonds, and cash equivalents. You make this decision based on your goals, tolerance for risk, and time horizon.

asset allocation fund. A mutual fund that typically includes a mix of stocks, bonds, and cash equivalents to meet its objective. This type of fund helps you diversify among classes with one investment.

asset class. A broad investment category such as stocks, bonds, and cash equivalents.

automatic investment plan (AIP). An agreement between you and a brokerage firm in which you authorize regular investments to be made through payroll deductions or automatic transfers from your checking account.

automatic reinvestment. An agreement by which all dividends produced by your investments are reinvested; that is, they are used to buy more shares of the same or another investment.

back-end load. A sales charge on a mutual fund that's applied when you sell shares of the fund (as opposed to a FRONT-END LOAD, applied when you buy shares).

balanced fund. A mutual fund that buys a combination of stocks, bonds, and cash equivalents to provide both income and capital appreciation while avoiding excessive risk.

bear market. A declining market in which prices are falling for a sustained period of time.

benchmark. A standard used for comparison. For example, the performance of large-cap stock funds is often compared to the performance of the S&P 500 Index, which serves as a benchmark.

bid and ask. The buy and sell prices for securities, representing the spread in the market. You buy at the ask, and sell at the bid.

bid price. The highest price anyone is willing to pay for the security at a given time.

block. A large order or transaction, generally involving 10,000 or more shares, or shares in excess of $200,000 in value.

blue chip stock. Generally speaking, the stock of a large, well-established company.

bond. A type of investment that's like an IOU from a corporation or a municipal or federal government. You loan the borrower some money, and in return it promises to repay the full amount on a specific date, and to pay you interest in the meantime.

bond fund. A mutual fund that includes only bonds—typically corporate, municipal, or U.S. government bonds.

bond maturity. The lifetime of a bond, concluding when the final payment of that obligation is due.

broad-based index fund. An index fund based on an index that includes a large portion of the market, rather than being narrowly focused.

brokerage. A securities firm that sells stocks, mutual funds, and other securities.

brokerage account. An account with a brokerage firm that allows you to buy and sell securities.

bull market. A rising market in which prices are going up for a sustained period of time.

buy-and-hold. An investing strategy that encourages investing for the long term by buying and then "holding," meaning not selling, rather than selling based on the market's day-to-day ups and downs. Buying and then trying to sell based on the movement of the market is the opposite investment strategy and is called MARKET TIMING.

capital appreciation. An increase in the market price of an asset.

capital gain. The profit you receive when you sell an investment for more than you paid for it. For example, if you purchased stock for $1,000 and sold it for $1,500, your capital gain would be $500. Capital gains are taxable income, and must be reported to the IRS on your tax return.

capital gains distribution. A payment you receive when your mutual fund makes a profit by selling some of the securities in its portfolio. Capital gains distributions are usually made annually, often at the end of the calendar year.

capitalization. The total stock market value of all shares of a company's stock, calculated by multiplying the stock price by the number of shares outstanding.

capital loss. The amount of money you lose when you sell an investment for less than you paid. Capital losses may be deducted from your annual income and must be reported on your tax return.

capital return. The capital gain or loss realized from the market appreciation or depreciation of your investment.

cash equivalent. An investment that can easily be converted into cash, such as a money market fund or Treasury bill.

certificate of deposit (CD). An investment made with a financial institution, such as a bank or savings and loan, in which you deposit a specified amount for a specific period of time, at a preset, fixed interest rate. CDs are FDIC-insured.

closed-end mutual fund. A mutual fund that distributes a fixed number of shares that trade much like stocks. They are usually listed on a major exchange, and they may trade in the market at a premium or discount to NET ASSET VALUE (NAV).

commission. The fee paid to a brokerage firm for executing a transaction.

commodities. Goods such as agricultural products, metals, or financial instruments traded on a separate commodities exchange. Commodity contracts state a future date of delivery or receipt of a certain amount of the product. Speculators generally invest in these contracts at a price that they hope they can turn into a profit when the actual commodities are delivered.

common stock. Securities that represent an ownership interest in a company (as opposed to PREFERRED STOCK, in which, for example, stockholders receive dividend payments before such payment is made to common stockholders).

compounding. Generally speaking, the growth that results from investment income being reinvested. Compound growth has a snowball effect because both the original investment and the income from that investment are invested.

concentrated equity position. Holding a large amount of one company's stock in your portfolio. A concentrated equity position is often due to company stock options, but it can also be the result of inherited stock or holding too much company stock in a 401(k) plan.

Core & Explore®. Schwab's investment philosophy that strives to minimize a stock portfolio's risk of lagging the market, while increasing its probability of outperforming it. The Core & Explore portfolio seeks both to capture the benefits of holding a diversified Core of U.S. companies and to retain the potential of beating the market with high-quality, more specialized Explore holdings.

cost basis. What you paid for an investment, as opposed to its current market value. This number, which is used for tax purposes, includes any dividends that have been reinvested, and any capital gains distributions.

country risk. The potential for volatility in the price of a stock sold in a foreign country. The volatility may have a variety of causes, such as political or economic events.

Coverdell Education Savings Account (ESA). An account (formerly called an "Education IRA") established to help pay the education expenses of a child, grandchild, or other designated beneficiary who is a minor. The contributions aren't deductible; however, earnings are free from federal income tax as long as you use the money for qualified expenses.

credit risk. The possibility that the issuer of a bond—the borrower—will default, meaning the issuer fails to repay the principal or interest owed on a bond, either at the agreed-upon time or at all. Also called default risk.

currency risk. The possibility that the price in dollars of an international stock may fluctuate as a result of changing currency exchange rates.

current yield. The amount of annual interest on a bond divided by the amount paid for it, expressed as a percentage. For example, if you receive $80 a year from a bond that has a current price of $900, the current yield is 8.9% ($80 divided by $900).

custodial account. An account set up and managed by an adult for the benefit of a minor. It is set up in the name of a child, with a parent or trustee as custodian. Assets placed in the account are considered an irrevocable gift and belong solely to the child, with the custodian being in control of the account until the child reaches the age of majority (18, 21, or 25, depending on state law).

day order. An order to buy or sell a security that automatically expires if it is not executed at the day's market close.

defined benefit plan. An employer-sponsored retirement plan in which a retired employee receives a specific amount based on salary history and length of employment.

defined contribution plan. An employer-sponsored retirement plan in which you, your employer, or both of you contribute to your retirement account. Unlike defined benefit plans, these plans allow you, the employee, to have some say in how and where your money is invested. In some cases, the employee is responsible for all of those decisions. These plans include 401(k)s and 403(b)s.

deflation. A decrease in the cost of goods and services as measured by the consumer price index (CPI).

diversification. Spreading your investment dollars across and within different asset classes such as stocks, bonds, and cash equivalents, thereby helping to lower your risk.

dividend. The payment to shareholders declared by a company's board of directors. In general, dividends are paid quarterly in the form of cash, but they can also be in the form of stock or other property. Recent tax legislation has reduced the tax for qualified dividends to a maximum of 15%.

dollar cost averaging. Investing the same dollar amount in the same securities at regular scheduled intervals over the long term, with the aim of stabilizing your returns.

domestic fund. A mutual fund that invests only in stocks issued by U.S. companies. These funds are classified according to size (large-cap, mid-cap, and small-cap) and style (growth and value).

Dow Jones Industrial Average (DJIA or "the Dow"). One of the most commonly used measurements of the performance of the U.S. stock market. It includes 30 blue chip stocks, which are primarily industrial stocks considered leaders in the market.

earnings. A company's net income or profit, usually quoted in millions of dollars.

earnings per share (EPS). A company's total earnings for a period (its net income minus preferred dividends), divided by the number of common shares outstanding.

Education IRA. See COVERDELL EDUCATION SAVINGS ACCOUNT.

Employee Stock Ownership Plan (ESOP). A plan in which you acquire your company's stock through a company retirement plan that invests in and pays benefits in the form of company stock instead of cash contributions.

employer-sponsored retirement plan. A retirement plan offered and sponsored by the company that employs you.

equity. Another name for stock, representing ownership of a corporation. Also, the money value of a property or of an interest in a property in excess of all claims or liens against it.

ESOP. See EMPLOYEE STOCK OWNERSHIP PLAN.

ex-dividend. For stocks, the period between the announcement of a dividend and payment of that dividend. When a stock is trading ex-dividend, new buyers do not receive the dividend. An "x" in newspaper listings denotes a stock that is ex-dividend.

expense ratio. For mutual funds, the percentage of a fund's average net assets that is used to pay fund expenses. This percentage accounts for management fees, administrative fees, and any 12(b)-1 fees.

face value. The value appearing on the face of a bond, indicating the principal amount that the issuer will pay when the bond matures and the amount on which interest is calculated. Face value is not an indication of market value.

Federal Deposit Insurance Corporation (FDIC). A U.S. government agency that insures cash deposits, including certificates of deposit, that have been placed in member institutions, for up to $100,000.

fee-based management. A method of compensation in which you are charged for professional financial help. With fee-based management, you are charged a percentage of the assets in the manager's control, usually around 1% or 2%.

fixed-income investment. An investment such as a bond, money market instrument, or preferred stock that pays a specific interest rate. The borrower, called the ISSUER, can be a government—municipal, state, or federal—a corporation, or a bank or savings and loan.

foreign fund. A mutual fund that invests only in companies outside of the United States.

front-end load. A sales charge on a mutual fund that is applied when you buy shares of the fund (as opposed to a BACK-END LOAD, applied when you sell shares).

fund family. A group of mutual funds from the same organization. Investing in funds from the same fund family usually gives you exchange privileges between the funds, and you receive one statement for all of the funds in the family.

good-till-canceled (GTC). An order to buy or sell stock that remains valid until executed or canceled by the customer.

growth fund. A stock fund that seeks long-term capital appreciation. Growth funds generally buy common stocks of companies that advisers believe have long-term growth potential.

growth stock. The stock of a company that has seen rapid growth in revenue or earnings and is expected to see similar growth in the future. Generally speaking, growth stocks pay relatively low dividends and sell at a relatively high price, considering their earnings and book value.

income fund. A mutual fund that seeks current income over capital growth, often by investing in bonds and high-yielding stocks.

index. A statistical composite that measures changes in the economy or financial markets. Well-known market indexes include the S&P 500 Index, the Dow Jones Industrial Average, and the NASDAQ Composite Index.

index fund. A mutual fund that seeks to track the performance of a market index, such as the S&P 500 Index, by investing in the stocks or other securities that constitute that index. When you invest in index funds, you are essentially seeking to "buy the market" and not trying to outperform it.

Individual Retirement Account (IRA). A self-funded tax-deferred retirement plan (a plan that you, not your employer, establish and fund). There are several different types of IRAs, including traditional IRA, rollover IRA, and Roth IRA.

inflation. An increase in the cost of goods and services, which in turn decreases the buying power of money over time. Inflation is usually measured by the Consumer Price Index and classified according to its severity. Mild inflation occurs when the price level—an average of all prices—rises from 2% to 4%. Moderate inflation refers to an inflation rate of 5% to 9%, and severe inflation (or "double-digit inflation") refers to an inflation that threatens a country's economy, in which money loses its value and people turn to barter rather than relying on currency.

initial public offering (IPO). The first time a company makes its shares available for sale to the public.

international fund. A mutual fund that invests outside of the United States. International stock funds can include world funds, which invest in securities issued throughout the world including the United States, or foreign funds, which invest only in companies outside of the United States.

issuer. The corporation, municipality, or government agency that issues a bond or security; in other words, the borrower.

Keogh plan. A tax-deferred, qualified retirement account for self-employed persons and employees of unincorporated businesses. Contributions and earnings are deductible from gross income and grow tax-deferred until withdrawn (certain restrictions apply). Qualified plans meet the requirements of the Internal Revenue Code, making them eligible for favorable tax treatment.

laddering. A strategy of buying bonds with staggered maturities.

large-cap fund. A mutual fund that invests primarily in stocks of companies with a market capitalization in the top 5% of domestic companies.

large-cap stock. The stock of a company whose market capitalization is in the top 5% of domestic companies.

limit order. An order to buy or sell a security at a specified price or better. A limit order to buy sets a maximum purchase price. A limit order to sell sets a minimum sell price.

liquid investment. An investment that can be easily converted to cash.

liquidity. The ability of an asset to quickly be converted into cash. Generally, the greater the number of buyers and sellers of a particular asset, the more liquid it is considered to be.

load. A commission or sales fee on a mutual fund. A mutual fund that assesses this charge is a load fund. One without this charge is a no-load fund.

long-term capital gain. Gain from the sale or exchange of a capital asset held more than one year (at least one year and one day from the purchase date). Long-term capital gains are taxed at more favorable rates than short-term gains.

lump sum. An amount of money you receive (from a pension plan, divorce, or inheritance, for example) all at once, rather than in periodic payments.

management fee. The amount a mutual fund pays its managers to oversee the fund.

margin account. A type of brokerage account that allows certain securities to be used as collateral for a loan. You will be able to use margin after signing a margin agreement and meeting regulatory requirements. All trades using borrowed money will be conducted through the margin account.

market capitalization. The total value of a company's stock, calculated by multiplying the number of outstanding shares by the price per share.

market order. An order to buy or sell a security at the best price available at the time the order is received.

market timing. An investing strategy that attempts to predict and profit from future market directions, as opposed to buy-and-hold.

market value. For a stock, the total number of shares outstanding multiplied by the price per share.

maturity date. For a fixed-income investment, the date when a debt becomes due for payment.

mid-cap stock. The stock of a company whose market capitalization falls between LARGE-CAP (top 5%) and SMALL-CAP (bottom 80%).

money market mutual fund. A mutual fund that invests solely in short-term securities that can easily be turned into cash, such as Treasury bills, certificates of deposit (CD), and short-term loans. Money market funds are designed to maintain a stable $1 share value, but there is no guarantee that they will do that.

municipal bonds (or "munis"). Debt securities issued by state and local governments and their agencies. Munis typically pay interest at a fixed rate twice a year, and the issuer promises to return the principal at maturity. In general, interest paid on municipal bonds is exempt from federal taxes. When a muni is purchased by a resident of the state that issued the bond, the interest payments are also generally exempt from state tax.

mutual fund. A type of investment that pools the money of many investors to buy various securities, including stocks, bonds, and/or cash equivalents. Mutual funds can offer diversification and professional management within a single investment. See also PROSPECTUS.

mutual fund supermarket. A service provided by a brokerage firm through which you have access to a variety of mutual funds from different fund families, instead of having to go to the individual funds. There is often no transaction fee.

NASDAQ. Acronym for National Association of Securities Dealers Automated Quotation System, a computerized system for reporting current price quotations on active OVER-THE-COUNTER securities. The system provides price quotations and permits execution of small customer orders. Large orders are executed by separate negotiations.

net asset value (NAV). The market value of a single share of a mutual fund, calculated at the end of each business day by adding up the value of all the securities in the fund's portfolio, subtracting expenses, and dividing the sum by the number of shares outstanding. Mutual funds are traded based on their NAVs. Funds with an offer price identical to the NAV are either no-load, or they are load funds carrying a contingent deferred sales charge.

net profit. The profit on an investment that remains after you deduct all expenses.

New York Stock Exchange (NYSE). The oldest and largest stock exchange in the United States.

no-load mutual fund. A mutual fund that does not carry a sales charge or commission. The initials "NL" in the offer price column of a mutual fund table indicate no-load funds. You buy and sell these funds at the price listed in the NAV (NET ASSET VALUE) column.

odd lot. A trade involving fewer than 100 shares.

open-end mutual fund. A mutual fund that continuously sells its shares to the general public. An open-end fund issues additional shares as new investors ask to buy them, so the number of shares outstanding changes daily, as investors buy new shares or redeem old ones.

open order. A buy or sell order that has not yet been executed or canceled.

operating expense ratio (OER). A mutual fund's annual expenses (operating expenses, management fees, and 12(b)-1 fees, if any) expressed as a percentage of the fund's average net assets. These expenses are deducted before calculating the fund's NAV.

operating expenses. Costs incurred by a mutual fund in its day-to-day operations. Every fund is subject to some degree of operating expenses, which usually include management fees, annual fees, administrative costs, and maintenance fees.

over-the-counter. A market of securities that are not listed on an exchange but trade only in the over-the-counter network (via telephone or a computer network, instead of on an exchange floor).

par. For common stocks, the dollar value assigned to the stock when the stock is issued. Par value is used chiefly for bookkeeping, rather than for figuring the stock's market value. For preferred stocks, par is the amount used to calculate the investor's dividend. For a bond, the par value is the face amount.

penny stock. A low-priced stock, generally selling below one dollar per share.

portfolio. The group of stocks, bonds, and cash-equivalent investments held by an individual investor, a mutual fund, or a financial institution.

portfolio manager. The person in charge of managing a mutual fund's holdings.

preferred stock. A class of stock that pays dividends at a specified rate and has preference over COMMON STOCK in the payment of dividends and the liquidation of assets. Preferred stockholders may have different voting rights. Not all securities have preferred stocks.

pretax rate of return. The return you're getting on your investment without taking taxes into account, as opposed to an AFTER-TAX RATE OF RETURN.

price/earnings ratio (P/E). A measurement that represents the relationship between the price of a company's stock and its earnings for the past year. To get a company's P/E, divide its current price by its EARNINGS PER SHARE.

principal. The amount of money that is financed, borrowed, or invested.

prospectus. A legal document that describes a mutual fund and offers its shares for sale. It contains information required by the SEC and state securities regulators, including the fund's investment objectives and policies, risks, investment restrictions, fees and expenses, and how shares can be bought and sold. Every mutual fund is required to publish a prospectus and provide it to investors free of charge. Always read the prospectus carefully before investing.

rebalancing your portfolio. Changing the way in which your investments are allocated among asset classes.

redemption fee. A fee charged by some mutual funds when you sell shares, usually within a short period of time.

reinvesting. Using dividends from an investment to buy more shares of that investment.

retirement plan distribution. A withdrawal of funds from a retirement plan.

rollover IRA. A transfer of assets from a qualified plan to an Individual Retirement Account without tax. If you change jobs, retire, or get a divorce settlement that includes a distribution from a company retirement plan, you can "roll it over" into an IRA to preserve your capital and keep its tax-deferred status.

Roth IRA. A tax-deferred retirement plan. Although contributions are not deductible, if you meet certain qualifications, your withdrawals—including interest—are without tax.

round lot. The basic unit of trading for a particular security, usually 100 shares.

secondary market. A market where previously issued securities are traded, usually a stock exchange or the OVER-THE-COUNTER market.

sector/specialty fund. A mutual fund that invests in a specific sector of the economy, such as communications, finance, health, technology, or utilities.

securities. Stocks that signify ownership interest in a company, or bonds that indicate a credit relationship with a borrower, such as a company or government agency. Some other types of securities are options, warrants, and mutual funds.

Securities and Exchange Commission (SEC). A federal government agency established by Congress to regulate and protect investors against malpractice in the securities markets.

SEP-IRA. An acronym meaning Simplified Employee Pension—Individual Retirement Account. A SEP-IRA is an alternative for those who are self-employed or who own a small business with employees.

settlement. The close of a securities transaction, when you pay your brokerage firm for the securities you've purchased, or when you deliver securities you've sold and receive the proceeds from the sale.

settlement date. In a securities transaction, the date when payment is due either to the customer or to the broker, and/or the date when the certificates must be in the broker's possession.

share. A unit of ownership in a stock or mutual fund.

short-term capital gain. A profit on the sale of a stock or mutual fund that the investor owned for less than one year.

SIMPLE IRA. Stands for Savings Incentive Match Plan IRA. A retirement plan for employees of companies that do not have a 401(k) plan and employ fewer than 100 people.

small-cap fund. A mutual fund that invests in stocks of companies with a market capitalization in the lower 80% of the largest domestic companies.

small-cap stock. The stock of a company with a relatively small total market value, meaning a market capitalization in the lower 80% of the largest domestic companies. Small-cap companies tend to be more volatile than larger companies.

Social Security. Money paid out by the U.S. government's social insurance program of the same name, especially during an individual's retirement. The amount of your monthly benefit is based on the contributions you've made and the age at which you retire.

spousal IRA. An IRA established for a nonworking spouse.

Standard & Poor's 500 (S&P 500) Index. A well-known capitalization-weighted index consisting of 500 of the country's most widely traded companies that are listed on the New York Stock Exchange (NYSE) or the American Stock Exchange (AMEX).

stock. A type of investment that represents a share of equity ownership in a company.

stock split. An action from the company's board of directors, with the approval of company shareholders, that increases the total number of outstanding shares. The goal is often to reduce the price per share of a high-priced stock, making it easier to trade. The outstanding shares of the corporation are simply multiplied. There is no increase in capital, and the proportionate ownership of the company's equity remains the same.

stop-limit order. A combination of a LIMIT ORDER and a STOP ORDER used to protect a profit or limit a loss. This is a request to buy or sell a security at a specified limit price or better, but only after the specified stop price has been reached or passed. Even if the stop price is triggered, a stop-limit order guarantees the limit price but not the execution.

stop order. An order to buy or sell a security once it reaches or trades through a set market price, called the stop price. Once this happens, your pending stop order becomes a market order—which guarantees execution but not price. For comparison, see STOP-LIMIT ORDER.

STRIPs. An acronym for "separate trading of registered interest and principal" securities. STRIPs are Treasury ZERO-COUPON BONDS, which are bonds that don't pay interest until maturity.

tax deferral. The postponement of a tax obligation until sometime in the future.

ticker symbol. An abbreviation of a security's name used to identify it for trading purposes and in printed and online price quotations.

trade date. The actual date on which a security is bought or sold. The purchase price is determined by the closing NET ASSET VALUE on this date. The trade date also determines whether you are eligible for dividends.

traditional IRA. A self-funded tax-deferred retirement plan. Contributions are tax-deductible if you do not participate in an employer-sponsored retirement plan or if you meet certain income limitations. You have complete control over how you invest your IRA money.

Treasuries (or "Treasurys"); Treasury bill (T-bill), note, or bond. Securities issued by the U.S. government. T-bills are short-term obligations that mature in 90 days to one year; Treasury notes mature between one and ten years; Treasury bonds mature in over ten years.

turnover rate. The rate, in a percentage, at which a mutual fund annually buys and sell securities. For example, if a fund whose assets totaled $200 million bought and sold $100 million worth of securities in a year, the fund's turnover rate would be 50%.

unrealized capital gain. A gain that would be realized if securities were sold.

value fund. A mutual fund that invests in companies whose assets are considered undervalued, or companies that have turnaround opportunities, with lower price/earnings ratios.

value stock. A stock that is considered to be a good stock at a very good price.

volatility. The magnitude and frequency of changes in securities' values. The more volatile an investment, the higher its risk and return potential.

world fund. A mutual fund that invests in both U.S. and non-U.S. companies. By contrast, a foreign fund invests only in companies outside of the United States.

yield. The annual rate of return on an investment, expressed as a percentage.

yield to maturity. The average annual return on a bond, assuming the bond is held to maturity and all interest payments are reinvested at the same rate. It includes an adjustment for any premium or discount from face value. Comparing yield to maturity is the most common way to compare the value of bonds.

zero-coupon bonds (or "zeros"). Bonds that do not pay interest during their terms but are sold at a discount from their face value. A zero-coupon bond generally increases in value as it approaches maturity, and the return comes solely from its appreciation. The dollar amount difference between the purchase price and the maturity value represents the yield or accretion value. Maturities range from one to 30 years. There are three types of zeros: corporate, municipal, and Treasury.

Appendix C

Important Legal Information

The information provided in *Charles Schwab's New Guide to Financial Independence* is for general informational purposes only and should not be considered an individualized recommendation or personalized investment advice. The securities mentioned and investment strategies discussed may not be suitable for everyone. Each investor needs to review and decide, based on his or her own particular situation, the type of investments and investment strategies that will best meet individual investment objectives. Third-party Web sites referenced in this book are not affiliated with, sponsored by, or endorsed by Charles Schwab & Co., Inc. Schwab has not reviewed these sites and makes no representations about their content. The information should not be considered either as a recommendation by Schwab or as an offer to purchase or sell any securities.

Charles Schwab's New Guide to Financial Independence discusses, in part, mutual funds. As mentioned in the book, mutual fund prospectuses should be obtained and read carefully before investing. They contain more complete information, including management fees, charges, and expenses, and are available from Charles Schwab & Co., Inc., by phoning 800-435-4000. Past performance is no indication of future results. Fund investment values will fluctuate and shares, when redeemed, may be worth more or less than original cost.

In particular it should be noted that an investment in a money market fund is not insured or guaranteed by the FDIC or any other government agency. Although the fund seeks to preserve the value of your investment at $1 per share, it is possible to lose money by investing in the fund. Small-cap funds and stocks are generally subject to greater volatility than investments in other asset categories. International investing involves additional risks such as currency fluctuation, political instability, and the potential for illiquid markets. Indexes are unmanaged; do not incur management fees, costs, and expenses; and cannot be invested in directly. Income from municipal securities (bonds or bond funds) may be subject to the federal Alternative Minimum Tax. Bond fund shares are not guaranteed and will fluctuate with market conditions and interest rates. Shares, when redeemed, may be worth more or less than their original cost. Certificates of deposit offer a fixed rate of return and are FDIC-insured. The value of "guaranteed" securities fluctuates due to changing interest rates or other market conditions, and investors may experience a loss or may, due to prepayment of obligations, receive back part of their investment before redemption.

The Schwab Equity Ratings are generally updated weekly, so you should review and consider any recent market or company news before investing. The Schwab Equity Ratings and other information presented are general information that does not take into account your individual circumstances, financial situation, or needs, nor does it represent a personalized recommendation of a particular stock or stocks to you. Stocks can be volatile and entail risk, and individual stocks presented may not be suitable for you. You should not buy or sell a stock without first considering whether it is appropriate for you and your portfolio.

Charles Schwab & Co., Inc., receives remuneration from companies that participate in the Mutual Fund OneSource program for record-keeping and shareholder services, and other administrative services.

Epilogue

Dear Reader,

There, you've done it: In these pages, you've learned what it takes to be a successful, long-term investor, and it's my great hope that you feel confident and encouraged. All that remains is to get started.

If you're not yet an active investor, take heart. I know it can be hard to get started, especially today when so many things are vying for your attention. Maybe you're one of those people who know they haven't done enough about investing for their futures, but just can't seem to do anything about it. There are many reasons for investing to sink to the bottom of a person's list. Time is a big factor; a lot of people feel that they just don't have the time to learn, or once they do learn, they don't stay with it. Fear is another reason. Some find the whole thing intimidating; investing seems like too difficult a skill to master on your own. Other people avoid it because they don't like thinking about the future or about changing and getting older. And others are afraid to invest because they think they'll lose their hard-earned money.

While all of those reasons are understandable, none of them

should keep you from investing. First, as you've seen, anyone can learn to invest wisely without making it a second career. While a lot of brokers work very hard and make a lot of money trying to convince people otherwise, the fact is that it's not that hard. It's like buying a car: You don't want to do it on a whim, or without some research, but it's certainly doable. You just have to do a little homework, and the main thing you need is something you've already got: simple common sense. Add to that some guidance from this book, and you're well on your way. And once you've gotten started, investing becomes a matter of maintenance, like going for a checkup, or having the oil changed, or taking the dog to the vet. It's just something you do on a regular basis.

As for fears about the future, it *can* be hard to talk about the future, and to think about getting older. But facing those concerns is a lot better than stuffing them in the closet. And in the long run, it's easier. It takes a lot of effort to ignore what you don't want to deal with.

Finally, there's the fear of losing money. A look at history helps with that one. We've seen ten recessions since the end of World War II, and we've recovered from each of them. Not only recovered—we've gone on to reach new highs. It's always tempting to stay on the sidelines and wait until the time is right, especially during a bear market, but time and again, I've learned that the potential rewards of participating in the market outweigh the risk of waiting for the right time. Investing isn't about timing the market; it's about time *in* the market. Eventually things turn positive. Markets recover and individuals are able to rebuild their wealth. And over the long term, investors who participate in the market, regardless of timing, have been shown to realize the best results.

So if you've been avoiding this part of your life, whatever your reason, I urge you to do what it takes to make investing a priority. It's just too important to ignore, because investing is about your *life* and about taking action now so that you'll have choices later on. *That's* the reason to invest: to avoid getting caught unprepared. And while you may have to give a little—to cut back on the annual getaway or the impromptu spending—you'll get a lot more. You'll rest easier as you learn that this is an area of your life where you have some control. And you'll know that by planning for your future, you're doing the right thing.

In these pages, you've learned how to begin or continue to invest for your future. *Start investing now,* you've read; *diversify; invest steadily; be patient; take the long view.* Discipline yourself to hold on to or add to your investments through down markets as well as up, and when you hit a down market, take a walk or head to the driving range—whatever will settle your nerves and take your mind off the market. But don't panic, and don't let some bad times chase you out of the market. Cultivate patience, the art of hanging in there, but never confuse patience with complacency. Patience means not acting on emotion. Complacency means not acting at all.

Investing is a commitment. Sign it in stone, cross your heart, do whatever it takes to commit yourself to long-term investing. It's not about making money overnight, and you have to understand that or you'll find yourself wanting to jump ship at the first sign of a down market. Instead, learn to close your eyes and resist the urge to sell; learn to ride through those down markets. Once you do, the next one won't be quite as bad, and the one after that will be a little better. But I have to be honest: It never gets easy. Every down market can rattle you if you let it, whether you've been at this for 5 years or 50. Those downward turns never quite lose their edge. The only antidote is a steeliness that, while it may not come naturally, will come if you're patient.

So choose a starting place, and develop a plan to continue. You know enough to get started, and you know how to get help if and when you need it. The only thing that remains is to begin. I wish you all the best as you set out.

With my best regards,

Charles R Schwab

Permissions

Grateful acknowledgment is made to the following for permission to reprint previously published material.

Doris S. Michaels Literary Agency, Inc.: Excerpt from *The Neatest Little Guide to Mutual Funds* by Jason Kelly. Reprinted by permission of the Doris S. Michaels Literary Agency, Inc.

International Creative Management, Inc.: Excerpt from "Why Women Fear They Will End Up Living in a Box Outside Bergdorf 's" by Gail Sheehy, originally from *Money Magazine*. Copyright © by Gail Sheehy. Reprinted by permission of International Creative Management, Inc.

Nightly Business Report: Excerpt from "Commentary on Staying Involved" by Irving R. Levine from the *Nightly Business Report,* January 30, 2003. Reprinted by permission of the Nightly Business Report.

Index

Actively managed mutual funds, 80,
  89, 100–101, 103, 106,
  113–14, 117, 162, 264
Active market, 264
ADRs. *See* American Depository
  Receipts
Advice. *See* Financial advisor
After-tax rate of return, 261, 264
Aggressive growth fund, 264
AIP. *See* Automatic investment plan
Alternative Minimum Tax (AMT),
  124, 162, 264, 280
American Depository Receipts
  (ADRs), 86, 264
AMT. *See* Alternative Minimum Tax
Annual report, 108, 117, 239, 264
Annuity, 149
Ask price, 264
Asset, 264
Asset allocation:
  and buy-and-hold strategy, 30
  changing, 246–47
  definition of, 29, 264

funds, 64–65, 264
international, 85–89
looking at current, 244–45
and lump sum investing, 150
pie charts, 61–64, 140–41,
  228–29
rebalancing, 243–47
Asset class, 29–30, 82, 264
Automatic investment plan (AIP),
  48–49, 188, 265
Automatic reinvestment, 265
Average cost basis, 165
Average cost per share, 165

Back-end load, 106, 265
Balanced fund, 265
Bally Manufacturing Company, 184
Bear market, 224–25, 228, 241,
  252, 265, 282
Benchmarks, 216
  in bear market, 224–25
  blended, 229, 262

Benchmarks (*cont.*)
  in bull market, 223–24
  definition of, 216, 265
  finding appropriate, 217–20,
    226–27
  and indexes, 217–22
  underperforming, 224, 230, 235
Bid and ask, 265
Bid price, 265
Blended benchmark, 227–29, 262
Blend fund, 83
Block, 265
Blue chip stock, 265
Bond fund, 127–28, 163, 265, 280
Bonds:
  advantages of, 118–19
  choosing, 118–29
  corporate, 122
  definition of, 121–22, 265
  funds, 127–28, 163, 265, 280
  evaluating, 122
  individual, 128
  laddering, 123
  maturity, 146, 265
  municipal, 121, 122–23, 124,
    272
  narrowing search for, 121–22
  pros and cons of, 25
  risk and return, 31–33
  risk of, 119–20
  selling before maturity, 120
  TIPs, 124–25
  U.S. Treasury, 122–24
  zero-coupon, 126
Broad-based index fund, 265
Brokerage firm:
  account, 144–45, 265
  choosing, 144
  definition of, 265
  order confirmation, 147–48
Buffett, Warren, 210
Bull market, 241, 252, 266
Buy-and-hold strategy, 29–30, 37,
    102, 161, 237, 240, 266

Capital appreciation, 266
Capital gains, 149, 162, 163, 165,
    250, 266
Capital gains distribution, 114, 266
Capital growth, 33
Capitalization, 81, 266
Capital loss, 239, 266
Capital return, 266
Cash-equivalent investment, 29, 32,
    130–35, 266
Cash flow, 259, 261
Caution, 55, 119–21
CDs (certificates of deposit), 26,
    32, 134, 135, 266, 280
Certificates of deposit. *See* CDs
Change, 56, 70, 92, 236, 239, 242
Charles Schwab & Co., Inc., 280
Children, 197–207
  Coverdell Education Savings
    Account, 205–6, 267
  custodial accounts, 206–7
  and estate planning, 210–11
  financing early education, 205–6
  investments for future, 201–7
  saving for college (529 plans),
    203–5
  tax considerations, 207–10
  teaching about finances, 197–201
Choice, 42
Closed-end mutual fund, 266
Coca-Cola, 27
College education, 201–5
Commission, 266
Commoditites, 266
Common stock, 267
Companies:
  concentrated equity portfolio,
    248–49, 267
  foreign, 85–88
  knowing about, 95
  small, 93–94
Compounded return, 23
Compound growth, 49–50, 192,
    193, 267

Concentrated equity portfolio, 248–50, 267
Consumer Price Index (CPI), 124, 125
Control, 43–45
Core and Explore®, 65, 84–85, 90, 103, 267
Corporate bonds, 122
Cost basis, 161, 163, 165, 267
Country risk, 267
Coverdell Education Savings Account (ESA), 205–6, 267
CPI. *See* Consumer Price Index
Credit risk, 119, 122, 267
Currency risk, 88, 267
Current yield, 267–68
Custodial account, 206–7, 268

Day order, 146, 268
Default risk. *See* Credit risk
Defined benefit plan, 185, 268
Defined contribution plan, 185, 269
Deflation, 26–27, 268
Delegator, 67, 70
Dickson, Joel, 161
Diversification:
  with bonds, 118
  definition of, 268
  in foreign companies, 86
  with mutual funds, 80, 103
  of portfolio, 20–21, 28–33, 40
  of stocks, 84, 90
Dividend(s), 23, 98–99
  definition of, 268
  from mutual funds, 163, 165
  from stocks, 117
  reinvesting, 146–47
  tax rate, 98–100
  yield, 98
Divorce settlements, 149
DJIA. *See* Dow Jones Industrial Average

Dollar cost averaging, 153, 155, 268
Dollar-weighted return, 257–59
Domestic fund, 268
Dow Jones Industrial Average, 104, 218, 268
Down market, 36, 37, 216, 234, 241
Dyslexia, 43–45

Earnings, 23, 95–96, 268
Earnings per share (EPS), 95–96, 116, 269
Education IRA. *See* Coverdell Education Savings Account
EFT. *See* Electronic funds transfer
EIRA. *See* Coverdell Education Savings Account
Electronic funds transfer (EFT), 153
Emotions, 21, 35–37
Employee Stock Ownership Plan (ESOP), 186, 269
Employer-sponsored retirement plan, 183–86, 188, 269
EPS. *See* Earnings per share
ESA. *See* Coverdell Education Savings Account
ESOP. *See* Employee Stock Ownership Plan
Estate planning, 210–11
ETFs. *See* Exchange traded funds
Exchange traded funds (ETFs), 104
Ex-dividend date, 269
Expense ratio, 269

Face value, 269
Falling prices. *See* Deflation
Families, 46, 197–212
FDIC. *See* Federal Deposit Insurance Corporation

Fear, 54–56, 282
Federal Deposit Insurance
    Corporation (FDIC), 134, 269,
    280
Federal Reserve, 27
Fee-based management, 71, 269
FIFO. *See* First-in first-out (FIFO)
    rule
Finances:
    control of, 43–45
    family picture, 46
    safety net for, 47–48, 72
    women's, 46–47
Financial advisor, 71, 73, 231–34,
    235
Financial aid, 201–2, 204
Financial objectives, 21, 33–35
Financial values, 198
First-in first-out (FIFO) rule, 165,
    251
529 plans, 203–5, 263
Fixed-income investment, 269
Foreign fund, 81, 87, 88, 269
Fortune magazine, 93
401(k) plan, 48, 72, 158, 174, 177,
    184, 185, 186, 263
403(b) plan, 48, 72, 174, 184, 185,
    186, 263
Front-end load, 106, 269
Fund family, 270

GARP. *See* Growth at a reasonable
    price, 98
GICS. *See* Standard & Poor's
    Global Industry Classification
    Standard
Gift tax, 203, 206, 209–10
Global fund. *See* World fund
Goals, 34, 52–53
Good-till-canceled (GTC) order,
    146, 270
Government bond, 121, 122–23

Grandchildren, 210
Growth:
    capital, 33, 105
    compound, 49–50
    investing for, 20, 22–28, 61
    long-term, 23–25, 28, 105
    stock market, 72
Growth at a reasonable price
    (GARP), 98, 117
Growth fund, 105, 270
Growth stock, 270
GTC. *See* Good-till-canceled
    (GTC) order
Guideline of 300, 189–90

HOPE Scholarship tax credit, 208

Iacocca, Lee, 201
I-bonds. *See* Inflation-indexed
    savings bonds
Income fund, 270
Income investment, 33
Income tax, 209
Independent investor, 66
Index, 102, 110–112, 217–22,
    270
Index fund(s), 100–104
    broad-based, 106, 117
    choosing, 109–10
    definition of, 80, 89, 117, 270
    measuring sticks for, 110–12
    performance, 110
    and taxation, 160
Individual retirement accounts.
    See IRAs
Industries, 83
Inflation:
    and bonds, 120
    definition of, 270
    figuring into goals, 154
    keeping up with, 124–25

and retirement, 171
and wise investing, 26–28, 40
Inflation-indexed savings bonds
  (I-bonds), 125
Inheritance, 149, 210
Initial public offering (IPO), 270
Insurance, 48
Interest rates, 120, 122
International stocks/funds, 81,
  85–89, 271
Internet, 105, 219, 220
"Investing Personality"
  Questionnaire, 67–70
Investment manager. See Financial
  advisor
Investment(s):
  automatic and systematic, 153,
    155
  basics of, 20–40
  cash-equivalent, 29, 32, 130–35,
    266
  choosing, 142–43
  diversifying portfolio, 20–21,
    28–33, 40
  and families, 197–212
  and financial objectives, 21
  getting started on, 42–73
  for growth, 20, 22–28, 49
  income, 33
  and inflation, 26–28, 40
  initial, 145–46
  international, 85–89
  language of, 263–77
  learning about, 45
  lump sum, 149–50
  monitoring, 37–38, 215–35
  monthly amounts, 151–53
  online, 144–45, 148
  perspective on, 21, 35–37
  plan, 140–42, 155
  for retirement, 189–94
  risk and return, 30–33, 34, 40
  selling, 237

staying involved with, 21, 34,
  37–39
staying on track, 236–53
and taxation, 157–66
wise, 19–41
See also Bonds; Mutual funds;
  Stock(s)
"Investor Profile Questionnaire,"
  56–60, 62
Investor(s):
  delegator, 67, 70, 73
  independent, 66, 73
  personality, 51–60
  profile, 51–60
  style, 65–70, 81–82
  types, 66–67, 73
  validator, 66–67, 73
Investor's Business Daily, 96
Involvement, 21, 34, 37–39
IPO. See Initial public offering
IRAs (individual retirement
  accounts), 175–83
  contributing early in year, 176
  definition of, 270
  as investment priority, 176
  maximum contributions to, 48,
    72, 175
  mutual funds in, 178–79
  rollover, 183, 274
  Roth, 175, 177–78, 180–82, 195,
    207, 274
  SEP-IRA, 174, 187, 275
  SIMPLE IRA, 174, 186–87, 275
  and taxation, 149, 158, 175, 177
  traditional, 175, 179–80, 182,
    195, 276
Irrevocable trust, 209
Issuer, 271

Jobs and Growth Tax Relief
  Reconciliation Act of 2003, 12,
  99–100

Keogh, Eugene, 187
Keogh plan, 174, 187, 271

Laddering, 123, 271
Large-cap (capitalization)
    stock/fund, 81, 117, 271
Learning, 43–45, 197–201
Legal information, 279–80
Lehman Brothers Aggregate Bond
    Index, 219–20, 226–27
Levine, Irving R., 39
Life insurance, 48
Lifetime Learning tax credit,
    208–9
Limit order, 145–46, 271
Liquid assets. *See* Cash-equivalent
    investment
Liquid investment, 271
Liquidity, 271
Load, 271
Load fund, 106, 271
Long-term capital gain, 271
Long-term growth, 23–25, 28,
    105
Long-term view, 35
Low-load fund, 106
Lump sum, 149–50, 271
Lynch, Peter, 150

MAGI. *See* Modified adjusted gross
    income
Margin account, 271–72
Market capitalization, 81, 93, 272
Market fluctuation, 30
Market order, 145–46, 272
Market timing, 272
Market value, 272
Market volatility, 35
Maturity date, 272
Measurable outcomes, 215
Mid-cap (capitalization) stock/fund,
    81, 272

Modified adjusted gross income
    (MAGI), 182
Momentum investing, 96
Money market mutual fund,
    132–33, 147, 272, 280
Morgan Stanley Capital
    International MSCI® EAFE
    Index, 112, 219, 220, 227
Municipal bond, 121, 122–23, 124,
    272
Mutual funds:
  actively managed, 80, 89,
    100–101, 103, 106, 113–14,
    117, 162, 264
  advantages of, 79–80, 89
  asset allocation fund, 64–65
  bond, 127–28
  broad-based, 105
  categories of, 81–83
  changes in objectives, 242
  choosing, 100–116
  closed-end, 266
  definition of, 272
  diversification with, 80, 103
  domestic, 81
  foreign, 87, 88
  index, 80, 100–104, 109–12
  international, 81, 86–88
  in IRAs, 178–79
  low performance over time,
    241–42
  management changes, 242
  money market, 132–33, 147, 272,
    280
  narrowing search for, 104–5
  no-load, 106–7, 108, 273
  open-end, 273
  prospectus, 108–9
  record keeping, 163, 164–65,
    250–51
  risk and return, 32
  selling, 237–38, 240–42, 250
  stock, 79–83, 100–116
  supermarket, 272

tax implications, 109, 114, 117, 160, 161–62, 163, 164–65, 250–52
world, 87
See also Index fund(s)

NASDAQ (National Association of Securities Dealers Automated Quotation System), 104, 112, 218, 272
NAV. *See* Net asset value (NAV)
Net asset value (NAV), 106, 273
Net profit, 273
New York Stock Exchange (NYSE), 273
New York Times, 219
No-load funds, 106–7, 108, 273
Nonqualified plans, 185
NYSE. *See* New York Stock Exchange

Objectivity, 21, 115
Observation, 92
Odd lot, 273
OER. *See* Operating expense ratio
O'Neil, William J., 96
Online investing, 144–45, 148
Open-end mutual fund, 273
Open order, 273
Operating expenses, 273
Operating expense ratio (OER), 107, 273
Order confirmation, 147–48
Oversaving, 131
Over-the-counter, 273

Par, 273
Patience, 37, 283
Payroll deduction, 153
P/E. *See* Price/earnings ratio

Penny stock, 83, 273
Pensions. *See* Retirement plans
Performance:
asset class, 82
during down market, 234
mathematics of measurement, 257–62
monitoring, 215–17
mutual fund, 113–14, 241–42
vis-à-vis advice, 231, 232
Personality, 51–60, 67–70, 72
Perspective, 21, 35–37
Portfolio:
bonds in, 118
building, 144–50
building stock portion of, 84–85
checking funds and other large holdings, 220–23, 234
concentrated equity, 248–50
definition of, 274
diversification of, 20–21, 28–33, 40
looking at entire, 223–29
in mutual funds, 88, 117, 234, 220–23
rebalancing, 243–48, 274
Portfolio manager, 274
Preferred stock, 274
Preparation, 36
Pretax rate of return, 161, 274
Price/earnings ratio (P/E), 96–98, 116, 239, 273
Prices, 93, 94
Principal, 274
Product stocks, 93
Professional advice. *See* Financial advisor
Prospectus, 108–9, 117, 274
Publications, 104–5

Qualified plans, 185
Quarterly report, 108, 117, 239

Rebalancing, 243–48, 274
Redemption fee, 274
Reinvestment, 274
REIT (real estate investment trust), 85, 139
Research, 115
Retirement, 53
  funds needed for, 169, 171–72, 189–91
  goals, 189–95
  investments for, 189–94
  planning for, 167–96
  redefining, 168–72
Retirement plans, 174–87, 195
  benefits office of employer, 188
  distribution, 274
  employer-sponsored, 183–86, 188, 269
  for self-employed, 186–87
  and taxation, 149, 158–61, 174–83
  See also IRAs and specific plans
Return, 23, 31–33, 40
Risk:
  attitude toward, 52
  of bonds, 119–20
  currency, 88, 267
  definition of, 40
  and foreign investments, 87–88, 267
  and return, 30–33
  tolerance for, 34, 54, 64
  unnecessary, 31, 33
Rollover IRA, 183, 274
Roth, William V., Jr., 180
Roth IRA, 175, 177–78, 180–82, 195, 207, 274
Round lot, 274
Rule of 72, 50
Russell 1000 Index, 219
Russell 2000 Index, 110, 112, 219, 220, 227
Russell 3000 Index, 219

Safety net, 47–48, 72
Savings accounts, 31, 131
Schwab Center for Investment Research, 84, 108, 242–43
Schwab Equity Ratings (SER), 94, 240, 280
SchwabFunds®, 79
Schwab Learning, 44–45
Schwab 1000 Index®, 106, 112, 116
Schwab model portfolios, 61–64, 140–41, 228–29
Schwab's Mutual Fund Marketplace®, 79
Schwab Mutual Fund OneSource®, 79, 143, 280
Schwab's Mutual Funds *Select List™*, 108
SEC. *See* Securities and Exchange Commission
Secondary market, 274–75
Sector, 83
Sector/specialty fund, 275
Securities, 275
Securities and Exchange Commission (SEC), 275
SEP-IRA (Simplified Employee Pension-Individual Retirement Account), 174, 187, 275
SER. *See* Schwab Equity Ratings
Settlement, 275
Settlement date, 275
Share, 275
Sharpe, William F., 30
Sheehy, Gail, 46–47
Short-term capital gain, 275
Short-term redemption fee, 143
Shoven, John, 161
Simple Dietz method, 259
SIMPLE (Savings Incentive Matching Plan for Employees) IRA, 174, 186–87, 275
Small-cap (capitalization) stock/fund, 81, 117, 275, 280

Small companies, 93–94
Social Security, 124, 171, 172–73, 275
Specific shares method, 165
Spiders (exchange traded funds), 104
Spousal IRA, 275
Standard & Poor's 100 Index, 110
Standard & Poor's 500 Index, 38, 80, 106, 110–11, 116, 218–25, 275–76
Standard & Poor's Global Industry Classification Standard (GICS), 83
Standard & Poor's Small-Cap 600 Index, 112, 219
Stock fund. See Actively managed mutual funds, Domestic fund, Index fund, International stocks/funds, Large-cap stocks/funds, Small-cap stocks/fund
Stock market:
    down market, 36, 37, 216, 234, 241
    fluctuations, 30
    following the crowd, 36–37
    growth, 72
    volatility, 35
Stock(s):
    basics of investing in, 89–90
    blue chip, 265
    building with Core & Explore®, 84–85, 90
    categories of, 80–83
    choosing, 91–100
    common, 267
    concentrated equity portfolio, 248–50
    definition of, 276
    genetics of, 22–23, 25
    and growth, 23–24, 26, 28, 61, 270

individual, 77–79, 91–100
    and inflation, 27, 28
    international, 81, 85–89, 271
    narrowing search for, 91–94
    options, 184
    past performance of, 24–25
    penny, 83, 273
    product, 93
    research basics, 115–16
    risk and return, 31–33
    Schwab Equity Ratings, 280
    selling, 237–40
    small company, 93
Stock split, 276
Stop-limit order, 276
Stop order, 276
STRIPs (separate trading of registered interest and principal), 126, 276

Taxation:
    alternative minimum tax, 124
    and bond funds, 163
    capital gains, 149, 162, 163, 165, 250, 266
    deductions versus credits, 208–9
    dividend rate, 98–100
    and 529 plans, 203, 204
    and foreign investment, 87
    gift tax, 206, 209–10
    income tax, 209
    and index funds, 160
    and investment, 157–66
    and investments for children, 207–10
    and lump sum investing, 149
    and mutual funds, 109, 114, 117, 160, 161–62, 163, 164–65, 250–52
    and retirement plans, 149, 158–61, 174–83
    tax-advantaged accounts, 158–61, 177–78

Taxation (*cont.*)
  tax-free securities, 162
  and Treasuries, 123
  and tuition deductions and
    credits, 208–9
  Treasury Inflation-Protected
    Securities, 125
Tax deferral, 276
Tax efficiency, 159, 160, 177
Taxpayer Relief Act (1997), 180
Tax Reform Act (1986), 176, 209
Tax Relief Reconciliation Act
  (2003), 12, 99–100
1099–DIV form, 263
Ticker symbol, 276
Time frame, 34, 52, 64
Time-weighted return, 257–62
TIPS (Treasury Inflation-Protected
  Securities), 124–25
Trade date, 276
Traditional IRA, 175, 179–80, 195,
  276
Treasury bill, 123, 133–34, 135,
  227, 276
Treasury bond, 31, 123, 124, 276
Treasury Inflation-Protected
  Securities. *See* TIPS
Treasury note, 122, 123, 276
Treasury zeros. *See* STRIPs
Trends, 92
Tuition credits, 208–9
Tuition deductions, 208
Turnover rate, 276–77
12(b)-1 fees, 263

UGMA. *See* Uniform Gifts to
  Minors Act

Underperformance, 224, 230, 235
Uniform Gifts to Minors Act
  (UGMA), 207
Uniform Transfers to Minors Act
  (UTMA), 207
Unnecessary risk, 31, 33
Unrealized capital gain, 277
U.S. Treasury bills. *See* Treasury
  bill
U.S. Treasury bonds. *See* Treasury
  bond
UTMA. *See* Uniform Transfers to
  Minors Act

Validator, 66–67
Value stock/fund, 83, 277
Volatility, 35, 277

Wait-and-see approach, 36, 83
Wall Street Journal, 219
Web sites. *See* Internet
"Why Women Fear They Will End
  Up Living in a Box Outside
  Bergdorf's" (Sheehy), 46
Wilshire 5000 Equity Index, 80,
  103, 110, 112, 219, 226
Women, 46–47
World fund, 81, 87, 277

Yield, 277
Yield to maturity, 277

Zero, 51
Zero-coupon bond, 122, 126, 277

About the Author

Charles R. Schwab is founder and Chairman of the Board of The Charles Schwab Corporation. He started investing in 1957, and in 1974 he became a pioneer in the discount brokerage business, guided by the vision of empowering average Americans with information, investment tools, and easy, low-cost access to the stock market. Today, Charles Schwab & Co., Inc., is one of the nation's largest full-service financial services firms. Mr. Schwab is currently a member of the board of directors of Siebel Systems, Inc., and is the founder and chairman of two nonprofit organizations, Schwab Foundation for Learning and All Kinds of Minds Institute, both committed to helping students with learning difficulties. The father of five children, he lives with his wife, Helen, in the San Francisco Bay Area.

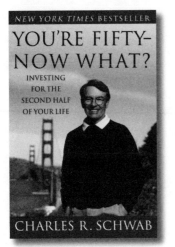
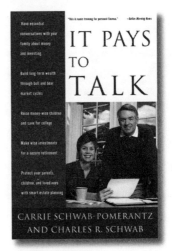